National Intergovernmental Programs

National Intergovernmental Programs

ROBERT JAY DILGER
University of Redlands

PRENTICE HALL, Englewood Cliffs, New Jersey 07632

LIBRARY OF CONGRESS
Library of Congress Cataloging-in-Publication Data

Dilger, Robert Jay, (date)
    National intergovernmental programs / by Robert Jay Dilger.
        p.   cm.
    Includes index.
    ISBN 0-13-609462-7
    1. Grants-in-aid--United States. 2. Intergovernmental tax
relations--United States. 3. Federal government--United States.
HJ275.D55 1989
336.1'85--dc19   88-19605
                                                          CIP

Cover design: Wanda Lubelska Design
Manufacturing buyer: Peter Havens

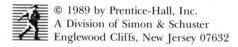 © 1989 by Prentice-Hall, Inc.
A Division of Simon & Schuster
Englewood Cliffs, New Jersey 07632

Printed in the United States of America

10 9 8 7 6 5 4 3 2 1

ISBN 0-13-609462-7

Prentice-Hall International (UK) Limited, *London*
Prentice-Hall of Australia Pty. Limited, *Sydney*
Prentice-Hall Canada Inc., *Toronto*
Prentice-Hall Hispanoamericana, S.A., *Mexico*
Prentice-Hall of India Private Limited, *New Delhi*
Prentice-Hall of Japan, Inc., *Tokyo*
Simon & Schuster Asia Pte. Ltd., *Singapore*
Editora Prentice-Hall do Brasil, Ltda., *Rio de Janeiro*

Dedicated to Gloria, Anne, and Alex

Contents

Preface

The primary objective of *National Intergovernmental Programs* is to provide undergraduate and graduate students with a broad and general understanding of the structure, function, and operation of contemporary American intergovernmental grants-in-aid programs, their historical development, and the politically and ideologically charged controversies that surround them. To accomplish this objective, eight of the most expensive nationally financed intergovernmental programs and two of the most expensive national tax expenditures that affect state and local governments were selected for in-depth analysis. The eight intergovernmental spending programs account for more than $70 billion or approximately 70 percent of the total national funding for intergovernmental programs. These eight programs also constitute a representative sample of intergovernmental grant types and purposes.

The book also discusses three prescriptive theories of intergovernmental relations and asks students to consider which of the three is the most appropriate, given what they have learned about the eight intergovernmental spending programs and two national tax expenditures.

The first of these prescriptive theories, best represented by the writings of Daniel Elazar, suggests that the national government should treat state and local governments as equal partners in domestic governance. However, advocates of this theory are convinced that many contemporary intergovernmental programs treat state and local governments as little more than administrative appendages of the national government rather than as equal partners in governance. To rectify this situation, this theory suggests that the responsibility for some intergovernmental programs should be turned over to the states and localities and that coercive administrative regulations that relegate state and local governments to a subservient role in policymaking should be eliminated in the many programs that should remain intergovernmentally financed and administered.

The second prescriptive theory, best represented by the writings of David Walker, suggests that governmental performance would be enhanced greatly if domestic policy responsibilities that are currently shared through intergovernmental programs were sorted out, with the national government assuming total responsibility for some intergovernmental programs (especially income maintenance programs) and the states and localities assuming total responsibility for the remaining programs.

The third prescriptive theory, best represented by the writings of Thomas Anton and Richard Nathan, suggests that contemporary intergovernmental relationships have been, on the whole, successful and are not in need of the major reforms suggested by the first two prescriptive theories. Instead, they suggest more modest reforms such as efforts to target available resources to areas and people of greatest need.

Finally, the book argues that the traditional arguments that have been used for the past 40 years in the debate over the proper role of the national government in intergovernmental relations have been supplemented by a new set of arguments that are based in a new macroeconomic theory of intergovernmental relations. This new theory has emerged out of the contemporary political and ideological debate over national economic policy and budget priorities. Its emergence represents a major new challenge to those who advocate a strong role for the national government in intergovernmental relations.

ACKNOWLEDGMENTS

I would like to thank Thomas Anton, Timothy Conlan, Daniel Elazar, Daphne Kenyon, Donald Kettl, Christopher Leman, William McCarthy, Richard Nathan, Michael Pagano, Michael Rich, and David Walker for making valuable comments and suggestions on this book's manuscript and for sending me copies of their latest work on intergovernmental relations. I have incorporated many of their suggestions into the book and have learned much from their enlightened scholarship. I would also like to thank the thoughtful reviewers who lent their time and energy to this project. Their constructive criticisms were very helpful and greatly appreciated. Michael Lawson and Susannah E. Calkins, staff members at the U.S. Advisory Commission on Intergovernmental Relations, deserve recognition for helping me find various statistics on intergovernmental programs. The following students at the University of Redlands who undertook an exhaustive article, book search, and photocopying mission for their professor also deserve mention: Kevin Adamson, Philip Fischer, David Gutknecht, Davina Haimov, Jeffrey Leon, John Rice, Jennifer Shannon, and Michael Woods.

I would also like to acknowledge the contributions of a number of people who provided moral, intellectual, or economic assistance that allowed work on this manuscript to proceed and reach completion. I am especially thankful that my colleagues in the Department of Political Science at the University of Redlands—Graeme Auton, Gordon Lloyd, Michael Ng-Quinn, and Arthur Svenson—continue to provide a strong intellectual environment that encourages active scholarship. I am also grateful to the University of Redlands Personnel Committee for awarding me a modest travel grant in 1986. I used the funds to travel to Washington, D.C., where I interviewed a number of public interest group lobbyists, academics, and bureaucrats who deal with the intergovernmental programs examined in this book. I also appreciate the continuing economic support the Lincoln Institute of Land Policy has provided me over the past several years. It was at one of their Roundtable of Governments meetings that I listened to a high-ranking Reagan administration official argue that most nationally financed housing programs were unnecessary because national economic indicators pointed to an economic recovery. I became convinced by that speech that the Reagan administration had embraced the macroeconomic theory of intergovernmental relations.

Finally, I would like to thank my family—Gloria, Anne, and Alex—for putting up with someone who spent many evenings and weekends in his office working on his book instead of staying at home with his family.

CHAPTER 1

Introduction

As Richard Leach pointed out in 1970, the framers of the U.S. Constitution clearly intended that both the national and the state governments would exercise power in domestic policy at the same. However, the framers failed to make clear exactly what the precise relationship between the two levels of government ought to be.[1] Some passages in the Constitution seem to indicate that the national government should play the dominant role in domestic policy. In Article VI, the framers clearly indicated that the national government's laws "shall be the supreme Law of the Land, and the Judges in every State shall be bound thereby, any Thing in the Constitution or Laws of any State to the Contrary notwithstanding."[2] Moreover, the "necessary and proper" clause found in Article I, Section 8, of the Constitution suggests that the U.S. Congress can take almost any action that is necessary and proper to carry out its assigned duties. On the other hand, the framers carefully enumerated the national government's powers in Articles I, II, and III. This has suggested to many people over the course of our history that the framers intended the national government's powers to be limited to those actually listed in the Constitution. Moreover, the Constitution's Tenth Amendment explicitly guarantees that all powers not specifically granted to the national government are reserved to the states or to the people. Some people have argued that the Tenth Amendment's reference to powers being reserved to the states clearly indicates that the states were expected to play the dominant role in domestic governance. Others have argued that the Tenth Amendment's reference to powers being reserved to the people clearly indicates that the national government, which represents all of the people, was expected to play a prominent, if not dominant, role in domestic governance.

[1] Richard Leach, *American Federalism* (New York: W. W. Norton, 1970), p. 8.

[2] "The Constitution of the United States," in *The Federalist Papers*, ed. Clinton Rossiter (New York: New American Library, 1961), p. 540.

STATES' RIGHTS VERSUS THE NATIONALIST
INTERPRETATION OF THE CONSTITUTION

The constitutional ambiguities concerning American intergovernmental relations have led to the emergence of a large number of competing theories throughout our history concerning the proper relationship between the national government and the states and localities. Historically, these theories have had important implications for the distribution of powers among the three levels of government and, because each governmental level has historically displayed different approaches to solving societal conflict, for the distribution of goods and services within our society. Many of our domestic political battles during the 1800s, for example, involved the debate between those who believed in the states' rights interpretation of the Constitution and those who believed in the nationalist interpretation. Advocates of the states' rights, or compact, theory of intergovernmental relations included, among many others, Thomas Jefferson, Andrew Jackson, and John C. Calhoun. This theory suggests that since the Constitution was ratified by the states, it is a compact among the states, and the national government cannot interfere with the powers reserved to the states by the Tenth Amendment. Advocates of the nationalist interpretation of the Constitution included Alexander Hamilton, John Marshall, and Abraham Lincoln. It suggests that the Constitution is a compact among the American people. As a result, the national government receives its authority from the people, not from the states, and is free to do whatever is necessary and proper to carry out its enumerated powers.

THREE MODERN PRESCRIPTIVE THEORIES
OF INTERGOVERNMENTAL RELATIONS

The battle over the proper roles for each level of government in domestic governance is still going on. But the nature of intergovernmental relationships has changed dramatically during the 1900s. Starting with the adoption of the New Deal programs during the 1930s (especially the Social Security Act of 1935) and accelerating with the adoption of the Great Society programs during the 1960s (especially Medicaid and the civil rights acts), and nearly 200 national intergovernmental regulations during the 1970s, the national government has clearly moved to the forefront of domestic policy. The national government's budget now exceeds $1 trillion annually, more than twice the combined budgets of all the states and localities.[3] It directly influences state and local decisions by spending more

[3]U.S. Advisory Commission on Intergovernmental Relations, *Significant Features of Fiscal Federalism, 1988 Edition* (Washington, DC: U.S. Government Printing Office, 1987), p. 2.

than $100 billion annually on national grants-in-aid programs, subsidizing certain state and local activities with $36 billion annually in special tax incentives, reissuing hundreds of regulations mandating state and local officials to take certain predetermined actions, supplying states and localities with over $500 million annually in loans for approved activities, and providing nearly $200 million annually in loan guarantees.[4]

Since the issue over which level of government ought to dominate intergovernmental relations has been largely determined by the politics of the 1900s, most intergovernmental scholars have devoted their energies to devising models that describe intergovernmental relationships rather than to devising theories that prescribe what those relationships ought to be.[5] Nevertheless, a number of prescriptive theories have emerged in recent years. Each acknowledges the national government's tremendous growth since the 1930s in determining the nature of domestic policy.[6] Each also offers a different view concerning the appropriateness of the national government's increasingly powerful role in domestic policy and its use of intergovernmental programs, regulations, and administrative conditions to achieve that dominance.

One of the leading prescriptive theories is best represented by the writings of Daniel Elazar. He views the national government's contemporary role in domestic governance as a usurpation of legitimate and necessary state and local powers. Although Elazar is critical of the performance of many national intergovernmental programs, his objections to the national government's programs are based primarily on conceptual and constitutional considerations, not the effectiveness or ineffectiveness of the programs themselves. He is convinced that the national government has overstepped boundaries that were established by the framers of the Constitution to protect states and citizens from governmental tyranny. Elazar has written that American federalism has been reduced to a "half-baked theory

[4]U.S. Office of Management and Budget, *Special Analyses, Budget of the United States Government, FY 1988* (Washington, DC: U.S. Government Printing Office, 1987), pp. H-2 to H-4.

[5]Some of the leading descriptive theories or models of intergovernmental relations include dual and cooperative federalism—see Daniel Elazar, *The American Partnership* (Chicago: University of Chicago Press, 1962); Morton Grodzins, *The American System* (Chicago: Rand McNally, 1966); Harry N. Scheiber, "The Condition of American Federalism: An Historian's View," a study presented to the Subcommittee on Intergovernmental Relations of the Committee on Government Operations, U.S. Senate, 89th Cong., 2nd sess. (15 October 1966); and Deil Wright, *Understanding Intergovernmental Relations*, 3rd ed. (Pacific Grove, CA: Brooks/Cole, 1988); picket fence federalism, see Terry Sanford, *Storm over the States* (New York: McGraw-Hill, 1967); technocratic federalism, see Samuel Beer, "The Modernization of American Federalism," *Publius* 1, no. 3 (Fall 1973): 57–63; and regulatory federalism, see George F. Hale and Marian Lief Palley, *The Politics of Federal Grants* (Washington, DC: Congressional Quarterly Press, 1981).

[6]For an overview of the national government's increasing influence over intergovernmental relations, see Robert Jay Dilger, "The Expansion and Centralization of American Governmental Functions," in *American Intergovernmental Relations Today: Perspectives and Controversies*, ed. Robert Jay Dilger (Englewood Cliffs, NJ: Prentice-Hall, Inc., 1986), pp. 5–29.

of decentralization" that is "vulgar."[7] He is particularly concerned that many policymakers have a hierarchical view of federalism in which power flows from the national government to the states and localities. These policymakers tend to view states as the middle level of the federal system. Following a chain-of-command philosophy, they treat states as administrative arms of the national government rather than as independent and equal partners in domestic governance.

Elazar is convinced that the framers intended the states and the national government to provide public goods and services in the context of a cooperative partnership bounded by the legal framework of the Constitution. To return American federalism to its original intent—a diffusion of governmental powers marked by active cooperation in many areas of domestic governance—he has advocated a significant reduction in the national government's coercive role in domestic policymaking through the elimination of some national intergovernmental programs and the removal of many administrative regulations in those that remain. By enhancing the domestic policymaking powers of state and local governments, he contends, policy implementation will be improved because the number of decision makers and the amount of administrative red tape will be reduced. Political accountability will be enhanced because citizens will have fewer public officials to deal with, making it easier for them to figure out whom to blame when programs fail and whom to praise when programs work. He is also convinced that citizens will become more active in the political process because they will see that their political participation can have an immediate and visible impact on the conduct of public officials and the operations of public programs.[8]

Another leading prescriptive theory is best represented by the writings of David B. Walker. It also views the national government's array of intergovernmental programs and regulations with great alarm.[9] But, unlike Elazar, Walker bases his objections primarily on the performance of national intergovernmental programs, not on conceptual and constitutional considerations. He is convinced that the large number of national intergovernmental programs and the intrusive nature of many inter-

[7]Daniel J. Elazar, "Is the Federal System Still There?" in *American Intergovernmental Relations Today: Perspectives and Controversies*, ed. Robert Jay Dilger, pp. 281–289.

[8]See the following by Daniel Elazar: "Cursed by Bigness or Toward a Post-Technocratic Federalism," in *The Federal Polity*, ed. Daniel J. Elazar (New Brunswick, NJ: Transaction Books, 1974); "The New Federalism: Can the States Be Trusted?" *The Public Interest* 35 (Spring 1974): 89–102; "Federalism vs. decentralization: The drift from authenticity," *Publius* (1976):9–19; "Reagan's New Federalism and American Federal Democracy," paper prepared for the American Enterprise Institute's Public Policy Week, Washington, DC, December 1982; and *American Federalism: A View from the States*, 3rd ed. (New York: Harper & Row, 1984).

[9]See David B. Walker, *Toward Functioning Federalism* (Cambridge, MA: Winthrop Publishers, 1981); U.S. Advisory Commission on Intergovernmental Relations, *The Federal Role in the Federal System*, 11 vols. (Washington, DC: U.S. Government Printing Office, 1980); and *An Agenda for American Federalism: Restoring Confidence and Competence* (Washington, DC: U.S. Government Printing Office, 1981).

governmental regulations have diminished the capacity of government as a whole to provide needed public services in an efficient and cost-effective manner. He argues that intergovernmental relations have become dangerously overloaded and have permitted the national government to avoid some of its most basic domestic responsibilities while cluttering up its agenda with issues that more properly belong at the state and local levels.[10]

In Walker's view, the best way to improve governmental performance is to allow the national government to perform the functions it does best and to allow the states and localities to perform the functions they do best. Specifically, since the states' fiscal resources are so varied, the national government should be responsible for those programs where uniform levels of benefits or services are desirable. Walker cites income maintenance programs, such as Medicaid (medical care for the poor), Aid to Families with Dependent Children (cash assistance for the poor), and Food Stamps (food for the poor) as examples of programs that should be nationalized. Administrative and financing responsibilities for programs in areas that address issues where conditions and needs vary considerably from one geographic area to another—such as education, economic development, and law enforcement—should be turned over to the states and localities. In addition, any program with an annual appropriation of $100 million or less should be turned over to the states and localities.[11]

A third prescriptive theory of intergovernmental relations is best represented by the writings of Richard Nathan and Thomas Anton. They are not alarmed by the national government's expanded role in domestic governance and the contemporary status of intergovernmental grant-in-aid programs and regulations.[12] Anton has argued that many intergovernmental programs have been very successful, and that Walker's concern that the contemporary intergovernmental system is dysfunctional and overloaded is based largely on conceptual inadequacies concerning how one measures program success and system overload.

Moreover, both Anton and Nathan argue that the federal system has always been a system of shared responsibilities. Nathan suggests that the idea of achieving political equilibrium between the national government and the states and localities "should not be jettisoned on the grounds that

---

[10]U.S. Advisory Commission on Intergovernmental Relations, *Hearings on the Federal Role* (Washington, DC: U.S. Government Printing Office, October 1980), p. 50.

[11]Ibid., p. 53.

[12]See the following by Richard Nathan: "Federal Grants—How Are They Working?" in *Cities Under Stress: The Fiscal Crisis of Urban America*, ed. Robert W. Burchell and David Lincoln (Piscataway, NJ: Center for Urban Policy Research, Rutgers University, 1981); "'Reforming' the Federal Grants-in-Aid System for States and Localities," *National Tax Journal* 34, no. 3 (1981): 321–327; "The Role of the States in American Federalism," paper prepared for the Annual Meeting of the American Political Science Association, Chicago, September 4, 1987; and Thomas Anton, "Decay and Reconstruction in the Study of American Intergovernmental Relations," in *American Intergovernmental Relations Today: Perspectives and Controversies*, ed. Robert Jay Dilger, pp. 268–280.

the modern world doesn't permit the luxury of sometimes slow and often untidy decisionmaking."[13] Operating grants for local mass-transit systems, for example, would, under Walker's theory, be considered a local function that ought to be the responsibility of state and local governments. Nathan argues that these grants are one of the most important sources of external support for the nation's older urban centers. Since these urban centers have serious fiscal, economic, and social problems, they should continue to receive national assistance for local mass-transit systems on equity grounds.[14]

Anton and Nathan also strongly dispute the notion that contemporary intergovernmental programs promote a lack of accountability by confusing citizens. They are not convinced that national intergovernmental red tape necessarily hinders efficient and effective program implementation. Instead, they cite evidence to support the notion that states and localities have a large capacity to manage intergovernmental programs and to influence their operations.[15] As a result, they reject both the significant reduction in national powers advocated by Elazar and the sorting out of functions advocated by Walker. Instead, they see elements of strength, health, and dynamism in contemporary intergovernmental relationships and firmly support a continuation of shared governance in domestic policy. Instead of major reforms, they advocate the relaxation of coercive national regulations and a greater effort to target available resources to areas of greatest need.

HOW DO WE KNOW WHICH THEORY IS CORRECT?

Given these competing views of the best course of action for enhancing governmental performance, it is difficult for anyone, particularly students who are just beginning to understand what intergovernmental relations are all about, to determine which of these prescriptive theories, if any, is correct. The first step in making such a determination is to gather as much information about the workings of American intergovernmental relations as possible. In an earlier book, I attempted to provide a general understanding of the historical development and contemporary political dynamics of intergovernmental relations as a system of programs and regulations.[16] This book extends that discussion by examining specific intergovernmental programs in detail. Although political scientists often speak of an inter-

[13]Richard Nathan, "'Reforming' the Federal Grants-in-Aid System for States and Localities," p. 324.

[14]Ibid.

[15]See U.S. Advisory Commission on Intergovernmental Relations, *The Question of State Government Capability* (Washington, DC: U.S. Advisory Commission on Intergovernmental Relations, January 1985).

[16]Robert Jay Dilger, ed., *American Intergovernmental Relations Today: Perspectives and Controversies* (Englewood Cliffs, NJ: Prentice-Hall, Inc., 1986).

governmental "system," intergovernmental relations is actually a conglomeration of individual programs and regulations that sometimes work in unison and sometimes work against each other. It is necessary, therefore, to examine individual intergovernmental programs as well as the overall pattern of intergovernmental relations to get a good idea of what contemporary intergovernmental relations are all about.

As Tables 1.1, 1.2, and 1.3 suggest, studying the contemporary intergovernmental "system" of grant-in-aid programs is significantly more difficult today than it was in 1960. In 1960 there were only 132 intergovernmental programs, and just two programs (Federal Aid to Highways and Aid to Families with Dependent Children) accounted for 70 percent of all national intergovernmental expenditures. Thus, after examining the role of intergovernmental regulations, it was possible to get a pretty good idea of what intergovernmental relations were all about in 1960 by studying just two intergovernmental programs. Today, it is necessary to look at a number of intergovernmental programs to achieve any significant understanding of intergovernmental relationships. Although the number of intergovernmental programs peaked at 539 in 1981 and at the latest count now stands at 435, there are still more than three times as many intergovernmental programs in operation today as there were in 1960. Moreover, most of the reduction in the number of intergovernmen

TABLE 1.1 National Grants-in-Aid: Number and Expenditure (billions of dollars)

YEAR	NUMBER	EXPENDITURE
1987	435	$108.4
1984	405	97.6
1983	410	92.5
1982	441	88.2
1981	539	94.8
1978	498	77.9
1975	448	49.8
1968	387	18.6
1964	181	10.1
1960	132	7.0

Sources: U.S. Office of Management and Budget, *Special Analyses, Budget of the United States Government, FY 1989* (Washington, DC: U.S. Government Printing Office, 1988), p. H-21; U.S. Advisory Commission on Intergovernmental Relations, *A Catalog of Federal Grants-in-Aid Programs to State and Local Governments, Grants Funded FY 1987* (Washington, DC: U.S. Government Printing Office, 1987), p. 1; Robert Jay Dilger, "The Expansion and Centralization of American Governmental Functions," in *American Intergovernmental Relations Today: Perspectives and Controversies*, ed. Robert Jay Dilger (Englewood Cliffs, NJ: Prentice-Hall, Inc., 1986), p. 18; and U.S. Advisory Commission on Intergovernmental Relations, *Significant Features of Fiscal Federalism* (Washington, DC: U.S. Government Printing Office, 1985), p. 21.

TABLE 1.2   Ten Most Expensive Intergovernmental Programs, 1960 and 1970 (budget outlays in billions of dollars)

	1960	1970
	highways ($2.9)	AFDC ($4.7)
	AFDC (2.0)	highways (4.3)
	impact aid (.23)	Medicaid (2.7)
	unemployment services (.21)	compens. education (1.5)
	health resources (.19)	urban renewal (1.0)
	child nutrition (.15)	health resources (.9)
	agric. price support (.14)	Food Stamps (.6)
	public housing (.12)	community action (.6)
	urban renewal (.10)	impact aid (.6)
	job training (.10)	social services (.5)
No. exceeding $1 billion	2	5
Total Dollars:	$7 billion	$23.9 billion

Source: U.S. Office of Management and Budget, *Historical Tables, Budget of the United States Government, FY 1989* (Washington, DC: U.S. Government Printing Office, 1988), Table 12.3.

TABLE 1.3   Ten Most Expensive Intergovernmental Programs, 1980 and 1990 (budget outlays in billions of dollars)

	1980	1990 (est.)
	Medicaid ($13.9)	Medicaid ($35.8)
	Food Stamps (9.1)*	highways (12.6)
	highways (8.6)	Food Stamps (12.5)
	AFDC (7.2)	AFDC (10.7)
	GRS (6.8)	subsidized housing (6.2)
	CETA (6.1)	child nutrition (4.8)
	sewage treatment (4.3)	compens. education (4.5)
	CDBG (3.9)	CDBG (2.9)
	compens. education (3.5)	social services (2.7)
	child nutrition (3.2)	JTPA (2.7)
No. exceeding $1 billion	16	25
Total Dollars:	$100.1 billion	$133.1 billion

*Funding for Food Stamps includes both Food Stamp benefit payments and administrative grants. OMB excludes Food Stamp benefit payments in its tables.

Source: U.S. Office of Management and Budget, *Historical Tables, Budget of the United States Government, FY 1989* (Washington, DC: U.S. Government Printing Office, 1988), Table 12.3.

tal programs since 1981 has resulted from the elimination of relatively small, inconsequential programs (with the notable exception of general revenue sharing in 1987). In addition, although the dramatic growth of intergovernmental regulations has been slowed in recent years, these regulations are far more pervasive and intrusive today than they were in 1960.[17] Furthermore, since 1960 the U.S. Supreme Court has sanctioned a tremendous growth of the national government's role in many areas that were previously reserved to the states and localities.[18] Thus, it is much more difficult to reach any definitive answers about intergovernmental relations today than it was in 1960.

A REPRESENTATIVE SAMPLE

Where do we begin? Given time and space limitations, which of the 435 national intergovernmental programs should be picked for inclusion in this book? First, the programs selected for analysis should be representative of the two different types of grants-in-aid programs currently in existence: categorical grants and block grants. Categorical grants, designed to aid a particular activity and subject to relatively stringent administrative conditions, account for the vast majority (422 out of 435) of all national grants-in-aid programs. Any representative sample of national grants-in-aid programs must include a relatively large proportion of categorical grants.

There are four types of categorical grants. A representative sample of national grants-in-aid programs should also include more than one type of categorical grant. Project categorical grants, the most used grant mechanism, generally have relatively small budgets. States and localities receive project grant funding only after applying to the national bureaucracy that administers the program. Funds are then allocated among those states and localities according to criteria specified by Congress and at the discretion of national bureaucrats. Formula categorical grants are automatically distributed to eligible states and localities according to a formula that has been predetermined by national policymakers. The most common criteria used in these formulas are population and per capita income. Formula/project categorical grants are allocated among recipient governments according to

[17]See U.S. Advisory Commission on Intergovernmental Relations, *Regulatory Federalism: Policy, Process, Impact and Reform* (Washington, DC: U.S. Government Printing Office, 1984); and David R. Beam, "Washington's Regulation of States and Localities," in *American Intergovernmental Relations Today: Perspectives and Controversies*, ed. Robert Jay Dilger, pp. 227–243.

[18]See Cynthia Cates Colella, "The United States Supreme Court and Intergovernmental Relations," in *American Intergovernmental Relations Today*, ed. Robert J. Dilger, pp. 30–71; Paul J. Hartman and Thomas R. McCoy, "Garcia: The Latest Retreat on the States' Rights' Front," *Intergovernmental Perspective* (Spring/Summer 1985): 8–11; and A. E. Dick Howard, "Garcia: Federalism's Principles Forgotten," *Intergovernmental Perspective* (Spring/Summer 1985): 12–14.

factors specified by national policymakers. Usually a formula allocates the program's funding among the states and territories, and then local governments apply on a competitive basis to their state's appropriate bureaucracy for funding. Open-ended reimbursement categorical grants reimburse states and localities, usually on a percentage basis, for undertaking certain predetermined activities.[19]

There are 13 national block grants, accounting for approximately 12 percent of all national intergovernmental grants-in-aid expenditures.[20] Since block grants are so different from categorical grants (instead of funding a single activity, the national government provides funding for a number of functionally related activities, allows states and localities to use their own discretion concerning which of the listed activities to fund, and attaches relatively few administrative conditions to the grant), at least one block grant program should be selected for analysis to make certain that all grants-in-aid types are represented and comparisons can be made.

Intergovernmental grants-in-aid programs are also differentiated according to the nature of the grant's recipients. Approximately 60 percent of all national intergovernmental funding is provided to individuals in the form of a direct cash or an indirect in-kind subsidy. Among the most expensive of these programs are Medicaid, Aid to Families with Dependent Children, and Food Stamps (See Table 1.3). Most of the remaining funds are allocated to state and local governments to build public works projects such as highways, subways, and wastewater treatment plants, or to provide public services such as remedial education for the poor. A representative sample of national intergovernmental programs should, therefore, include grants that provide benefits to individuals and grants that help states and localities build public works projects and provide public services. Finally, a representative sample of national intergovernmental programs should cover each of the six major functional categories of assistance: transportation; income security; education, employment, and social services; health; community development; and natural resources and the environment.

Transportation programs still account for a significant portion of the national government's intergovernmental expenditures (see Table 1.4). An examination of the most expensive program in this category, Federal Aid to Highways ($12.6 billion in FY 1990), should provide a good idea of what programs in this functional area are like. Moreover, Federal Aid to Highways is one of the few intergovernmental programs that has revenues set aside for it in a special trust fund. Proceeds from excise taxes on gasoline

[19]In 1987 there were 288 project categorical grants, 94 formula categorical grants, 23 formula/project categorical grants, and 17 open-ended reimbursement categorical grants. See U.S. Advisory Commission on Intergovernmental Relations, *A Catalog of Federal Grant-in-Aid Programs to State and Local Governments: Grants Funded FY 1987* (Washington, DC: U.S. Government Printing Office, 1987).

[20]U.S. Office of Management and Budget, *Special Analyses, Budget of the United States Government, FY 1988*, p. H-25.

TABLE 1.4 Percentage Distribution of National Grants-in-Aid Funding, by Functional Category: 1960–1990

CATEGORY	1960	1970	1980	1990 (EST.)
Transportation	43%	19%	14%	15%
Income security	38	24	20	26
Education, employment and social services	7	27	24	19
Health	3	16	17	31
General fiscal assistance	2	2	9	1
Community development	2	7	7	3
Natural resources and environment	2	2	6	3
Agriculture	3	3	1	1
Energy	—	—	1	—
Other	—	—	1	1
Total	100	100	100	100

Source: U.S. Office of Management and Budget, *Special Analyses, Budget of the United States Government, FY 1989* (Washington, DC: U. S. Government Printing Office, 1988), p. H18.

and other automotive products are earmarked for the trust fund and cannot be used for any other purposes. The highway program offers a rare opportunity to compare programs that must compete for their share of the national government's general revenues and those financed through a trust fund.

The income security area continues to account for a substantial amount of national intergovernmental expenditures. Aid to Families with Dependent Children ($10.7 billion in FY 1990) and Food Stamps ($12.5 billion in FY 1990) were selected to represent the programs within this functional category. Although the national government's commitment to its intergovernmental programs in the education, employment, and social services area peaked in the 1970s, they nevertheless have experienced significant growth since 1960. An analysis of the Jobs Training Partnership ($2.7 billion in FY 1990) and Compensatory Education for the Disadvantaged programs ($4.5 billion in FY 1990) should provide some useful insights concerning the intergovernmental programs in this area.

National intergovernmental programs in the health area have experienced the largest expenditure growth since 1960. Spending for the Medicaid program ($35.8 billion in FY 1990), which subsidizes health care expenses for the poor, increased dramatically during the 1980s (see Tables 1.2 and 1.3). Nearly one out of every three dollars spent by the national government on intergovernmental programs is now spent on Medicaid. Obviously, Medicaid needs to be examined. Although the community development area represents only 3 percent of all intergovernmental expenditures, the Community Development Block Grant (CDBG) program ($2.9 billion in FY 1990) is one of the few major intergovernmental programs that bypasses state governments and provides financial assistance directly to localities. Since it is one of the most important intergovernmental programs from the perspective of the nation's cities, an analysis of CDBG makes sense, especially since it should also provide a very good indication of what intergovernmental programs in the community development area are like. Another expensive intergovernmental program that is important to cities is the Wastewater Treatment Construction Grants program ($2.4 billion in FY 1990). It was selected to represent programs in the natural resources and environment functional category.

These eight intergovernmental programs are expected to account for approximately 70 percent of all national intergovernmental expenditures during the 1990s. Since they are representative of the national government's major efforts in intergovernmental relations' primary functional categories and include grants targeted to individuals and to state and local governments, they should provide an excellent idea of what national intergovernmental programs are all about. Moreover, the sample includes three open-ended reimbursement categorical grants (Medicaid, AFDC, and Food Stamps), two formula categorical grants (Compensatory Education for the Disadvantaged and Federal Aid to Highways), two block grants (Job Training Partnership and Community Development Block Grants) and one formula/project categorical grant (Wastewater Treatment Construction Grants). Thus, the only type of intergovernmental grant program not studied is the project categorical grant. Ironically, this is the most numerous of all the grant types. Since the sample does not include a project categorical grant, it can be argued that the eight selected programs may not be perfectly representative of all national intergovernmental grants. However, while project categorical grants are numerous, they have relatively small budgets and collectively account for only a small fraction of total national intergovernmental funding.

To broaden the scope of the analysis beyond the examination of the national government's spending programs, a chapter dealing with the impact of the national income tax code on intergovernmental relations is included. As mentioned previously, the national government provides state and local governments tax subsidies amounting to more than $36 billion annually. Moreover, the national income tax code has a tremendous impact on private investment in states and localities, on the types of taxes that states and localities impose on their citizens, and on their decisions concerning what governmental services will be offered at the state and local levels. For example, partially as a result of the national government either freezing or reducing the budgets of many intergovernmental programs, and partially because of state and local fiscal limitations that have been imposed by either public referenda or constitutional changes, many states and localities have increased their reliance on tax-exempt bonds to finance their governmental services. An examination of the national government's policy of exempting the interest earned on most state and local bonds from the national income should provide a good idea of how the national income tax code impacts intergovernmental relations. Another tax issue that will be discussed is the national government's policy of allowing itemizers to deduct most of their state and local tax obligations from their taxable income. The deductibility of state and local taxes influences the types of taxes employed at the state and local levels and the willingness of state and local taxpayers to accept state and local tax increases. Each of these programs will be examined separately in nine individual chapters.

THE BOOK'S OBJECTIVES

The book has three prime objectives. First, it carefully examines these intergovernmental programs to determine what they are designed to accomplish, whom they benefit, what they cost, where they came from, and where are they going. To answer these questions, each chapter is organized within the context of a five-part, sequential model of the national policymaking process.[21] The first stage of the policymaking model consists of problem definition and agenda setting. Thus, the book attempts to provide the reader with some insight into the rationales (political and ideological) that led the national government to put these programs on the public agenda in the first place.

The second and third stages of the policymaking model are policy formation (the development of appropriate and acceptable proposals for addressing programs on the public agenda) and policy adoption (the actions of decision makers on the proposals). The book provides an extensive legislative history of each of the intergovernmental programs, to make certain that the reader understands the political, ideological, and economic forces that shaped the programs' administrative structures, financing mechanisms, and programmatic objectives during these two stages.

The final two stages of the policymaking model are policy implementation (the day-to-day administrative operations of the program) and policy evaluation (appraisals of the program's effectiveness). The book examines the latest literature concerning each of the program's day-to-day operations to see if national intentions are being met. It also reviews the evaluative studies that have been done on each of the programs to determine if they have achieved their goals. Finally, it examines the political demands that have arisen to change the program's administrative structures, financing mechanisms, and/or programmatic goals because of those evaluative studies.

The book's second objective is to examine the emergence of the macroeconomic theory of intergovernmental relations and the new set of arguments it presents opposing the national government's strategic intervention in the affairs of states and localities. Since the 1930s, New Deal liberals (those who advocate an active national government that regulates the economy and promotes economic and social equality through

---

[21]See James E. Anderson, ed., *Cases in Public Policy-Making* (New York: Holt, Rinehart and Winston, 1982), pp. ix, x.

nationally financed social welfare programs) have cited one or more of the following seven arguments to justify the establishment and continuation of nationally financed intergovernmental grants and regulations. Some of these arguments are based on ideological considerations, some on economic considerations, and others on administrative considerations:

1. The national government's fiscal resources are superior to those of the states and localities; therefore nationally financed intergovernmental grants are justified to ensure uniform levels of essential governmental services in areas such as education and health, especially since state and local fiscal resources vary so much.

2. Since the national government is providing the financing for these intergovernmental programs, and state and local participation in these programs is voluntary, the national government has the right to determine which governmental services are essential and deserving of assistance.

3. States and localities are unable to levy sufficient taxes to provide acceptable levels of governmental services because they compete with other states and localities for businesses and taxpaying residents.

4. The national government has the right and the obligation to promote through the carrot of intergovernmental grants and the stick of intergovernmental regulations certain fundamental national goals, such as civil rights, equal employment opportunities, and care for the poor and aged, because it is difficult to achieve change when reform-minded citizens must deal with 50 state governments and over 79,000 local governments.

5. The national government has the right and the obligation to protect the poor and disadvantaged by providing them a minimum standard of living and equal access to those governmental services (such as education) that are essential to economic success. States and localities will not protect the poor and disadvantaged because they lack either the fiscal resources or the political will to do so.

6. There are some governmental services that have either costs or benefits that spill over onto other localities or states. Water and air pollution controls, for example, benefit not only the local community that pays for the air and water pollution controls, but all of the communities that are located downwind or downstream from that community. Since local and state taxpayers are generally reluctant to pay for programs whose benefits go to others, local and state jurisdictions often underfund programs with significant spillover effects. Nationally financed intergovernmental grants are justified to encourage states and localities to fund these programs at logical levels.

7. The national government has the right to offer nationally financed intergovernmental programs to demonstrate new approaches to solving domestic policy problems.[22]

[22]U.S. Advisory Commission on Intergovernmental Relations, *Categorical Grants: Their Role and Design* (Washington, DC: U.S. Government Printing Office, 1978), pp. 50–58; Claude E. Barfield, *Rethinking Federalism: Block Grants and Federal, State, and Local Responsibilities* (Washington, DC: American Enterprise Institute, 1981), pp. 4–8; and Thomas R. Dye, *Understanding Public Policy*, 6th ed. (Englewood Cliffs, NJ: Prentice-Hall, Inc., 1987), p. 300. The ACIR study points out that there are also a number of political reasons for Congress and interest groups to advocate intergovernmental grants. For a thorough discussion of these political reasons, see David R. Mayhew, *Congress: The Electoral Connection* (New Haven: Yale University Press, 1974), pp. 52–61, 129; and Morris P. Fiorina, *Congress: Keystone of the Washington Establishment* (New Haven: Yale University Press, 1977), pp. 87–93.

Since the 1930s, New Deal conservatives (those who oppose an active national government that regulates the economy and promotes economic and social equality through nationally financed social welfare programs) have generally argued, with limited success, that most national intergovernmental programs and regulations are not necessary because:

1. Active state and local governments promote a sense of state and community responsibility and self-reliance.
2. State and local governments are closer to the people and better able to adapt public programs to state and local needs and conditions.
3. State and local governments encourage participation and civic responsibility by allowing more people to become involved in public questions.
4. The existence of active state and local governments encourages experimentation and innovation in public policy.
5. Active state and local governments reduce the administrative work load on the national government and reduce the political turmoil that results from single policies that govern the entire nation.[23]

In recent years the nature of the liberal/conservative cleavage has become much more complex. This complexity, in turn, has had a direct impact on the arguments currently being put forth in the debate over the appropriateness of national intergovernmental programs. Instead of classifying people as liberals or conservatives on all issues, we now classify them as liberal or conservative on various issues, usually dealing with the economy, questions concerning social issues such as civil rights and race relations, and public or private conduct (such as legalization of marijuana and homosexual rights). It is not uncommon for a person to hold what is considered to be a liberal view in one issue area and a conservative view in another.[24] This inconsistency in ideological views has come about, at least in part, because the New Deal liberals' Keynesian economics failed to live up to expectations and the New Deal conservatives' free-market alternative has not been applied since the 1920s.

Embraced by New Deal liberals, Keynesian economics, named after economist John Maynard Keynes, argued that a short-term economic downturn (a recession) can become long-term (a depression) because during a short-term economic downturn businesses tend to reduce production and lay off workers to cope with weakened demand for their products. As more people are laid off during the short-term economic downturn, there is less demand for businesses' goods and services because people have less money to spend. As demand falls, businesses continue to lay off workers and a vicious downward economic cycle ensues. To prevent this, Keynesians believed that the national government should step in during an economic downturn and increase demand for goods and services by increasing

[23]Thomas R. Dye, *Understanding Public Policy*, 6th ed., p. 301.

[24]James Q. Wilson, *American Government: Institutions and Policies*, 3rd ed. (Lexington, MA: D.C. Heath, 1986), pp. 114, 115.

government spending, even if it meant incurring a deficit. In the long run, this meant higher national government taxes and borrowing to pay for increased government spending.

One of the beneficiaries of the Keynesians' pro-spending stance was national intergovernmental grants. They were convenient vehicles for New Deal-era liberals to satisfy their desire to stimulate the economy and to address social problems at the same time. Unfortunately, Keynesian economics assumed that prices would remain constant during the period of government spending. Instead, prices rose. Thus, Keynesian economics has been blamed for causing inflation, higher interest rates, and the higher levels of unemployment that accompany the economic slowdown caused by higher interest rates.

There are now three major alternative economic theories vying with Keynesian economics for acceptance: monetarism (the money supply should be kept at a constant rate to prevent alternate economic booms and busts), neoclassical economics (based on recent experiences, the national government should play a very passive role in regulating the economy), and supply-side economics (the national government should increase the supply of goods and services in the economy by reducing marginal income tax rates, so that people will have an incentive to work and invest more).

The confusion over economics has led to increased complexity in the use of the terms "liberal" and "conservative" and has had a direct impact on the contemporary debate over national intergovernmental programs. In the past, all liberals were drawn to support national intergovernmental programs because they believed that these programs not only helped to address specific economic and social inequalities but also helped to promote a robust economy. The current uncertainty about Keynesian economics has made liberal support for intergovernmental grants vulnerable to attack on economic grounds. Advocates of both neoclassical and supply-side economics have stated that the first six arguments used by New Deal liberals to justify funding for national intergovernmental programs no longer apply because:

1. The national government's fiscal resources are not necessarily superior to those of the states and localities, especially given the size of the national deficit that was brought about, at least in part, by Keynesian economics.

2. States and localities are just as capable as the national government of determining which governmental services are essential and deserving of assistance.

3. States and localities would be capable of levying sufficient taxes to provide acceptable levels of governmental services if the national government reduced its taxes and let the states and localities determine for themselves what is an acceptable level of governmental services.

4. The national government's two primary goals are promoting a strong national defense and a strong economy. Many intergovernmental programs, particularly those aimed at helping the poor, are expensive and ineffective. As a result, these programs weaken the national economy by fostering higher levels of taxation and borrowing to pay for them.

5. The best way to protect the poor and disadvantaged and to promote social equality is to provide them with a strong and vibrant national economy that will give them a permanent job. The way to do that is to turn back many intergovernmental programs to the states and localities, and to use the saved revenue to reduce national taxes, which, in turn, will stimulate the economy.

6. Although programs with significant economic spillovers (such as Federal Aid to Highways and the Wastewater Treatment Construction Grants programs) may be underfunded by states and localities without national fiscal assistance, the national government's fiscal difficulties preclude funding for these programs at this time, especially since most states are currently running budgetary surpluses.

Although the advocates of neoclassical and supply-side economics have never coined a term to justify their demands for significant reductions in national intergovernmental expenditures and the turning back of national intergovernmental programs and revenues to the states and localities, their efforts clearly go beyond attempts, as many social liberals view it, to balance the national government's budget on the backs of the poor.[25] For lack of a better term, these new economic conservatives have been promoting a macroeconomic theory of intergovernmental relations that is based on their respective theories of economics. This new intergovernmental theory diminishes the role of national intergovernmental programs and regulations in achieving "good" domestic public policies and, instead, highlights the national government's role in fostering overall economic growth by balancing its budget and reducing economic, social, and administrative regulations on both business and individuals.

Congressmen who still advocate traditional New Deal liberal views on social and economic issues, those who adhere to Keynesian economics, and those with constituencies that benefit from particular national intergovernmental programs oppose this new way of thinking about national intergovernmental programs. They claim that the economic conservatives' "macroeconomic theory of intergovernmental relations" is just a new and convenient way to justify the elimination of programs for the poor that conservatives have never liked. Neoliberals (who want the national government to play a limited role in regulating the economy and a major role in protecting civil liberties) and neoconservatives (who want the national government to leave the economy alone but are willing to allow it to play a role in protecting civil liberties) are caught in the middle. They want to promote social equality directly, by supporting national intergovernmental programs that address the needs of the poor and the disadvantaged, but worry that by doing so, they may hurt the economy and the availability of jobs for the poor and the disadvantaged.

Finally, the book's third objective is to help students, politicians, lobbyists, and scholars to reach a conclusion concerning which of the three

---

[25]Social liberals advocate the use of national powers to promote economic and social equality in society. They advocate laws such as affirmative action to help minorities gain equal treatment in employment situations.

leading prescriptive theories of intergovernmental relations discussed earlier is correct. Although I have my own opinion, this book is not designed to convince you that the Elazar, Walker, or Anton/Nathan theory is the "right" one. My hope is that you will find this book useful in making your own determination.

THE BOOK'S ORGANIZATION

I have organized the book according to funding expectations in 1990 as reported in Table 1.4. Medicaid is the first intergovernmental program discussed because health programs are expected to account for the largest percentage of national intergovernmental funding in 1990. Chapters 3 and 4 examine the Aid to Families with Dependent Children and Food Stamp programs, respectively, because income security programs are expected to account for the second largest percentage of national intergovernmental funding in 1990. Discussing these three programs sequentially also makes sense because Medicaid eligibility is linked to AFDC eligibility, and Food Stamp eligibility is linked to AFDC benefit payments. Education, employment, and social services programs are expected to account for the third largest percentage of national intergovernmental funding in 1990. As a result, Chapters 5 and 6 analyze the Job Training Partnership and Compensatory Education for the Disadvantaged programs. Transportation programs are expected to receive the fourth largest allocation of national intergovernmental funding in 1990. Chapter 7 examines the Federal Aid to Highways program. It is followed by chapters on Community Development Block Grants, Wastewater Treatment Construction Grants, and national tax expenditures. The last chapter of the book attempts to summarize what has been learned about intergovernmental relations by examining these intergovernmental programs and national tax expenditures.

CHAPTER 2

Medicaid

Medicaid is an open-ended reimbursement categorical grant that helps states pay for certain health care expenses incurred by low-income individuals who are in families with dependent children or are aged, blind, or disabled. Created in 1965, it has quickly grown into the national government's most expensive intergovernmental program. The national government's share of providing medical assistance to an anticipated 23 million Medicaid recipients in 1990 is expected to exceed $35 billion.[1]

The national government's matching grants start at 50 percent of eligible medical expenses for states with relatively high per capita incomes. The matching grant increases beyond the 50 percent figure for states that have relatively low per capita incomes. In this way, states with relatively poor fiscal resources are given an added incentive to participate in a program that for many of them represents one of the largest single items in their budgets. The nation's poorest state, Mississippi, receives the national government's maximum matching grant of 79.6 percent of eligible medical expenses. The average matching grant to the states is 56 percent of eligible medical expenses. (see Table 2.1).

Medicaid's variable matching grant feature has apparently succeeded in attracting the states' interest in the program. All of the states, the District of Columbia, Puerto Rico, Guam, and the Virgin Islands participate in the Medicaid program, making it an integral part of the nation's welfare system.

Since Medicaid is the national government's most expensive intergovernmental program and it is an integral part of the nation's welfare system, it should come as no surprise that it is surrounded by political controversies. After outlining the program's legislative history, this chapter examines three of these controversies.

First, there is considerable disagreement concerning Medicaid's intergovernmental structure. At the present time states not only administer the program but also have some leeway in determining eligibility criteria, the

---

[1]U.S. Office of Management and Budget, *Budget of the United States Government, FY 1988, Supplement* (Washington, DC: U.S. Government Printing Office, 1987), pp. 5-106, 5-108.

TABLE 2.1   Total Medicaid Expenditures: States Ranked by National Reimbursement Rate, FY 1988

STATE	REIMBURSEMENT RATE	STATE	REIMBURSEMENT RATE
1. Mississippi	79.6%	26. Ohio	59.1%
2. West Virginia	74.8	27. Wisconsin	58.9
3. Arkansas	74.2	28. Wyoming	58.0
4. Utah	73.7	29. Pennsylvania	57.3
5. South Carolina	73.5	30. Texas	56.9
6. Alabama	73.3	31. Michigan	56.5
7. Kentucky	72.3	32. Rhode Island	55.8
8. New Mexico	71.5	33. Florida	55.4
9. Tennessee	70.6	34. Kansas	55.2
10. Idaho	70.5	35. Minnesota	54.0
11. South Dakota	70.4	36. Hawaii	53.7
12. Montana	69.4	37. Washington	53.2
13. North Carolina	68.7	38. Delaware	51.9
14. Louisiana	68.3	39. Virginia	51.3
15. Maine	67.1	40. Nevada	50.2
16. Vermont	66.2	41. Alaska	50.0
17. North Dakota	64.8	42. California	50.0
18. Georgia	63.8	43. Colorado	50.0
19. Indiana	63.7	44. Connecticut	50.0
20. Oklahoma	63.3	45. Illinois	50.0
21. Iowa	62.7	46. Maryland	50.0
22. Arizona	62.1	47. Massachusetts	50.0
23. Oregon	62.1	48. New Hampshire	50.0
24. Nebraska	59.7	49. New Jersey	50.0
25. Missouri	59.3	50. New York	50.0
National average	56.0		

Note: The District of Columbia is reimbursed for 50 percent of its Medicaid expenses. Guam, Puerto Rico, and the Virgin Islands receive a 75 percent reimbursement.

Source: U.S. Department of Health and Human Services, *Social Security Bulletin, Annual Statistical Supplement, 1987* (Washington, DC: U.S. Government Printing Office, 1987), p. 60.

kinds of medical services covered, overall expenditure levels, and administrative guidelines. Presidents Nixon and Reagan, however, both asked Congress to nationalize Medicaid. They proposed that the national government administer the program and determine all of its operational features, including eligibility standards, kinds of medical services covered, financing levels, and administrative procedures. On both occasions Congress refused to abandon the program's intergovernmental structure or to significantly infringe further on the states' role in determining Medicaid's operational features. The rationales, concerns, and impact of nationalizing the program versus maintaining its intergovernmental structure are presented.

Second, Medicaid's costs are already high and are growing at such a rapid pace that many analysts believe the program is out of control. Four factors that contribute to Medicaid's escalating cost and the efforts that are being made by national and state policymakers to reduce expenditures without jeopardizing the availability of free health care for the poor are analyzed.

Third, there is considerable disagreement concerning the program's eligibility criteria. Thirty-two million Americans had incomes below the national government's official poverty level in 1987.[2] Yet only 21 million of the nation's poor are provided Medicaid benefits.[3] Although many policymakers, lobbyists, and concerned citizens would like everyone who has an income below the official U.S. poverty level to have access to free medical care, most of them agree that the cost of enrolling all of the poor in Medicaid is prohibitive. The debate over which of the excluded poor, if any, can be added to the Medicaid eligibility rolls, given the national government's budgetary difficulties, is examined.

MEDICAL CARE FOR THE POOR: THE NATIONAL GOVERNMENT'S ROLE PRIOR TO MEDICAID

During the 1800s the provision of medical care for the poor was primarily the responsibility of private charities, churches, and local governments. Most towns housed the poor in public almshouses, where they were provided with free room and board and, if there was a doctor in the town, with free medical care. Not all of the poor, however, were offered public assistance. Following the English tradition, most towns offered public assistance only to those who were judged to be incapable of work. Widows, orphans, and the mentally or physically handicapped usually qualified. Others were deemed to be undeserving of assistance and were turned away.

During the early 1900s some states established public hospitals for the poor, but on the whole the provision of medical care for the poor was rudimentary at best, and varied enormously from state to state and from town to town.[4] Some bills were introduced in Congress during the early 1900s to rectify this situation by offering a system of national health insurance that would guarantee access to medical care for everyone in the United States, regardless of ability to pay. National health insurance was not approved at that time because many in Congress were concerned about its potential cost, given the national government's limited fiscal resources (the income tax amendment was not approved until 1913 and did not

[2]"Poverty Rate Drops to Lowest Since 1980," *Los Angeles Times*, July 31, 1987, p. 13.

[3]Many Medicaid recipients have incomes above the national government's official poverty line. Included in this group are the medically and categorically needy.

[4]Robert Stevens and Rosemary Stevens, *Welfare Medicine in America: A Case Study of Medicaid* (New York: The Free Press, 1974), pp. 5–7.

generate significant amounts of revenue until the 1920s), and most people viewed welfare as a state and local responsibility.

During the Great Depression the national government did enact legislation to subsidize state and local programs that provided cash assistance to the poor who were blind or disabled, children, or old (see Chapter 3). But it did not enact legislation to supplement state and local efforts to provide free medical care for the poor. One reason for this was that the American Medical Association (AMA) strongly protested any national system of health assistance, on the grounds that such assistance was a prelude to controls over the way its members practiced medicine. The AMA adroitly exploited the public's dislike of Germany by pointing out that America's enemy in World War I had national health insurance for its working class. It attacked any proposal involving the national government and health care as being German and, therefore, un-American.[5]

To accommodate the health care needs of the millions of Americans who were out of work during the Great Depression, states and large cities greatly expanded the number of public hospitals in the United States. In 1935 New York City owned and operated 23 public hospitals out of a total of 200 hospitals in that city.[6] Public hospitals at that time were used exclusively by the poor. As a result, a two-class system of medical care began to emerge in the United States. Those who could afford to pay for their medical care received that care at a private hospital, while those who could not afford to pay their medical bills went to a public hospital. Given the limited fiscal resources of cities and states, the public hospitals were often underfunded and could not provide the quality of care that was offered at the private hospitals.

Many New Deal liberals were convinced that quality medical care was a right, not a commodity to be purchased only by those who could afford it. But public support for a national system of health insurance was eroded as private health insurance, especially Blue Cross (for hospitals) and Blue Shield (for physician bills), increasingly became a part of employee benefit packages during the 1940s.[7] Thus, the majority of Americans were not particularly interested in spending their tax dollars on a program that showed little promise of ever providing any benefits to them. Moreover, during the 1940s World War II forced the national government to focus most of its fiscal resources on defense, leaving little budgetary room for domestic programs that did not have widespread public support.

After the war the national government found itself in a relatively strong fiscal position. An expanding economy coupled with higher income tax rates caused national tax revenue to remain relatively high, while the

[5]Ibid., p. 10.
[6]Ibid., p. 16.
[7]Ibid., p. 19.

end of the war caused defense-related expenditures to fall. This left some room for increased domestic expenditures. Recognizing that the AMA and most conservatives (who advocated states' rights, a balanced national budget, and private health insurance) would not support a national health insurance program, liberals decided to offer a compromise that was adopted as part of the Social Security Amendments of 1950. This legislation gave the states the option of including medical care as part of their reimbursable expenses in the three nationally subsidized public assistance programs (old age assistance, aid to the blind or permanently disabled, and aid for dependent children).

Conservatives' fears concerning states' rights were minimized by making medical care an optional part of these three basic welfare programs. Their fears about costs were minimized because they recognized that the national government required the states to pay 20 to 50 percent of public assistance costs, that many states would choose not to offer the new benefit, and those that did, would contribute to its cost. State officials did not oppose the program because it was optional and it offered them an opportunity to pass on some of their welfare costs to the national government.

The AMA's fear of socialized medicine was minimized because the legislation did not create any government-owned and -operated hospitals, nor did it call for public employment of doctors. It did, however, require state welfare officials to reimburse medical care providers directly. The AMA liked this portion of the law because it knew that state welfare officials were more reliable than the poor when it came time to pay the poor's medical bills.

Liberals continued to advocate a national system of health care during the 1950s but conservatives, worried about costs and states' rights, and the AMA, worried about socialized medicine, were able to defeat all of their bills. It was not until 1960 that the liberals were able to get the national government to further increase its role in providing subsidized medical care for the poor. The Kerr-Mills Bill of 1960, named after Senator Robert Kerr (D–OK) and Representative Wilbur Mills (D–AK), created the Medical Assistance for the Aged program. It reimbursed states between 50 and 80 percent of the cost of providing medical care for the elderly who were medically needy. The medically needy were defined as aged persons who were not poor enough to qualify for public assistance for the aged unless their medical bills were deducted from their income.

The Kerr-Mills Bill was adopted primarily because health insurance for the aged had become a major political issue. Public opinion polls conducted throughout the 1940s and 1950s indicated that there was widespread support for government subsidies for the aged who could not afford to pay their medical bills. In 1960 there were still ten states that did not provide medical care to any of the poor, and medical services varied widely in states that did offer medical coverage. Some states covered hospitalization but not physician services, while others excluded hospitalization but paid for physician services, and so on.[8] Liberals, convinced that medical care is a right, successfully argued that the national government should step in and guarantee that the aged poor had equal access to medical care regardless of their home mailing address.

MEDICAID: AN INTERGOVERNMENTAL COMPROMISE

Without much debate Congress decided in 1965 to consolidate its four medical subsidy programs for the poor into a single intergovernmental grant called Medicaid.[9] It continued the long-standing policy of limiting national assistance for medical expenses to those incurred by the deserving poor (the blind or disabled, children and their abandoned or single mothers, and the aged). The new program did, however, increase the poor's access to medical care by requiring states that participated in the program to offer medical coverage for five essential services: hospital inpatient care, hospital outpatient care, laboratory and X-ray services, physician services, and skilled nursing home services. The new program continued as a voluntary, intergovernmental program, however. States were not required to participate, but were encouraged to do so by being reimbursed between 50 and 80 percent of covered expenses.

States also were given a significant role in determining the range of medical services provided to the poor. Although the law required states to provide Medicaid recipients with five basic medical services, the national government also offered to help pay for ten optional medical services. Pharmaceutical drugs, for example, were made an optional medical service even though they are recognized as an integral component of health care and, though relatively inexpensive compared with hospital care, are often too expensive for the very poor.[10] By limiting the number of mandatory medical services, the law allowed states to design their own packages of medical coverage for their poor that reflected their different values concerning welfare and their varying abilities to pay for welfare services.

States also were given considerable control over who qualified for Medicaid. While recipients of Aid to Families with Dependent Children (AFDC) were automatically eligible for Medicaid benefits, states played an

---

[8]Ibid., pp. 23, 26. Since the need for medical care was perceived as an unavoidable consequence of growing older, and most Americans viewed old age as a barrier to work, most Americans viewed the old poor as deserving governmental assistance. Younger adults who were poor, on the other hand, were expected to get a job and either to buy health insurance or to save enough money in advance to pay for their medical expenses.

[9]The four programs were medical assistance for the aged, medical care reimbursements for the blind and permanently disabled, aid for dependent children, and old-age assistance.

[10]Bruce Spitz and John Holahan, *Modifying Medicaid Eligibility and Benefits* (Washington, DC: The Urban Institute, 1977), p. 57.

important role in determining who qualified for AFDC. Moreover, states were given the option to provide coverage to the medically needy. Thus, states could alter Medicaid's eligibility criteria to match their views on providing welfare assistance and their ability to pay for welfare benefits.

The states' strong role in determining the range of medical services offered to the poor is still in force. Although states are now required to provide all Medicaid recipients with eleven basic medical services (hospital inpatient care, hospital outpatient care, physician services, skilled nursing facility care, laboratory and X-ray services, home health care services, rural health clinic services, nurse-midwife services, family planning services, pre-natal care, and early, periodic screening, diagnosis, and treatment services for children), they can now receive matching grants for 30 optional medical services, including mental hospital care, hospice care, free eyeglasses, pre-scription drug reimbursement, and dental services.[11] Thus, there is consid-erable state-by-state variation in the range of medical services offered to the poor and in the way offered medical services are rendered. Some states, for example, pay for necessary hospitalization without any limit on length of stay, while others pay for a maximum number of days and cut off support after that limit is reached.[12] As Table 2.2 indicates, the vast major-

TABLE 2.2 Number of Medicaid Recipients Using Available Medical Services, Selected Years, 1972—1986 (recipients in millions)

FY	TOTAL	HOSPITAL INPATIENT	NURSING HOMES	PHYSICIAN	HOSPITAL OUTPATIENT	PRESCRIBED DRUGS
1986	22.4	3.5	1.6	14.8	10.7	14.7
1984	21.4	3.6	1.5	14.2	9.8	14.0
1982	21.6	3.6	1.4	13.9	9.8	13.5
1980	21.6	3.7	1.5	13.7	9.7	13.7
1978	21.9	3.8	1.4	15.6	8.6	15.1
1976	22.8	3.6	1.4	15.6	8.4	14.8
1974	21.4	3.3	1.2	14.9	5.7	14.2
1972	17.6	2.8	.5	12.2	5.2	11.1

Note: The sums of the rows exceed the total number of users because many recipients use more than one available medical service.

Sources: U.S. Department of Health and Human Services, *Social Security Bulletin, Annual Statistical Supplement, 1987* (Washington, DC: U.S. Government Printing Office, 1987), p. 252; U.S. Health Care Financing Administration, "Medicaid Recipients by Type of Service and by Region and State: Fiscal Year 1985," staff report, U.S. Department of Health and Human Services (Baltimore, July 1986); and "Health Care Financing Trends," *Health Care Financing Review* 6:3 (Spring 1985):98.

[11]U.S. Department of Health and Human Services, *Social Security Bulletin, Annual Statis-tical Supplement, 1984–85* (Washington, DC: U.S. Government Printing Office, 1985), p. 39; and Randall R. Bovbjerg and John Holahan, *Medicaid in the Reagan Era: Federal Policy and State Choices* (Washington, DC: The Urban Institute Press, 1982), p. 2.

[12]Stephen M. Davidson, *Medicaid Decisions: A Systematic Analysis of the Cost Problem* (Cambridge, MA: Ballinger, 1980), p. 10.

ity of Medicaid recipients use the program to pay for visits to the doctor, for outpatient hospital services, and for prescription drugs. Most of Medicaid's budget, however, is spent on relatively high bills incurred by Medicaid recipients receiving nursing home and hospital inpatient care (see Table 2.3).

The states also retain a strong influence over eligibility criteria. Although 32 million Americans, 14 percent of the population, had incomes below the official poverty level in 1986 ($11,203 for a family of four), only 21 million of them were eligible for Medicaid.[13] Fourteen states, for exam-

TABLE 2.3   Total Medicaid Expenditures for Selected Services, Selected Years, 1972—1986 (billions of dollars)

FY	TOTAL	HOSPITAL INPATIENT	NURSING HOMES	PHYSICIAN	HOSPITAL OUTPATIENT	PRESCRIBED DRUGS
1986	$40.8	$10.3	$17.4	$2.5	$1.9	$2.7
1984	34.3	10.1	14.9	2.2	1.7	2.0
1982	29.4	8.6	12.8	2.0	1.4	1.6
1980	23.3	7.1	9.8	1.8	1.1	1.3
1978	18.0	5.6	7.4	1.5	.8	1.0
1976	14.1	4.4	5.3	1.3	.5	.9
1974	9.9	3.3	3.5	1.0	.3	.7
1972	6.3	2.6	1.4	.8	.3	.6

Note: Total expenditures reflect payments to health providers. Administrative grants awarded to the states are excluded.

Sources: U.S. Department of Health and Human Services, *Social Security Bulletin, Annual Statistical Supplement, 1987* (Washington, DC: U.S. Government Printing Office, 1987), p. 254; U.S. Health Care Financing Administration, "Medicaid Medical Vendor Payments By Type of Service and By HHS Region and State: Fiscal Year 1985," staff report, U.S. Department of Health and Human Services (Baltimore, July 1986); and "Health Care Financing Trends," *Health Care Financing Review* 6:3 (Spring 1985):95.

[13]Of the 21 million Medicaid recipients in 1985, approximately 10.8 million were enrolled in the Aid to Families with Dependent Children program, 3.7 million were enrolled in the Supplemental Security Income program (poor who are aged, blind, or disabled), 2.6 million were enrolled under the categorically needy option, and 3.4 million were enrolled under the medically needy option. See U.S. Health Care Financing Administration, "Medicaid Recipients by Maintenance Assistance Status and by Region and State, Fiscal year 1985," staff report, U.S Department of Health and Human Services (Baltimore, July 1986). The "categorically needy" are individuals who are excluded from either AFDC or SSI but are considered by the national government to be poor enough to justify their being given free medical care. The national government has established a number of categories to identify these individuals, and states have the option of extending Medicaid coverage to them. For example, 26 states offer Medicaid coverage to individuals who are eligible for AFDC or SSI benefits but are not enrolled in either program, and 15 states offer Medicaid coverage to individuals who are not eligible for AFDC benefits but would be eligible if their work-related child care expenses were deducted from their earnings. For more information see U.S. Health Care Financing Administration, *Health Care Financing: Program Statistics* (Baltimore: Health Care Financing Administration, 1985), pp. 20–28.

ple, have chosen not to offer medical coverage to the medically needy, and AFDC eligibility criteria vary considerably from state to state.[14]

CONTROVERSY #1: A NATIONAL OR INTERGOVERNMENTAL PROGRAM

Since its creation in 1965, the debate concerning Medicaid has essentially revolved around two questions: Do the poor have a fundamental right to equal access to medical care? If they do, which level of government is going to pay the bill? Liberals have generally advocated a stronger role for the national government in determining Medicaid's eligibility criteria and the range of medical services offered to the poor because they believe that the national government will use its fiscal resources to increase and equalize the poor's access to medical care. They point out that the capacity of state and local governments to finance major social programs is limited by constraints on their taxing capacity due to the national government's preemption of the income tax. They also point to the reluctance of state and local officials to increase taxes to pay for welfare benefits because businesses may relocate to states and localities that have lower tax rates.[15]

Conservatives, on the other hand, have generally opposed a stronger role for the national government in determining Medicaid's eligibility criteria and the range of medical services offered to the poor because they believe that the liberals are correct in assuming that the national government would make it easier to qualify for Medicaid and would increase the range of medical services offered to the poor. Although conservatives are just as concerned about the poor and their health care needs as are liberals, they are convinced that such actions would prove to be costly, leading to higher national taxes and a weakened economy. This, in turn, would lead to increased unemployment, more poor, and yet higher Medicaid expenses. Moreover, conservatives view the states' role in determining the program's eligibility criteria and range of medical services as a healthy reflection of federalism in action.

Congress and the executive branch have seriously considered altering Medicaid's intergovernmental structure on several occasions. In 1969 President Nixon surprised many liberals in Congress when he suggested that Medicaid be nationalized. Under his proposal, the national government would administer the program and determine its funding level, eligibility

---

[14]Janet Hook, "Congress Shies Away From Any Cap on Medicaid Outlays," *Congressional Quarterly, Weekly Report* (May 11, 1985): 894; and U.S. Department of Health and Human Services, *Social Security Bulletin, Annual Statistical Supplement, 1987,* p. 40.

[15]John Holahan, William Scanlon, and Bruce Spitz, *Restructuring Federal Medicaid Controls and Incentives* (Washington, DC: The Urban Institute, 1977), p. 51.

standards, and medical services coverage. The Medicaid proposal was part of Nixon's sweeping New Federalism program.

The key assumption driving Nixon's New Federalism was the perceived need to sort out and rearrange governmental responsibilities among national, state, and local governments and between the public and private sectors.[16] The Nixon administration was convinced that the national government had taken on too many responsibilities and was incapable of solving the nation's problems.[17] Nationally financed intergovernmental programs that involved services provided in local communities (where conditions and needs varied) were to be decentralized through the establishment of block grants (Nixon called them special revenue sharing programs). In this way, states and localities would have a greater influence over funding levels, eligibility criteria, and administration of those programs where local decision making was viewed as being most important. Nixon named education, social services for the poor, job training, community development, and law enforcement programs as ones that ought to be decentralized.

On the other hand, programs that involved transfers of money or in-kind services (in this case medical services) were to be nationalized to ensure that benefits remained uniform throughout the country. Intergovernmental programs having benefits that spilled over from one community to another, such as air and water pollution controls and highway programs, and intergovernmental programs (such as drug abuse prevention) that were designed to serve as pilot, demonstration programs to stimulate state and local governments to undertake their own programs also were slated for nationalization.[18]

Many liberals in Congress opposed Nixon's New Federalism because they were convinced that many state and local officials could not be trusted to treat minorities and the poor fairly once they were in control of the programs selected for decentralization. In addition, they were suspicious of Nixon's real intentions concerning the budgets of those programs selected for nationalization. They supported the nationalization of Medicaid in theory but were worried that President Nixon would use his veto to force liberals and moderates to cut the program's expenditure levels once it had been nationalized. Fearing the worst, the Democrat-controlled Congress defeated most of Nixon's New Federalism proposals, including his effort to nationalize Medicaid.

The next major effort to restructure Medicaid came in 1982, when President Reagan announced his own New Federalism program. Like

---

[16]Richard P. Nathan, *The Administrative Presidency*, 2nd ed. (New York: John Wiley and Sons, 1983), p. 19.

[17]Claude E. Barfield, *Rethinking Federalism: Block Grants and Federal, State, and Local Responsibilities* (Washington, DC: American Enterprise Institute, 1981), p. 16.

[18]Richard P. Nathan, *The Administrative Presidency*, 2nd ed., p. 19.

Nixon, Reagan was convinced that the national government had taken on too many responsibilities and was less capable than the states of solving the nation's domestic problems. Unlike Nixon, however, Reagan supported the notion of decentralizing nearly all nationally financed intergovernmental programs, including ones that transferred money and in-kind services. Only programs that had significant spillover effects (such as highways) and relatively inexpensive demonstration grants were to remain under the control of the national government.[19]

Recognizing that the Democrat-controlled House of Representatives would never adopt a proposal to decentralize nearly all nationally financed intergovernmental programs, President Reagan proposed a major New Federalism initiative in 1982 that included a $20 billion intergovernmental swap involving Medicaid. In return for nationalizing Medicaid, he asked Congress to allow the states to take over full responsibility for Aid to Families with Dependent Children (see Chapter 3) and Food Stamps (see Chapter 4).

Liberals in Congress quickly announced their opposition to the swap. They were concerned that many states lacked either the political will or the fiscal resources to keep AFDC and Food Stamp payments at what they considered to be acceptable levels. They were also concerned that Congress would be forced to set uniform eligibility and coverages for Medicaid once it was nationalized. Given the national government's fiscal difficulties, they were afraid that these new uniform standards would be at or below the current average standards employed by the states. Thus, Medicaid's nationalization would probably cause some Medicaid recipients living in states with relatively easy eligibility requirements to be thrown out of the program. Moreover, Medicaid recipients living in states that currently offer a relatively large number of optional medical services would be forced to pay for some of those services. For these reasons, representatives from states with relatively generous Medicaid programs announced their opposition to any plan to nationalize Medicaid that did not raise all the states' benefits to at least their states' levels.[20]

Recognizing that his swap proposal would generate considerable controversy, President Reagan decided to initiate a series of meetings between White House officials and representatives of the nation's governors, state legislators, mayors, and county officials. The goal of these meetings was to reach a consensus of realigning governmental responsibilities prior to the formal submission of legislation to the Congress.[21]

The governors' and local officials' initial reaction to the swap proposal

[19]Claude E. Barfield, *Rethinking Federalism*, pp. 23–34.

[20]Timothy J. Conlan and David B. Walker, "Reagan's New Federalism: Design, Debate, and Discord," in *American Intergovernmental Relations Today*, ed. Robert Jay Dilger, p. 194.

[21]Richard S. Williamson, "The 1982 New Federalism Negotiations," *Publius: The Journal of Federalism* 13 (Spring 1983):11.

was positive. They applauded the administration's intent to sort out governmental responsibilities. The National Governors' Association (NGA), for example, had called for a sorting out of these responsibilities in 1980. They were particularly pleased that the administration was willing to nationalize Medicaid because they were happy to rid themselves of their share of its huge and growing expense. However, they were opposed to the administration's desire to turn AFDC and Food Stamps over to the states.

The NGA, the National Conference of State Legislatures, the National League of Cities, and the U.S. Advisory Commission on Intergovernmental Relations had all previously adopted resolutions advocating the nationalization of all income maintenance programs as a means to equalize welfare benefits across the nation and to relieve the states and localities of the burden of financing their share of welfare expenditures. In addition, they argued that income maintenance costs are directly related to the vitality of the national economy. Since many economic factors are beyond the control of the states and localities, most state and local officials argued that the costs of welfare payments should be absorbed by the national government.[22] Moreover, city officials were more interested in protecting existing funding levels and preserving the direct national-local linkages than in sorting out governmental responsibilities.[23]

President Reagan strongly disagreed with the governors' and local officials' position on income maintenance programs. He was convinced that all of these programs should be turned over to the states because he believed the states were much better than the national government at targeting public assistance dollars to those individuals most in need of that assistance. Although a number of compromise counterproposals were discussed, including one that left the Food Stamp program as a national responsibility, this philosophical difference over income maintenance programs ultimately proved to be the key factor in the negotiations. Neither side was willing to compromise when it came to dealing with the Aid to Families with Dependent Children program. As a result, the negotiations collapsed and the swap proposal died.[24]

There were several other factors that contributed to the swap's demise. Many governors and congressmen were upset when the administration announced it would propose that the new, nationalized Medicaid program not include coverage of the medically needy. Moreover, the administration's call for deep cuts in other intergovernmental programs

[22]Ibid., p. 25; and Albert J. Davis and S. Kenneth Howard, "Perspectives on a 'New Day' for Federalism," *Intergovernmental Prespective* 8:2 (Spring 1982):11, 12.

[23]Richard S. Williamson, "The 1982 New Federalism Negotiations," p. 20.

[24]Ibid., pp. 24–26; and Stephen B. Farber, "The 1982 New Federalism Negotiations: A View from the States," *Publius: The Journal of Federalism* 13 (Spring 1983):36, 37.

during the negotiation process severely strained relations between the representatives of the intergovernmental lobby and White House officials.[25] Finally, many social welfare advocates and most of the nation's major newspapers opposed the swap because they viewed it as a retreat from the welfare state. Thus, despite a series of compromise offers from the Reagan White House, the swap proposal was never formally submitted to Congress for a vote.[26]

Another argument raised against the nationalization of Medicaid was that the wide range of political, economic, and social circumstances existing both among states and between localities within the states makes all nationalization proposals economically and politically inefficient. Presented by economists and academics who advocate what is known as public choice theory, the argument basically rests on the assumption that governmental policies should reflect taxpayers' demands. Since taxpayers in different states have different priorities, the establishment of uniform Medicaid eligibility criteria and medical services coverage violates the fundamental right of taxpayers to set their own communities' standards. For example, taxpayers in Wisconsin have historically demanded additional state and local taxes to expand Medicaid's eligibility and medical services coverages far above national averages. The nationalization of Medicaid, however, presumably would impose national standards of eligibility and medical services coverage that would fall below the standards currently in force in Wisconsin. Nationalization of Medicaid, therefore, would prevent taxpayers in Wisconsin from offering its citizens governmental services that they want and are prepared to pay for.

Similarly, taxpayers in Florida have historically refused to demand additional state and local taxes to expand either Medicaid's eligibility criteria or its medical services coverage much beyond the minimum required by the national government. The nationalization of Medicaid, however, presumably would impose uniform national standards for eligibility and medical services coverage that are more generous than those currently in force in Florida. Thus, the nationalization of Medicaid would impose additional governmental services on Florida's taxpayers although they neither want nor, if given the choice, will pay for those services.

In both cases, the national government is not responding to taxpayers' demands and, as a result, is promoting an action that is inefficient from the perspective of taxpayers' demands.[27]

[25]Richard S. Williamson, "The 1982 New Federalism Negotiations," p. 29.

[26]Timothy J. Conlan and David B. Walker, "Reagan's New Federalism: Design, Debate, and Discord," pp. 189–200; and Richard P. Nathan, *The Administrative Presidency*, 2nd ed., pp. 65–68.

[27]Thomas W. Grannemann and Mark V. Pauly, *Controlling Medicaid Costs* (Washington, DC: American Enterprise Institute, 1983), pp. 51, 52.

CONTROVERSY #2: COST CONTAINMENT

The second major controversy facing Medicaid is its cost. Medicaid is expensive. It is also one of the fastest-growing budgetary items for both state governments and the national government. Expenditures on the program have been rising at an average rate of 11 percent a year since 1980. Moreover, the Congressional Budget Office has estimated that rising medical costs and the aging of the population will cause Medicaid expenditures to continue to grow by at least 16 percent annually through 1992 unless the program is changed.[28] Given the national government's and many state governments' current budgetary difficulties, much of the debate about Medicaid has focused on finding ways to contain Medicaid's escalating costs without seriously jeopardizing the poor's access to medical care.

States are trying to reduce the growth of their Medicaid expenditures for a number of related reasons. Although each state has its own unique set of reasons and priorities that is driving its cost containment efforts, the following five reasons are shared by nearly all of them:

1. The general resistance of taxpayers to state tax increases, coupled with the requirement to have balanced state budgets, has forced many states to look seriously for ways to reduce expenditures in all state programs, including Medicaid.
2. The recession in the late 1970s, coupled with the slow economic recovery in the early 1980s, reduced many states' fiscal capacity to finance Medicaid at the level that they would like.
3. The purchasing power of state budgets has been reduced by inflation, forcing states to order priorities more systematically and to use their scarce resources for other purposes, such as education.
4. Reductions in funding for other nationally financed grants-in-aid programs, coupled with the elimination of the general revenue-sharing program, is forcing many states to order priorities more systematically and to use their scarce resources for other purposes.
5. The national government has reduced its funding commitment to the program and, as a result, has forced state governments to question their own funding commitments to the program.

State Efforts to Contain Costs

Lowering Medicaid expenditures is difficult because it is difficult to predict or control health care expenses. This is particularly true for a population of health care users that changes in composition and size according to factors that are only partially controlled by state and national

[28]Sen. David Durenberger, statement, U.S. Congress, Senate, Subcommittee on Health, Committee on Finance, *Medicaid Freedom of Choice Waiver Activities*, Hearings, 98th Cong., 2nd sess. (Washington, DC: U.S. Government Printing Office, March 30, 1984), p. 2. The aging of the population is expected to increase nursing home expenditures and generally increase the frequency of physician visits and other medical uses per Medicaid enrollee.

policymakers. For example, enrollments in the AFDC and SSI programs tend to fluctuate with the economy, with enrollments accelerating during periods of recession and leveling off during periods of economic growth. The same is true of the number of people who meet the categorically needy and the medically needy definitions.

Some commentators have argued that because states have considerable control over eligibility requirements for the AFDC program, they can contain Medicaid expenses by making it more difficult to qualify for AFDC. Others, however, argue that the states have already restricted AFDC eligibility requirements so tightly that it would be politically (and perhaps morally) impossible for them to reduce Medicaid enrollments by manipulating AFDC eligibility standards. Moreover, they point out that the national government sets SSI eligibility requirements. Each state's Medicaid enrollment figure, therefore, is subject to the potentially fluctuating commitment of national policymakers to the SSI program. In recent years, national policymakers have refused either to reduce the absolute number of SSI recipients or to slow the program's enrollment growth. Thus, the only thing that states can be certain of concerning SSI is that as the number of older Americans continues to grow, the national government is probably going to allow SSI enrollments (and therefore Medicaid enrollments) to increase as well. What the states do not know is exactly how fast SSI enrollments are going to grow.

Another factor making Medicaid expenses unpredictable and, to a certain extent, uncontrollable is inflation in the medical services industry. States cannot mandate the rate of inflation. However, the national government, recognizing that Medicaid's matching-grant feature causes national expenses to fall whenever states realize cost efficiencies, has taken steps to encourage states to buy medical items in bulk and to undertake other measures to combat inflation in the medical services industry. Specifically, under the provisions of the *Omnibus Budget Reconciliation Act of 1981*, states were granted the authority to arrange for competitive bidding for laboratory services or medical devices that are provided to Medicaid recipients. States also were allowed to apply for special waivers from the U.S. Department of Health and Human Services to restrict the ability of Medicaid recipients to receive care from the doctor or medical facility of their choice. The idea behind limiting the poor's freedom of choice was to reduce costs by avoiding doctors and medical facilities that had a record of charging above-normal fees or overutilized available services. States also were allowed to offer medical coverage to certain categories of the medically needy instead of having to offer coverage to either all or none of them.[29]

---

[29]As of March 31, 1984, 42 freedom-of-choice waivers had been received by the U.S. Health Care Financing Administration from 19 states. See U.S. Health Care Financing Administration, *Health Care Financing, Program Statistics* (Baltimore: U.S. Department of Health and Human Services, 1985), pp. 136–139.

These changes have helped states achieve a small measure of control over their Medicaid expenses. However, state policymakers recognize that the only way to save significant amounts of money is to make politically and morally difficult decisions concerning medical coverage for the categorically and medically needy and for the provision of optional medical services, such as eyeglasses and dental services. Until recently, most states have refused even to consider these options. The number of states offering Medicaid coverage to the medically needy, for example, increased from 16 in 1980 to 36 in 1988.[30]

States have been reluctant to tighten Medicaid eligibility requirements or to reduce the number of optional medical services available to the poor for a number of interrelated reasons. First, such actions are politically controversial. State legislators are naturally reluctant to open up a divisive issue where the only options available are ones that hurt constituents (both recipients and providers).

Second, somebody has to pay for the indigents' health care expenses. Under Medicaid, the states at least receive matching funds from the national government to help pay for these costs.

Third, local governments are strongly opposed to Medicaid cuts and are becoming increasingly vocal in their opposition to reductions in Medicaid funding. They argue that public hospitals, financed by local governments, are forced to provide the health care needs of the indigent because many private hospitals refuse to serve them. As a result, local governments end up paying for most of the health care expenses of people who are not covered by Medicaid. In their view, when state policymakers cut the program, it represents not cost savings, but cost shifting.

Fourth, private hospitals are strongly opposed to Medicaid cuts. In the past, they were able to shift the costs associated with providing health care for the indigent onto paying customers (insurance companies, noninsured patients, and Medicare), The Medicare program now requires hospitals to accept fixed payments for medical services, and many insurance companies are considering or already have implemented similar reimbursement procedures. Thus, it is increasingly difficult for private hospitals to shift the cost of caring for the indigent, which forces them either to absorb losses or to refuse to provide health care for nonpaying patients. Many of them have chosen the latter action.

Fifth, reducing Medicaid expenditures may serve to increase rather than decrease the nation's health care bill. People who cannot afford regular medical care tend to wait until they are very ill or injured before seeking medical assistance. This increases the government's expense because early diagnosis of an illness usually results in significant cost sav-

---

[30]U.S. General Accounting Office, *Medicaid and Nursing Home Care: Cost Increases and the Need for Services Are Creating Problems for the States and the Elderly* (Washington, D.C.: U.S. Government Printing Office, 1983), p. ii; and U.S. Department of Health and Human Services, *Social Security Bulletin, Annual Statistical Supplement, 1987*, p. 40.

ings. Moreover, the indigent tend to visit hospital emergency rooms, the most expensive source of health care.[31]

For all of these reasons, plus the fact that state administrators are given considerable flexibility in determining reimbursement rates, states have concentrated their cost containment efforts in recent years on controlling reimbursement rates for physicians, hospitals, and nursing homes. Since these rates are set by each state, there is wide state-to-state variation in the amount providers are paid for performing similar services.

Physician Reimbursement, PCNs, and Copayments

The average payment for a doctor's visit by a Medicaid recipient is only 60 to 65 percent of the amount charged for visits by other patients.[32] By keeping physician reimbursement rates low, states are able to reduce their Medicaid expenses. Unfortunately, because states pay so little, many doctors will not accept Medicaid patients, while others severely limit the number they will serve.[33] This often forces Medicaid recipients to travel farther than other patients to get care, to visit doctors they may not prefer, and to use types of providers, such as hospital outpatient departments, local clinics, or foreign medical school graduates, that will accept them.[34]

Another strategy to reduce physician Medicaid costs is the creation of primary care networks (PCNs). Sixteen states have received permission from the U.S. Department of Health and Human Services to form PCNs. These networks match Medicaid recipients with state-approved physicians who act as those recipients' case managers. The designated physician provides all of a recipient's primary health care needs and sends him or her to a state-approved specialist whenever necessary. The object of PCNs, which are modeled after the practices of health maintenance organizations, is to provide Medicaid recipients their own, personal doctors who not only know their medical history but also can be counted on to provide quality care at a reasonable cost. Although PCNs restrict Medicaid recipients' freedom of choice concerning their health care providers, recipients are allowed to choose among the approved PCN physicians in their area.[35]

Another option open to the states for reducing Medicaid expenses for physician care is the use of copayments. Since 1982 states have been

[31]Janet Hook, "Congress Shies Away from Any Cap on Medicaid Outlays," *Congressional Quarterly, Weekly Report* (May 11, 1985):895.

[32]Congressional Budget Office, *Medicaid: Choices for 1982 and Beyond*, pp. 18, 19.

[33]Over 25 percent of the nation's private physicians refuse to treat Medicaid patients. See U.S. Health Care Financing Administration, *Health Care Financing, Program Statistics* (Baltimore: U.S. Department of Health and Human Services, 1985), p. 101.

[34]Thomas W. Grannemann and Mark V. Pauly, *Controlling Medicaid Costs*, pp. 69–71.

[35]Jack A. Meyer, written testimony, U.S. Senate Subcommittee on Health, Committee on Finance, *Medicaid Freedom of Choice Waiver Activities*, Hearings, pp. 13, 14. For more information on innovative physician reimbursement plans, see Stephen M. Davidson, *Medicaid Decisions: A Systemtic Analysis of the Cost Problem*, pp. 121–152.

allowed to require Medicaid patients to pay a small fee for their medical care, typically $1 per physician visit or $1 per day for hospital care. Copayments' advocates argue that copayments discourage unnecessary doctor and hospital visits. The Congressional Budget Office has estimated that if all the states used copayments, Medicaid expenses could be reduced by as much as $100 million a year. Copayments' critics argue that even a $1 fee might deter some Medicaid recipients from seeking needed medical care. They fear that people will put off seeing a doctor or visiting the hospital, thereby preventing early diagnosis and treatment of illness. If this occurs, copayments may result in significant additional costs to Medicaid as patients' illnesses become more severe, requiring hospitalization and prolonged care.[36] At present, 26 states have decided to exercise this option.[37]

Nursing Home Reimbursement

Although the vast majority of individuals who are no longer capable of taking care of themselves currently receive needed financial support for medical and personal care services from friends or relatives, the government's costs of providing long-term health care through nursing home services is the largest and most rapidly growing component of Medicaid outlays. Medicaid now pays nearly 50 percent of the nation's nursing home bills.[38] Although less than 8 percent of Medicaid recipients are nursing home residents, nearly half of the program's budget is allocated to meet their needs.

According to the U.S. General Accounting Office analysis of the characteristics leading to nursing home use, the number of elderly "at risk" to enter nursing homes has been rising rapidly since the early 1970s and will continue to rise dramatically in the near future.[39] The U.S. Department of Health and Human Services' Health Care Financing Administration estimated in 1983 that the number of nursing home residents is likely to increase by over 50 percent by 1998 and by over 130 percent by the year

[36]Congressional Budget Office, *Reducing the Deficit: Spending and Revenue Options* (Washington, DC: U.S. Government Printing Office, 1984), p. 80; Thomas W. Grannemann and Mark V. Pauly, *Controlling Medicaid Costs*, pp. 78, 79; and Congressional Budget Office, *Containing Medical Care Costs Through Market Forces* (Washington, DC: U.S. Government Printing Office, 1982), p. x.

[37]U.S. Department of Health and Human Services, *Social Security Bulletin, Annual Statistical Supplement, 1987*, p. 41.

[38]Julie Kosterlitz, "The Graying of America Spells Trouble for Long-Term Health Care for Elderly," *National Journal* (April 13, 1985):799; and Julie Rovner, "Long-Term Care: The True Castastrophe?" Congressional Quarterly, *Weekly Report* (May 31, 1986):1228. Total expenditures for nursing home care increased approximately $1 billion annually during the early 1970s, from $4.7 billion in 1970 to $10.1 billion in 1975. These expenditures increased approximately $2 billion annually during the latter half of the 1970s, reaching $20.4 billion in 1980. Since then, they have been increasing approximately $3 billion annually, reaching $32 billion in 1984.

[39]U.S. General Accounting Office, *Medicaid and Nursing Home Care*, p. ii.

2030.[40] Furthermore, as the "baby boom" generation ages and life expectancy continues to increase, the share of Medicaid funding dedicated to the care of the elderly and disabled in nursing homes is expected to continue to grow. The latest projections of the U.S. Bureau of the Census indicate that by the year 2050, 21.7 percent of the population is likely to be over age 65, up from approximately 12 percent in the 1980s.[41] As one author put it, the demographic time bomb ticks loudly in the background whenever Medicaid's budget is debated.[42]

Although Medicare is the national government's principal health care program for the elderly, its coverage of nursing home care is limited to short-term care for patients who require daily delivery of skilled or rehabilitative care. It will pay for only the first 100 days of post-hospitalization care in a nursing home. The average nursing home stay is two and a half years![43]

Most private insurance companies do not offer policies that cover long-term nursing home expenses. The few policies available that do cover these expenses have premiums so high that most people cannot afford them. Thus, the vast majority of middle- and upper-class elderly cannot count on either private insurance policies or the government to cover their nursing home costs. Since the typical nursing home bill now exceeds $25,000 a year, most people who enter nursing homes on a long-term basis exhaust their savings within a year or two, ending up poor and dependent on Medicaid to pay their nursing home bills.[44] It has been estimated that approximately half of the Medicaid recipients in nursing homes were not initially poor, but lost all of their economic resources as a result of the high cost of nursing home care.[45] A 1985 study conducted for the House Aging Committee revealed that 63 percent of elderly individuals without a spouse impoverished themselves after only 13 weeks in a nursing home, and 83 percent become impoverished within a year.

In 1980 the national government relaxed stringent reimbursement rules that virtually forced states to pay whatever nursing homes charged. By 1984, 37 states had adopted a prospective reimbursement system for

[40]U.S. Senate Committee on Finance, *Staff Data and Materials Related to Medicaid and Long-Term Care*, Committee Print, 98th Cong., 1st sess. (Washington, DC: U.S. Government Printing Office, November 1983), p. 3.

[41]Ibid.; and Ross H. Arnett III, Carol S. Cowell, Lawrence M. Davidoff, and Mark S. Freeman, "Health Spending Trends in the 1980's: Adjusting to Financial Incentives," *Health Care Financing Review* 6:3 (Spring 1985):4.

[42]Janet Hook, "Growing Demand for Long-Term Care . . . Drains Medicaid Coffers Nationwide," Congressional Quarterly, *Weekly Report* (May 11, 1985):892, 893.

[43]U.S. General Accounting Office, *Medicaid and Nursing Home Care*, p. 4.

[44]Julie Rovner, "Long-Term Care: The True Catastrophe?" Congressional Quarterly, *Weekly Report* (May 31, 1986):1228.

[45]Janet Hook, "Growing Demand for Long-Term Care . . . Drains Medicaid Coffers Nationally," p. 892; and Pamela Doty, Korbin Liu, and Joshua Wiener, "An Overview of Long-term Care," *Health Care Financing Review* 6:3 (Spring 1985):74.

Medicaid recipients located in long-term, skilled-care nursing home facilities, and 41 states did so for recipients in intermediate-care nursing home facilities.[46] Under these payment systems, nursing homes receive a fixed amount per admittance. The payment is based on the nature of the care needed by the resident. Since each state has established its own reimbursement schedule, there now exist wide state-by-state variations in payments for ostensibly similar services. The long-term implications of these disparities for the quality of nursing home care is difficult to judge. Some analysts have argued that Medicaid recipients living in states that have relatively generous reimbursement rates, such as Wisconsin and New York, probably will receive better nursing home care than Medicaid recipients who live in states that have relatively low reimbursement rates, such as Florida and West Virginia.[47]

One of the more innovative reimbursement methods currently attracting considerable attention is the uniform prospective reimbursement method. Under this system, states set a daily fee that they will pay to nursing homes for caring for each Medicaid recipient served. The payment is based on the average daily fee for nursing home care in that particular area, not on the actual cost of caring for the patient. This prevents nursing homes from charging the government unusually large fees and encourages nursing homes to seek the most cost-conscious approaches to health care. Most of the states that use this reimbursement system annually adjust their payments for inflation and have enacted specific, predetermined cost ceilings to prevent expenditures from rising too rapidly during periods of high inflation.[48]

In response to these recent changes in reimbursement practices, some nursing homes have restricted the number of Medicaid patients they will serve, preferring to fill as many of their beds as possible with patients willing to pay whatever they charge. Since the average occupancy rate is over 90 percent, most nursing homes can exclude Medicaid recipients and still have a reasonable chance of filling enough beds to make a profit.[49] In many instances, excluding Medicaid recipients leads to enhanced profits because income rises and overhead expenses related to the volume of paperwork required by Medicaid administrators are reduced.[50] This practice also serves to increase the states' and national government's expenses

[46]Many of the remaining states are expected to abandon the cost-based retrospective reimbursement system by the end of the 1980s. See U.S. Health Care Financing Administration, *Health Care Financing, Program Statistics* (Baltimore: U.S. Department of Health and Human Services, 1985), pp. 104–112.

[47]U.S. General Accounting Office, *Medicaid and Nursing Home Care*, pp. iii, iv, 47, 48.

[48]Ibid., pp. 86–89; and Pamela Doty, Korbin Liu, and Joshua Wiener, "An Overview of Long-term Care," p. 74.

[49]U.S. General Accounting Office, *Medicaid and Nursing Home Care*, p. 17.

[50]Julie Kosterlitz, "The Graying of America Spells Trouble for Long-Term Health Care for Elderly," p. 799.

because many of the Medicaid recipients who cannot find a nursing home that will accept them are hospitalized until they are placed in a nursing home. It has been estimated that at least 1 million, and perhaps as many as 9 million, days of hospital care are paid by Medicaid every year for people waiting to be placed in a nursing home.[51]

Another strategy used to contain nursing home costs is the use of home- or community-based care. Over 50,000 Medicaid recipients are now cared for at home by relatives or community-based organizations. Medicaid reimburses these medical "providers" for their expenses. Advocates of the home-care option argue that many people have needlesslly entered expensive nursing homes because Medicaid would not pay for the few ancillary services needed for the person to live independent of institutionalized care. They argue that this alternative form of health care not only improves the Medicaid recipient's lifestyle but also will, in the long run, save the taxpayers billions of dollars. Critics of this option concede that the program does enhance the lifestyle of Medicaid recipients but doubt that it will save money. On the contrary, they point out that more than 70 percent of those requiring long-term health care are now getting that care outside of nursing homes. They are worried that many of the elderly who are currently being taken care of without public assistance will now request to be placed in a home or community-based care program. According to this view, the home-care option could result in a significant expansion of Medicaid costs.[52]

Hospital Reimbursement

Prior to 1982, states were required to reimburse hospitals for expenses incurred by Medicaid recipients according to the "reasonable costs" method used by the Medicare program. This generally meant that hospitals were paid whatever they charged. At this time the national government did allow states to form hospital rate review commissions and to limit payments to hospitals that habitually charged higher-than-average fees for their services, but these provisions did not have a significant impact on hospital costs.[53]

The national government repealed the "reasonable cost" reimbursement method for hospitals in 1981. Since then, states have been required to reimburse hospitals only to the extent that Medicaid patients continue to

---

[51]U.S. General Accounting Office, *Medicaid and Nursing Home Care*, p. v. Another strategy employed by states to reduce nursing home expenses is to impose nursing home construction and expansion limitations. The idea behind these limits is that an expansion in the number of nursing home beds will lead to an expansion in the number of nursing home residents and, ultimately, to an expansion in the number of Medicaid recipients and costs. See Ibid., pp. 79, 80.

[52]Ibid., p. 800.

[53]Ibid., p. 71.

have "reasonable access to services of adequate quality."[54] This new flexibility has allowed many states, led by New Jersey's example, to adopt one of the several different forms of the hospital "prospective payment" reimbursement system.[55] Under this system, hospitals receive a single fixed payment for each Medicaid patient's hospital admittance. The payment is based on the average cost of treating that particular patient's illness.[56]

Advocates of prospective payment systems argue that they give physicians and hospital administrators an economic incentive to keep hospital stays as short as possible and to perform only essential services. Their critics are concerned that the quality of health care provided Medicaid patients will drop as hospital administrators pressure doctors to keep the hospital stays of Medicaid recipients as short as possible, or when a doctor has to think twice about the cost of ordering additional diagnostic tests for a Medicaid patient. Its advocates counter this argument by claiming that the vast majority of doctors will not "shortchange" Medicaid patients, regardless of the unusual complications of their illness. They contend that both doctors and hospital administrators recognize that the hospital will receive a reasonable return on its expenses in the long run because it will receive more than actual costs for some patients and less for others.[57]

National Cost Containment Efforts

Given the size of the national government's annual and cumulative debt and recent increases in defense expenditures, many domestic spend-

[54]"Medicaid Spending Cut but Cap Rejected," Congressional Quarterly, *Almanac, 1981* (Washington, DC: Congressional Quarterly, 1981), p. 478.

[55]By 1984, 33 states had adopted a variant of the prospective payment reimbursement system for hospitals, and it is expected that many of the remaining states will abandon the retrospective cost-based method of reimbursement by the end of the 1980s. See U.S. Health Care Financing Administration, *Health Care Financing, Program Statistics* (Baltimore: U.S. Department of Health and Human Services, 1985), pp. 112, 116, 117.

[56]There are several different ways to determine the nature of (and, therefore, the reimbursable cost) of a patient's illness under the hospital prospective payment reimbursement system. The most common method is to classify a patient's illness into one of 23 major diagnostic categories and then into one of 467 diagnosis-related groups (DRGs). The DRGs are differentiated according to the presence or absence of certain procedures, the age of the patient, the presence or absence of specific complications, and a host of other medical factors. Other ways of determining the nature of the patient's illness include the diagnosis staging method, where each illness is assigned into one of more than 400 illness' progression, and the severity-of-illness index, which assigns each illness a severity score from 1 to 4 based on an analysis of the patient's medical chart. See Stephen F. Jencks, Allen Dobson, Patricia Willis, and Patrice Hirsh Feinstein, "Evaluating and Improving the Measurement of Hospital Case Mix," *Health Care Financing Review* (1984 Annual Supplement):2, 3; Jonathan E. Conklin, John V. Lieberman, Cathleen A. Barnes, and Daniel Z. Louis, "Disease Staging: Implications for Hospital Reimbursement and Management," Ibid., pp. 13–22; and Susan D. Horn, Roger A. Horn, and Phoebe D. Sharkey, "The Severity of Illness Index as a Severity Adjustment to Diagnosis-Related Groups," Ibid., pp. 33–46.

[57]Thomas W. Grannemann and Mark V. Pauly, *Controlling Medicaid Costs*, pp. 71–77.

ing programs have undergone extensive budgetary scrutiny in recent years. Medicaid, as the most expensive national intergovernmental program, was not immune to this scrutiny during the 1980s. Lacking a strong empathy for nationally financed welfare programs and seeing the need for a reordering of budget priorities, the Reagan administration argued in 1981 that Medicaid's open-ended matching grant feature encouraged states to be excessively generous to Medicaid recipients. To contain costs, the administration recommended that the national government's contribution to Medicaid costs be capped at a 5 percent growth rate beginning in FY 1982. Since medical costs were rising at approximately 15 percent a year, the administration's proposal represented an effective, programmatic cut of approximately 10 percent.[58]

Critics of the administration's cap proposal, led by liberals in Congress, argued that it would place tremendous pressure on all states, particularly the poor ones, to reduce their participation in the program. Inflation, they argued, forces states to continually increase expenditures just to maintain current service levels. Poor states, having fewer resources than other states, are particularly hard-pressed to keep up with these rising costs. Under an open-ended matching grant arrangement in which poor states receive a relatively large subsidy for every dollar expended, poor states find it relatively easy to keep up with rising costs. Mississippi, for example, received the maximum subsidy (78 percent) in 1980. This meant that it cost Mississippi only 22 additional cents instead of a full dollar to increase its Medicaid expenditures to keep up with inflation in 1980. In economic terms, the cap proposal would have raised Mississippi's marginal price for Medicaid by over 450 percent (increasing the cost of keeping up with inflation from 22 cents to 100 cents per additional Medicaid dollar).

The administration's critics also argued that the large differences in the number of optional medical services offered by the wealthy and the poor states would be "locked in," as the cost to the poor states of adding the optional services already provided by the wealthy states would be increased tremendously. Moreover, a cap would place an unfair burden on states (such as Arizona and Florida) that have a rapidly growing elderly population. These states would now have to pay for all of the costs associated with SSI enrollment growth, a growth mandated by national policymakers.[59]

Recognizing that a national spending cap would force them to make politically unpopular decisions concerning eligibility standards and medical coverage, almost all of the states' governors opposed the administration's proposal. They lobbied members of the House Commerce and Senate Finance committees (which have jurisdiction over Medicaid) and used their

[58]"Medicaid Spending Cut but Cap Rejected," p. 478.

[59]Thomas W. Grannemann and Mark V. Pauly, *Controlling Medicaid Costs: Federalism, Competition and Choice*, pp. 47, 48.

national organization, the National Governors' Association, as a forum to denounce the proposal.[60]

The governors were able to convince Congress to defeat the administration's cap, but Congress nevertheless took steps to reduce the growth of Medicaid expenses. In the Omnibus Budget Reconciliation Act of 1981, Congress reduced the national government's projected Medicaid costs by approximately $3 billion in FYs 1982–1984.[61] The national government still provided states with an open-ended matching grant inversely related to each state's per capita income. But after the national government's grant to each state was determined, the grant was reduced by a set percentage. In 1982, the national government's contribution to each state was cut by 3 percent; in 1983, by 4 percent; and in 1984, by 4.5 percent. Thus, Medicaid expenses incurred by poor states were still subsidized to a greater extent than expenses incurred by wealthy states. Poor states, therefore, were still encouraged to increase their Medicaid expenditures to keep pace with inflation. However, since the percentage reductions were applied in an across-the-board fashion and poor states were initially provided a larger subsidy than wealthy states, poor states realized a disproportionate reduction in their benefits. As a result, their capacity to respond to inflation's impact on the cost of maintaining program services at existing levels was weakened, but not to the extent threatened by a spending cap.[62]

The 4.5 percent reduction in each state's Medicaid reimbursement payment expired at the end of 1984. In its continuing effort to control Medicaid costs, the Reagan administration proposed in 1986 that the national government's contribution to Medicaid be cut by approximately $2.5 billion in FY 1987 (to $21.7 billion). It also renewed its plea for a spending cap. Instead of asking for an annual cap of 5 percent, as it had in 1981, the administration sought to limit Medicaid increases (starting in FY 1987) to the general rate of inflation for health care as measured by the Consumer Price Index.[63] The administration had estimated that this change would save an additional $6.5 billion over three years.[64] Once again, the states' governors and social welfare advocates rallied in opposition to the concept of a spending cap; Congress rejected the cap and the proposed funding cut, leaving the open-ended matching grant feature in place.

[60]Randall R. Bovbjerg and John Holahan, *Medicaid in the Reagan Era: Federal Policy and State Choices*, pp. 8, 9.

[61]Elizabeth Wehr and Janet Hook, "Reagan Again Seeks to Curb Medicare, Medicaid Growth," Congressional Quarterly, *Weekly Report* (February 9, 1985):243–244.

[62]Thomas W. Grannemann and Mark V. Pauly, *Controlling Medicaid Costs*, p. 48.

[63]Elizabeth Wehr and Janet Hook, "Reagan Again Seeks to Curb Medicare, Medicaid Growth," Congressional Quarterly, *Weekly Report* (February 9, 1985):243, 244.

[64]Julie Kosterlitz, "Reagan's Health Rx," *National Journal* (February 8, 1986):324.

CONTROVERSY #3: WHY NOT INCLUDE ALL
OF THE POOR?

The third major controversy involving Medicaid is its eligibility criteria. Approximately 12 million people with incomes below the national government's poverty level currently do not qualify for Medicaid benefits.[65] Many analysts, policymakers, and concerned citizens believe that all poor people should have Medicaid coverage. They are particularly concerned about the exclusion of some poor from the program because many individuals with incomes above the poverty line do receive Medicaid benefits (including the medically needy), and the percentage of people with incomes that fall beneath the poverty line who do receive Medicaid benefits has been falling in recent years. According to the Robert Wood Johnson Foundation, approximately 65 percent of those below the poverty line received Medicaid benefits in 1976. By 1985 that figure had fallen to 52 percent.[66] In their study of this issue, the National Governors' Association estimated that the proportion of the poor covered by Medicaid dropped from 63 percent in 1975 to less than 50 percent in 1985.[67]

This coverage gap consists primarily of poor individuals and families who do not qualify for AFDC or SSI assistance. This includes the poor who are able-bodied individuals between ages 21 and 64, childless couples, and children in two-parent families. In addition, because many states have income qualification limits for AFDC that are below the national government's official poverty level, many poor families who would qualify for Medicaid if they lived in a more generous state are denied coverage.

Extending coverage to the ineligible poor would require substantial increases in governmental expenditures. Using the National Governors' Association's estimate concerning the number of ineligible poor, the cost of Medicaid could double if they were all brought into the program. Given the fiscal difficulties facing both the national and many state governments, such expenditures are politically unthinkable.

Another way of examining the Medicaid coverage gap is to ask why the national government has decided to require states to enroll certain categories of the poor while excluding others. The answer appears to be that national policymakers have decided that those who qualify for AFDC and SSI assistance are more deserving of medical assistance than those who

[65]Janet Hook, "Congress Shies Away from Any Cap on Medicaid Outlays," p. 891; and Congressional Budget Office, *Medicaid: Choices for 1982 and Beyond* (Washington, DC: U.S. Government Printing Office, 1981), p. xii.

[66]Jack A. Meyer, testimony, U.S. Senate Subcommittee on Health, Committee on Finance, *Medicaid Freedom of Choice Waiver Activities*, pp. 4, 24.

[67]Janet Hook, "Congress Shies Away from Any Cap on Medicaid Outlays," pp. 893, 894.

do not qualify.[68] In other words, able-bodied individuals between the ages of 21 and 64 who do not have dependent children and families with two able-bodied parents present do not deserve free medical care. Presumably, exclusion of these people is justified on the grounds that they ought to suffer the consequences of their laziness. Moreover, governmental assistance to such people could encourage them to avoid work and accept a lifelong dependence on governmental handouts.

There are many national and state policymakers who do not agree with the logic of the preceding argument. They point out that there are many ineligible poor who work, or at least have made honest efforts to get work, yet are still denied Medicaid benefits because they do not meet the eligibility standards for AFDC or SSI. Moreover, there are many people who do qualify for AFDC who could work but have decided to remain on the public dole. Nevertheless, they concede that while the present Medicaid eligibility categories are less than perfect, the categories do reflect an honest effort, in a difficult fiscal setting, to focus benefits on individuals and families with the greatest demonstrable need.

CONCLUSIONS

Medicaid will continue to be a central concern of intergovernmental scholars, lobbyists, and policymakers for years to come. Given the number of people currently served by Medicaid; population demographics that suggest that its enrollments will continue to grow; the increased number of enrollments that will result from the recent enactment of an immigration bill that grants amnesty to many of the estimated 6 million illegal aliens residing in the United States; and the generally expensive nature of medical care, it will also continue to be the national government's most expensive intergovernmental program.

The continued financial difficulties of the national government and of many state governments suggest that cost containment will continue to dominate the political and academic debate over Medicaid's future. It seems clear that additional cost savings from physician, hospital, and nursing home reimbursement rates will not produce enough revenue to allow national, state, and local policymakers to continue to avoid making politically difficult decisions concerning Medicaid's eligibility criteria and medical services coverage. It is very likely that many states will be forced to reduce costs by dropping the eligibility of the categorically needy and/or the medically needy. Moreover, many states will be forced to reduce the number of optional medical services they currently offer their Medicaid recipients. It is important to recognize that the likelihood of these actions'

[68]Thomas W. Grannemann and Mark V. Pauly, *Controlling Medicaid Costs*, p. 21.

taking place does not change significantly according to which political party is in power in Washington.

While it is true that liberals are generally more reluctant to cut Medicaid's funding levels than are conservatives, the size of the national government's deficit and the perceived necessity of maintaining growth of national defense expenditures will force both conservatives and liberals in Congress to seek cost savings in all domestic programs. Since Medicaid is one of the most expensive nationally financed domestic programs, it is a natural target for budget cutters at the national level. In addition, it is unlikely that state and local taxpayers' resistance to higher taxes will abate significantly in the 1990s, or that state and local fiscal stress will evaporate overnight. As a result, state policymakers also will find Medicaid a tempting target for savings.

Another set of cost-saving strategies that may be pushed by liberals during the 1990s is the imposition of nationally enforced controls on the prices charged by health care providers. They also may ask for additional national intergovernmental funding for the construction of medical schools and the subsidization of medical students' educational expenses. The idea would be to increase the supply of physicians, which would promote greater competition in the medical care industry. Given the economic theory of supply and demand, this would moderate anticipated increases in future medical care costs.[69] Conversely, conservatives are likely to stress the role of private insurance to cope with the rising cost of medical and nursing home care.[70]

The debate over which of these cost-saving strategies is the best will be decided largely by determinations of their relative adverse impacts on the health care of the poor. This debate will, without a doubt, become a prime political issue in Washington and in the 50 state capitals throughout the 1990s.

On a related issue, the Reagan administration's attempt in 1982 to nationalize Medicaid and to turn the AFDC and Food Stamp programs over to the states raises a fundamental question about the national government's use of intergovernmental programs to influence the direction of domestic policy in the United States. Traditionally, nationally financed intergovernmental programs were justified according to one or more of the seven arguments presented in this book's introduction (superior fiscal resources, the pursuit of generally accepted national goals, subsidizing programs with significant spillover benefits, and so on).

The 1982 swap proposal was the first instance in which the admin-

---

[69]In 1986 there were 5,800 private hospitals and 520,000 physicians in the United States. See John K. Iglehart, "In a Land of Medical Plenty, More and More Are Going Hungry," *Washington Post*, National Weekly Edition, January 12, 1987, p. 23.

[70]Approximately 37 million Americans did not have health care insurance in 1986. See Ibid.

istration applied its macroeconomic theory of intergovernmental relations in a wholesale fashion. Even President Nixon, considered one of the most conservative presidents in the twentieth century, agreed that programs that transfer money or in-kind benefits should not be turned over to the states or localities, because their varying fiscal capacities and political wills concerning aid to the poor and disadvantaged would result in widely divergent treatment of the poor from state to state and from locality to locality. Yet the Reagan administration was convinced that turning over AFDC and Food Stamps to the states would improve the condition of the poor. Although his swap proposal was rejected by Congress, the logic underlying the proposal (the national government's fiscal resources are not necessarily stronger than the states' and localities' fiscal resources; state and local administrators are better than national administrators in identifying and correcting domestic problems; and the national government is best able to promote good domestic public policies by focusing its attention on improving the macroeconomic condition of the national economy) will be seen time and time again in the Reagan administration's proposals concerning the rest of the intergovernmental programs examined in this book.

CHAPTER 3

Aid to Families with Dependent Children

Created by the Social Security Act of 1935, Aid to Families with Dependent Children (AFDC) is one of the most talked-about and criticized national intergovernmental programs. Designed to provide children with a guaranteed source of income in the event of the death, absence, or physical or mental incapacitation of one or both parents, AFDC is the program most people have in mind when they speak of "welfare."[1] It is an open-ended reimbursement categorical grant program that provides states with matching grants to provide income to the very poor. Administered by state and local welfare agencies, it is currently the national government's fourth most expensive intergovernmental program. Total national and state AFDC expenditures currently exceed $19 billion annually. The national government provides approximately 56 percent of that amount ($10.7 billion).[2] The total number of AFDC recipients has remained fairly stable at about 11 million since 1975 (see Table 3.1).[3]

To encourage states to participate in the AFDC program, the national government reimburses them 75 percent of their administrative expenses plus at least half of all benefit payments made to individuals enrolled in the program (see Table 3.1 for average monthly payment rates per recipient). The exact reimbursement rate for benefit payments is tied to the state's fiscal ability to pay for those benefits. Although states are given a choice between two reimbursement mechanisms, all of them have chosen to receive the same percentage of total payments that they get from Medicaid

[1]Clarke E. Cochran, Lawrence C. Mayer, T. R. Carr, and N. Joseph Cayer, *American Public Policy: An Introduction* (New York: St. Martin's Press, 1982), p. 210.

[2]U.S. Office of Management and Budget, *Budget of the United States Government, FY 1988, Supplement* (Washington, D.C.: U.S. Government Printing Office, 1987), p. 5-123.

[3]Approximately 70 percent of AFDC recipients are children. See U.S. Department of Health and Human Services, *Social Security Bulletin* 49:5 (May 1986):56. Approximately 43 percent of AFDC recipients are black, 42 percent white, 14 percent Hispanic, and 1 percent other. Fathers are present in only 9 percent of AFDC homes. See Sar A. Levitan, *Programs in Aid of the Poor*, 5th ed. (Baltimore: Johns Hopkins University Press, 1985), p. 38.

TABLE 3.1   **Number of AFDC Recipients and Their Average Monthly Payments, Selected FYs, 1936—1990**

YEAR	RECIPIENTS	AVERAGE MONTHLY PAYMENT*
1990 (est.)	11,095,000	-------
1985	10,855,000	$116.65
1980	10,774,000	96.49
1975	11,346,000	67.65
1970	8,466,000	47.77
1965	4,329,000	31.96
1960	3,005,000	27.75
1955	2,214,000	23.26
1950	2,205,000	17.64
1945	907,000	13.75
1940	1,182,000	9.43
1936	534,000	7.75

*Per recipient.

Source: U.S. Office of Management and Budget, *Special Analyses: Budget of the United States Government, FY 1988* (Washington, DC: U.S. Government Printing Office, 1987), p. A-11; U.S. Department of Health and Human Services, *Social Security Bulletin, Annual Statistical Supplement, 1987* (Washington, DC: U.S. Government Printing Office, 1987), p. 294.

(one of the two reimbursement choices) because it provides a higher reimbursement rate (see Table 2.1 for the rates).[4]

The national government also gives states considerable flexibility in determining AFDC's eligibility criteria and monthly benefit payment rates.[5] Given the diversity of views among the states on welfare policy, eligibility standards and benefit payment rates vary significantly from state to state. Liberals oppose this variation, claiming that the national government has the responsibility to ensure that the poor are treated equally no matter where they live. Conservatives disagree. They argue that variation in welfare eligibility standards and benefit levels is a natural and healthy byproduct of American federalism.

In a bizarre way, AFDC has emerged as one of the great unifying issues in American politics. Nearly everyone thinks that it does not accomplish its objective of helping the poor escape poverty, and wants to change it. The problem is that people want to change it for different reasons and in different ways. As Lester Salamon has written, "Recipients complain about benefit adequacy, taxpayers about excessive costs, state officials about cum-

[4]U.S. Department of Health and Human Services, *Social Security Bulletin* 50:4 (April 1987):58.

[5]"Public Assistance: Major changes, 1935–64," in *Congress and the Nation, 1945–1964* (Washington, DC: Congressional Quarterly Service, 1965), p. 1273.

bersome red tape in Washington, federal administrators about non-compliance by the states, policy analysts about inequities, and congressmen about work disincentives."[6] Since many of these concerns are in conflict, consensus on the need to reform AFDC has not led to a consensus on how to reform it.[7]

This chapter provides a brief outline of the history of the national government's role in providing direct, public assistance to the poor. It then examines several major controversies involving AFDC's intergovernmental structure, eligibility criteria, benefit levels, and impact on the poor. In the past, the debate over these controversies generally found liberals on one side of the issue and conservatives on the other. In recent years, however, this liberal/conservative dichotomy has blurred as the solutions to poverty have proved elusive and increasingly complex. The chapter concludes with an examination of recent proposals offered by both liberals and conservatives to cure the "welfare mess" and the political obstacles that continue to stand in the way of efforts to achieve significant change in the AFDC program.

GOVERNMENT AND THE POOR: THE ENGLISH TRADITION

America's welfare policies developed out of the English tradition. England's Poor Law of 1601 established four welfare principles that influenced both the structure and scope of our contemporary welfare programs. First, it created a decentralized structure to deal with the poor. Localities were responsible for financing the program and administering it. Second, localities were allowed to establish their own residency requirements. This was designed to minimize welfare costs. Third, of the three categories of the poor to be provided public assistance—children, the able-bodied, and the mentally or physically incapacitated—children and the able-bodied were to be provided employment or were expected to find employment as a condition of assistance. Fourth, a distinction was made between the deserving and the undeserving poor, the latter being denied assistance. The subjective determination of who was deserving of assistance and who was not was left to the localities.[8]

Each of these English principles was incorporated into American welfare policies during the 1800s and early 1900s. Aid to the poor was considered the responsibility of the church, private charities, and, as a last resort, local governments. To save money, most American towns and cities estab-

[6]Lester M. Salamon, *Welfare: The Elusive Consensus* (New York: Praeger Publishers, 1978), p. 4.

[7]Ibid.

[8]U.S. Advisory Commission on Intergovernmental Relations, *Public Assistance: The Growth of a Federal Function*, (Washington, DC: U.S. Government Printing Office, 1980), p. 6.

lished long residency requirements to qualify for public assistance and based that assistance on the English concept of indoor relief.[9] Although poorhouses were never as widespread in the United States as they were in Great Britain, most towns and cities in the United States provided the poor with free room and board either in the home of a private citizen or in a public almshouse. They generally offered public assistance only to individuals who were considered deserving of assistance, primarily those who were unable to care for themselves, such as widows, orphans, and the mentally or physically handicapped.[10] The distinction between the deserving and undeserving poor reflected the assumption that public assistance undermined the moral character of people by discouraging work and saving. Thus, it was necessary to devise a welfare system that met both the demands of compassion for those who could not help themselves and the sterner demands of a public morality that was based on hard work and thrift.[11]

GOVERNMENT'S ROLE IN ASSISTING THE POOR: 1800 TO THE NEW DEAL

During the 1800s, state governments' role in providing assistance to the poor remained very limited. By midcentury most states were reimbursing cities and towns for the care of drifters who failed to meet local residency requirements for assistance if they were judged by local authorities to be indigent or a threat to society. Some states were also providing public assistance for the deaf, blind, mentally ill, and abandoned or orphaned children. But for the most part, church and private charities continued to play the lead role in helping the poor. The national government continued its hands-off approach to welfare. In 1854, a bill to provide land grants to the states for the founding of mental hospitals was vetoed by President Franklin Pierce on the grounds that it violated states' rights.[12]

It was not until 1907 that any state offered cash assistance to individuals who were not confined to the home of a private citizen or the public poorhouse. Wisconsin offered this "outdoor" aid to the blind. In 1911 Illinois and Missouri adopted the first state programs that offered outdoor aid to poor mothers. By 1919, 39 states had adopted programs to assist poor mothers who were not confined to the poorhouse. In 1923 Montana and Nevada became the first states to offer outdoor public assistance to the aged. By 1934, one year before the creation of the national government's

---

[9]Christopher K. Leman, *The Collapse of Welfare Reform: Political Institutions, Policy, and the Poor in Canada and the United States* (Cambridge, MA: MIT Press, 1980), p. 24.

[10]Ibid.

[11]Charles Murray, *Losing Ground* (New York: Basic Books, 1984), pp. 16, 17.

[12]Ibid., p. 237.

AFDC program, 24 states offered outdoor aid to the blind, 28 states offered outdoor aid to the aged, and 42 states offered outdoor aid to mothers. Despite this, localities, churches, and private charities continued to provide the lion's share of the cost of assisting the poor. Most of the state programs were poorly financed. During the 1920s less than half of the states with outdoor welfare programs appropriated any money for them and few directly supervised local administrating units. Moreover, localities continued to determine residency requirements, to require able-bodied adults and children to work, and to determine who deserved and who did not deserve aid.[13]

The stock market crash of 1929 and the economic depression that followed led to a fundamental change in public attitudes concerning the poor and the government's role in caring for them. Prior to the crash, most Americans divided the poor into two categories: a relatively small group who were poor due to reasons beyond their control, such as orphans, widows, and the mentally or physically incapacitated, and a larger group who were poor because of laziness. Most Americans believed that the first group deserved to receive assistance. They also believed that local welfare policies, combined with private and church charities, were equipped to handle that group's needs. The poor in the latter category were generally viewed with contempt. Most Americans felt that the poor in this group either should be confined to the poorhouse or should not be given any public assistance.

AFDC: NECESSITY IS THE MOTHER OF INVENTION

In 1933, 15 million able-bodied individuals, nearly one-third of the work force, could not find a job. Suddenly the traditional stereotype of most of the poor as lazy bums was shattered. The poorhouses were overflowing with men and women who wanted to work. The belief in the adequacy of local welfare policies and charities to care for the poor also was shattered. The states were the next logical level of government to handle the crisis, but as businesses closed and individuals reduced their consumption of private goods, state and local government revenue from business taxes and sales taxes fell. Most of the states lacked the fiscal capacity to provide help for all of the poor. Many of the states also were saddled with the responsibility of paying off relatively large debts that they had accumulated during the 1920s. That left only one level of government to turn to for help: the national government.[14]

When the Great Depression began, President Hoover and most of the

[13]U.S. Advisory Commission on Intergovernmental Relations, *Public Assistance: The Growth of a Federal Function*, pp. 6–8.
[14]Ibid., pp. 8, 9, 18–20.

states' governors strongly opposed the national government's direct involvement in public relief efforts. They believed that public relief was a state and local government responsibility protected by the Tenth Amendment to the Constitution. Despite the soaring unemployment rate, it was not until 1933, when the newly elected Democratic Congress and President Franklin D. Roosevelt took office, that the national government adopted legislation to provide significant amounts of public assistance to the poor. With the strong backing of the newly formed United States Conference of Mayors, whose urban constituencies were hit hardest by the Dpression, the Democrat-controlled Congress created the Federal Emergency Relief Administration. It provided emergency public assistance to able-bodied, employable individuals. Public assistance for individuals who were considered to be unemployable, such as widows, orphans, and the mentally and physically handicapped, remained the sole responsibility of private charities, churches, and state and local governments.[15]

As the Great Depression dragged on, the U.S. Conference of Mayors continued to call upon the national government to provide needed emergency relief to the nation's cities. It was particularly supportive of the national government's policy of providing assistance directly to the cities, bypassing state governments, which had, in general, exhibited a historical tendency to divert governmental assistance to rural areas.[16] The National Governors Conference, on the other hand, remained largely hostile to the national government, urging it to sever direct national-city links and to show restraint in infringing upon traditional state responsibilities.[17]

Recognizing the governors' concerns about states' rights and the public's uneasiness about big government in general, President Roosevelt indicated that once the Great Depression ended, the national government's role in public assistance ought to be limited to insuring individuals against the economic risks of old age and unemployment brought about by economic forces that were largely beyond the control of the affected individual. In other words, the traditional purpose of public assistance would remain the same: to help those who could not help themselves. Nothing in the New Deal provided assistance to people just because they were poor or hampered by social disadvantages.[18] The Social Security Act of 1935 was adopted to achieve these limited objectives.

AFDC was one of five income maintenance programs created by the

---

[15]Christopher K. Leman, *The Collapse of Welfare Reform*, p. 27.

[16]Much of this bias can be attributed to the disproportionate number of legislative seats apportioned to rural areas in most state houses of representatives and senates prior to the "one man, one vote" decisions by the U.S. Supreme Court in *Baker* v. *Carr* (1962) and *Reynolds* v. *Sims* (1964).

[17]Donald H. Haider, *When Governments Come to Washington* (New York: The Free Press, 1974), pp. 1–3, 20–22.

[18]Charles Murray, *Losing Ground*, p. 17.

Social Security Act of 1935. The Old-Age Insurance program, funded by business and personal payroll taxes, was designed to provide income to individuals after their forced retirement due to being considered too old to work. Unemployment Insurance, funded by a payroll tax, was to provide individuals with temporary income following a recession-induced layoff from work. Aid to the Blind, originally set up as an intergovernmental grant funded in part by the national government, provided income to blind adults who were unable to find work because of their physical handicap. The Old-Age Assistance program, also originally set up as an intergovernmental program funded in part by the national government, provided income to the indigent old who were unable to find work because of their age.[19] Aid to Dependent Children (changed to Aid to Families with Dependent Children in 1950, when mothers of eligible children were also provided assistance) was an intergovernmental program designed to provide mothers with income to support their children following the death, incapacity, or absence of the husband.[20] The national government paid one-third of the program's cost.

These five programs marked a significant development in the national government's role in both welfare policy and intergovernmental relations. Providing against the economic hardships of old age, unemployment, and abandonment was no longer considered the sole responsibility of the individual affected, his or her immediate family, or of private and church charities. However, the prevailing belief in states' rights and the perceived need for a balanced national budget, coupled with the relative political impotence of the poor, limited the national government's responsibility for public assistance to a select category of the poor for more than a quarter of a century. The ADC program, for example, prohibited assistance to poor families with two able-bodied parents until 1962, and even then that was made an optional feature of the program. In addition, the basic aim of these five programs was not to eradicate poverty but to prevent government dependency by providing temporary assistance for those who were down on their luck. ADC recipients were expected to grow up, enter the labor force, and become self-sufficient.[21] Moreover, the main governmental responsibility for welfare continued to rest with the states and localities.[22]

[19]Aid to the Blind and Old Age Assistance were merged in 1973 with the Aid to the Permanently and Totally Disabled program (created in 1950). This new program, called Supplemental Security Income, was, and still is, financed and administered by the national government. See "Welfare Legislation," in *Congress and the Nation, 1969–1972* (Washington, DC: Congressional Quarterly Service, 1973), p. 606.

[20]"Public Assistance: Major Changes, 1935–64," in *Congress and the Nation, 1945–1964*, p. 1273–1279.

[21]Charles V. Hamilton, "Social Policy and the Welfare of Black Americans: From Rights to Resources, " *Political Science Quarterly* 101:2 (1986):250–253.

[22]Christopher K. Leman, *The Collapse of Welfare Reform*, pp. 29, 30.

A NEW PURPOSE: THE LIBERAL ARGUMENT

AFDC initially enjoyed widespread public support. The idea of providing temporary assistance for widowed or abandoned mothers with dependent children fit the tradition of helping those who could not help themselves. It was expected that these women would be on welfare only until their children were old enough to work or until they remarried. But by the late 1950s public support for the program began to weaken as it became clear that many of the mothers receiving AFDC benefits were neither widows nor abandoned. Worst of all, these single women did not stop having illegitimate children after they started receiving benefits. In the public's eyes, the worst offenders seemed to be black women. Thus, the typical AFDC recipient was stereotyped as a single black woman with four or five children, all born out of wedlock, who had little, if any, intention of ever trying to get off of the public dole.[23]

Just as the public's support for AFDC began to decline, poverty suddenly became a hot political topic. In 1960 Edward R. Murrow's broadcast on "CBS Reports," titled "Harvest of Shame," revealed that tens of thousands of migrant workers were miserably paid, housed, and nourished. The American middle class was shocked that such conditions could exist in "the richest nation in the world." Newspapers and magazines began to feature stories on the poor, especially in Appalachia. In 1962 Michael Harrington's book, *The Other America*, argued that poverty is a widespread and largely ignored problem. He suggested that as many as 50 million Americans were living in poverty and that existing welfare programs, such as AFDC, did little to help the poor because they were based on the incorrect notion that it was relatively easy for any able-bodied individual to find work and to escape poverty. Harrington argued that for the most part, poverty was not caused by individual laziness but by the way the economic system distributed wealth in society. For Harrington and other liberals, the only way to combat poverty was to completely restructure the welfare system so that all of the poor were provided enough money to live on and were supplied with the necessary skills to compete in the economic marketplace.[24]

In general, liberals began to argue that most of the poor held the same values and attitudes as everyone else in America. They loved their children, wanted them to get the best possible education, to get a fulfilling

---

[23]Charles Murray, *Losing Ground*, pp. 18, 19. There is no statistical evidence to suggest that AFDC encourages poor single women to have children. See David T. Ellwood and Lawrence H. Summers, "Is welfare really the problem?" *The Public Interest* 83 (Spring 1986):68–73. For a counterargument see Charles Murray, "No, Welfare Isn't really the Problem," *The Public Interest* 84 (Summer 1986):3–11.

[24]Charles Murray, *Losing Ground*, pp. 26–29.

and well-paying job, to buy a home, and to lead a decent, moral life. Unfortunately, most of the poor lacked the opportunity to live the American dream because they were badly educated, did not get decent job training, were discriminated against because of their skin color or sex, and were raised in an environment where crime and drugs produced much larger economic returns than the minimum-wage jobs available to them.

The cure for poverty, therefore, was to provide the poor with the opportunity to act like middle-class Americans. They should be provided enough money to stay away from drugs, prostitution, and other forms of criminal behavior to earn a living. They should then be provided the best possible education and job training to give them an opportunity to compete for jobs that hold the potential for advancement and high income. They should also be protected by laws barring discrimination and punishing criminals and drug dealers. Since the states lacked the fiscal resources to provide the funds to educate and train the poor, the national government must step in and provide the poor with these opportunities.[25]

Liberals also argued that the national government's role in providing public assistance was justified because welfare has significant economic spillover effects that effectively prevent states from providing the poor with equitable levels of public assistance. States that offer relatively high welfare benefits must impose relatively high state taxes on individual taxpayers and on the business sector to pay for those benefits. Thus, any state that wants to provide its poor with relatively high welfare benefits is placed in a noncompetitive position with other states in its ability to attract and keep business investment. The only remedy for this situation is for the national government to help states and localities to finance their public assistance programs.

Moreover, welfare expenses are directly related to the health of the national economy. Since the economic factors that determine the health of the national economy are largely beyond the control of states and localities, the national government should pay for welfare benefits. Finally, liberals also cited the Constitution's general welfare clause as justification for the national government's role in combating poverty.[26]

[25]Clarke E. Cochran, T. R. Carr, Lawrence C. Mayer, and N. Joseph Cayer, *American Public Policy: An Introduction*, p. 204.

[26]Richard Nathan, *The Administrative Presidency* (New York: John Wiley and Sons, 1983), pp. 19–27; Richard Nathan, Robert R. Carlson, and Paul H. O'Neill, "Welfare Reform: Federalism or Federalization," *Common Sense* (Winter 1980): 1–30; President's Commission for a National Agenda for the Eighties, *A National Agenda for the Eighties* (Washington DC: U.S. Government Printing Office, 1980); U.S. Advisory Commission on Intergovernmental Relations staff, "Further Report on Illustrative Functional Trade-offs," in *ACIR Docket Book*, 73rd Meeting (Washington DC: U.S. Government Printing Office, 1981); and U.S. Advisory Commission on Intergovernmental Relations, *Public Assistance: The Growth of a Federal Function*, pp. 23–72.

THE CONSERVATIVE ARGUMENT

Conservatives generally disagreed with Harrington and the liberals' assessment of poverty's cause and solution. They worried about launching expensive social welfare programs that were designed to redistribute wealth from the rich to the poor. Specifically, they knew that higher domestic expenditures would lead to higher national taxes. They were convinced that these higher taxes would reduce the rich and the middle class's incentives to work and to invest. This, in turn, would lead to weakened economy and fewer jobs for the poor. Instead of spending more on government programs, conservatives generally believed that the government should provide tax incentives to businesses so that the economy would expand, thereby opening up more economic opportunities for the poor.

Many conservatives also held a different view of poverty's cause. They were convinced that many of the poor lacked middle-class values. Instead of working hard, demanding the best from themselves and others, and forsaking immediate pleasures for a better future, many of the poor purposively avoided work, competition, and self-sacrifice. They looked to the government for a handout or a safe, civil-service-protected government job. Some conservatives also speak of a culture of poverty that consists of a life of casual social relationships, irresponsibility, immediate gratification, and sexual license. They are convinced that there are lots of opportunities for those who are able-bodied and willing to work hard, save, and invest their earnings. In their view, people who do not take advantage of the many economic opportunities in our society do not deserve governmental assistance. Thus, the national government does not need to provide all the government-sponsored programs that the liberals talk about.[27] Moreover, some of the poor exhibit such different and hostile behavioral patterns that programs designed to enable them to better themselves are destined to fail.[28]

Most conservatives agreed with liberals that there were millions of people who deserved public assistance. In their view, the deserving poor included those who are unable to care for themselves because of their age, health, or mental and physical incapacities. However, they believed that these people could be adequately taken care of by state and local governments, churches, and private charities.

CONTROVERSY #1: AFDC'S INTERGOVERNMENTAL STRUCTURE

In the best of all possible worlds, neither liberals nor conservatives would have structured AFDC as an intergovernmental program. Citing welfare's economic spillover effects, the uneven fiscal capacities of state and local

[27]Clarke E. Cochran et al., *American Public Policy: An Introduction*, p. 203.
[28]Ken Auletta, "Dependency and Dignity," *New Republic* (7 February 1983): 33, 34.

governments and the necessity of providing every American with a minimum income regardless of his or her place of residence, liberals would have the national government financing the program, setting its eligibility standards and benefit payments, and administering it.

Representatives of state and local governments also would like to see AFDC nationalized, but not necessarily for the same reasons. Whether liberal or conservative, Democrat or Republican, state and local officials recognize that the burden of financing social services for the poor will ultimately fall on their shoulders if the national government withdraws its assistance for the poor. The more help the national government is willing to provide, the easier it is for these officials to continue to offer social services to the poor without having to ask for politically unpopular state and local tax increases. Thus, the National Governors' Association the National Conference of State Legislators, the U.S. Conference of Mayors, the National League of Cities, and the U.S. Advisory Commission on Intergovernmental Relations have all adopted resolutions calling for the nationalization of AFDC.[29]

Many conservatives disagree. They cite the principles of federalism, the inherent right of citizens to determine their communities' taxing and spending policies, the national government's fiscal difficulties, and AFDC's negative impact on the incentive to work as reasons to leave all public welfare decisions to state and local governments and private charities.

AFDC's intergovernmental structure was the result of political compromise. Liberals knew as they drafted its legislation in 1935 that they could not muster enough votes in Congress to create a nationally financed and administered welfare program. Conservatives knew that they could not stop the huge Democratic majorities that entered Congress following the congressional elections of 1932 from establishing a national role in welfare policy. The two sides compromised by giving AFDC an intergovernmental structure. Thus, liberals got the national government involved in the financing of welfare and in the setting of eligibility standards, and conservatives were able to give the states the right to refuse to participate in the program, considerable flexibility concerning AFDC's eligibility standards and benefit levels, and the right to administer the program.

Since the 1930s liberals have repeatedly tried to nationalize AFDC and conservatives have opposed them. The most recent attempt to change AFDC's intergovernmental structure was President Reagan's 1982 New Federalism swap proposal. He asked Congress to nationalize Medicaid and

[29]Richard S. Williamson, "The 1982 New Federalism Negotiations," *Publius: The Journal of Federalism* 13 (Spring 1983):15; U.S. Advisory Commission on Intergovernmental Relations, *Hearings on the Federal Role* (Washington DC: U.S. Government Printing Office, 1980), p. 53; and Albert J. Davis and S. Kenneth Howard, "Perspectives on a New Day for Federalism," *Intergovernmental Perspective* 8:2 (Spring 1982):11, 12.

to turn AFDC and Food Stamps over to the states (see Chapter 2).[30] Although neither side has succeeded in changing AFDC's intergovernmental structure, they have made a number of changes over the years in AFDC's eligibility requirements and in its provisions that influence the states' decisions concerning recipients' monthly benefits. As the next two sections indicate, liberals were able to expand eligibility standards and monthly benefits incrementally during the 1935–1980 period, and conservatives have been able to restrict them during the 1980s.

CONTROVERSY #2: WHO DESERVES HELP?

The Social Security Act of 1935 contained many provisions that restricted ADC enrollments and program costs. First, the law specifically indicated that only a needy child under the age of 16 who had been deprived of the support of a parent by death, incapacity, or absence could receive ADC benefits. If both parents were present in the home and at least one of them was able-bodied, the child was ineligible regardless of that family's financial status. Second, only children were eligible. The parent of the needy child was ineligible for public assistance even if he or she had no other source of income and was unable to work because of the lack of available child care. Third, states were allowed to determine the level of income and assets that determined who was poor enough to qualify for the program.[31]

Liberals have complained ever since ADC/AFDC was created that it does not cover enough of the poor. In 1939 they were able to pass legislation that extended coverage to needy children under the age of 18, and in 1950 to the eligible child's parent or guardian. Citing the worries of administrators that fathers were abandoning their families to allow them to get AFDC benefits, liberals tried unsuccessfully for years to enact legislation that would require states to offer AFDC benefits to poor families with unemployed fathers present in the household. Conservatives objected to this on the grounds that it violated the principles of federalism, was counter to the idea of assisting only the deserving poor, and would cost too much. In 1962, compromise legislation was enacted that created the optional unemployed parent program (AFDC-UP).[32] The optional nature of the AFDC-UP program appeased conservatives' concerns about the national government infringing upon states' rights. It was also viewed by

[30]See Timothy J. Conlan and David B. Walker, "Reagan's New Federalism," in *American Intergovernmental Relations Today: Perspectives and Controversies,* ed. Robert Jay Dilger (Englewood Cliffs, NJ: Prentice-Hall, Inc., 1986), pp. 189–200.

[31]"Public Assistance: Major Changes, 1935–64," in *Congress and the Nation, 1945–1964,* p. 1277.

[32]Despite the widespread belief that AFDC contributes to the breakup of poor families, there is no conclusive statistical evidence to prove the point. See David T. Ellwood and Lawrence H. Summers, "Is welfare Really the Problem?" pp. 67–70.

both liberals and conservatives as a relatively inexpensive means to provide additional fiscal relief to states that considered these families to be worthy of assistance.[33]

Liberals rejoiced in 1985 when legislation passed that would have made the optional AFDC-UP program compulsory starting in 1988. Their jubilation was short-lived, as the provision was deleted in 1986 to help reduce the national government's deficit that year.[34] Twenty-five states, the District of Columbia, and Guam currently offer this optional coverage.[35]

Liberals and representatives of the nation's cities, particularly the U.S. Conference of Mayors, also have complained over the years that many poor families are unjustly denied welfare benefits because most of the states have historically established an income threshold for qualifying for AFDC assistance that is far below the national government's poverty index.[36] As Table 3.2 indicates, in 1988 all of the states required AFDC applicants to have monthly incomes that fell below the national government's official poverty line before they could become eligible to collect AFDC benefits. Only Florida, Vermont, and Washington had a monthly income threshold that was at least 90 percent of the national government's official poverty line. Seventeen states required recipients to have incomes less than half of the national government's poverty income level before allowing them to collect AFDC benefits.

Liberals object to the states' low income thresholds because the thresholds exclude many of the poor from the program and weaken AFDC's ability to promote a more equal distribution of income in society. Many of the nation's mayors share the liberals' concerns about the states' low income thresholds because many of the excluded poor reside in metropolitan areas and impose relatively high expenses for social and medical services on city budgets.

In 1967, in an attempt to force states to provide AFDC assistance to a larger percentage of those people whose income falls below the national

[33]U.S. Advisory Commission on Intergovernmental Relations, *Public Assistance: The Growth of a Federal Function*, pp. 54, 55.

[34]"$18 Billion Deficit-Reduction Measure Clears," Congressional Quarterly *Weekly Report* (22 March 1986):682. Extending the unemployed parent program to all the states would have cost the national government approximately $410 million over fiscal years 1988–1990.

[35]U.S. Department of Health and Human Services, *Social Security Bulletin* 50:12 (December 1987):57. While 71 percent of welfare families live in jurisdictions offering AFDC-UP, only 6 percent of all recipients are AFDC-UP families because of various restrictions on earnings. See Julie Rovner, "Welfare for Two–Parent Families: An Old Issue," Congressional Quarterly, *Weekly Report* (April 23, 1988):1069.

[36]For a discussion of the national government's poverty index, see Clarke E. Cochran et al., *American Public Policy: An Introduction*, pp. 198–201; Martin Anderson, *Welfare: The Political Economy of Welfare Reform in the United States* (Stanford, CA: Hoover Institution, 1978), pp. 15–27; and Sar A. Levitan, *Programs in Aid of the Poor*, 5th ed., pp. 1–5. The state's income threshold is also called the state's standard of need.

TABLE 3.2   AFDC Applicant's Maximum Monthly Income Allowed: Family of Four, by State, 1988

STATE	NEED STANDARD	STATE	NEED STANDARD
1. Vermont	$997	26. Oklahoma	$583
2. Washington	941	27. North Carolina	582
3. Florida	933	28. Iowa	578
4. D.C.	870	29. Hawaii	574
5. Ohio	834	30. Rhode Island	546
6. Alaska	823	31. New Hampshire	541
7. Arkansas	820	32. Montana	523
8. Illinois	778	33. Colorado	510
9. California	753	34. Oregon	501
10. Louisiana	750	35. New Jersey	488
11. Arizona	748	36. Alabama	480
12. Wisconsin	772	37. South Carolina	467
13. Pennsylvania	724	38. North Dakota	454
14. Maine	702	39. Kansas	444
15. Michigan	698	40. Georgia	432
16. Texas	691	41. Mississippi	443
17. Nevada	650	42. Tennessee	431
18. New York	638	43. Nebraska	420
19. Massachusetts	635	44. South Dakota	408
20. Idaho	627	45. Wyoming	390
21. West Virginia	623	46. Virginia	386
22. Minnesota	621	47. Indiana	385
23. Connecticut	604	48. Delaware	374
24. Maryland	598	49. Missouri	365
25. Utah	586	50. New Mexico	317
		51. Kentucky	259

Note: The national government's poverty threshold for a nonfarm family of four was $1,000 per month in 1988.

Source: U.S. Department of Health and Human Services, "Aid to Families With Dependent Children: Need and Payment Amounts," Washington, DC, April 22, 1988.

government's poverty threshold, liberals successfully defended legislation that required states to disregard in their calculation of an applicant family's income all earnings of a child enrolled in a college or other school having a curriculum that leads to gainful employment. Liberals also were able to attract enough support from moderates to force states to disregard in their calculation of an applicant family's monthly income the first $30 earned plus one-third of the remainder.[37] Moderates supported the income disregards because they believed that by excluding the money spent by the poor to get to and from work ($30) and to eat (one-third of their earned income), the poor would be provided an incentive to seek work. Others supported the income disregards because they viewed them as a means to

[37]U.S. Department of Health and Human Services, *Social Security Bulletin, Annual Statistical Supplement, 1984–85* (Washington DC: U.S. Government Printing Office, 1985), pp. 49, 50.

reduce the likelihood of continued social turmoil as manifested in the mid-1960s', urban riots.[38]

Soon after these changes were enacted, AFDC enrollments began to increase dramatically. Between 1965 and 1970, AFDC enrollments more than doubled, from 4.4 million to 9.7 million recipients (see Table 3.1). Although a number of other factors, such as the increased awareness of the program by the poor and the erosion of the negative perception of being on welfare that resulted from the activities of welfare rights organizations, also contributed to this increase, conservatives targeted AFDC income disregards as the primary cause of these enrollment increases. They argued that income disregards changed AFDC's focus. Instead of a last resort "safety net" for the very poor, it was now a supplement program for those with marginal incomes. They also argued that the income disregards added too much to the cost of AFDC, given the difficulties in balancing the national government's budget; that they were counter to the basic principles of federalism, which suggest that the states should be allowed to determine their own income criteria; and that they had not proved to be a very effective work incentive.[39] Despite these concerns, the income disregards remained relatively unchanged until the 1980s.

President Reagan agreed with all of the conservative arguments against income disregards and was able to convince Congress to agree to a number of changes in 1981 that caused 687,000 households, approximately 6 percent of total 1980 recipients, to lose all or part of their AFDC benefits. The changes also promised to stabilize AFDC's enrollments at the 11 million level. President Reagan's intent was to target national welfare assistance to the truly needy.

Among the changes were the establishment of a monthly $75 standard work-expense income disregard and a $160 monthly income disregard for child or attendant care. The $30 plus one-third of earned income disregard was restricted to those enrolled in AFDC during at least one of the preceding four months. In addition, families with property resources (excluding the home and one automobile) whose equity value exceeded $1,000, that had total incomes in excess of 150 percent of a state's "standard of need," or had a parent participating in a labor strike were excluded from the program.[40]

[38]Benjamin I. Page, *Who Gets What From Government* (Berkeley: University of California Press, 1983), pp. 2, 3.

[39]Vernon K. Smith, *Welfare Work Incentives,* Studies in Welfare Policy, no. 2 (Lansing: Michigan Department of Social Services, 1974), pp. 226–227, cited in Lester M. Salamon, *Welfare: The Elusive Consensus,* p. 23.

[40]Sar A. Levitan, *Programs in Aid of the Poor,* pp. 36, 37. In 1984 the family gross income limit was changed to 185 percent of the state's standard of need, the $75 standard work expense disregard was extended to part-time workers, burial plots were exempted from property resources calculations, and the rules determining who qualified for the $30 plus one-third of earned income disregard were liberalized. See U.S. Department of Health and Human Services, *Social Security Bulletin: Annual Statistical Supplement, 1986* (Washington DC: U.S. Government Printing Office, 1986), pp. 52, 53.

States were required to adopt the monthly retrospective income accounting system for determining benefits. This system was expected to deter cheating and save both the national and the state governments millions of dollars by basing AFDC benefits on the recipient's actual, verifiable income earned during the month preceding the application date. Most states had used a prospective accounting system that based AFDC benefits on an estimate of the recipient's income for the month following the application date. Critics complained that AFDC recipients were understating their prospective income. To further ensure that people who were receiving benefits were not cheating, all recipients were required to file monthly income reports. In the past, recipients were required to notify state officials only when their income changed. Critics argued that many recipients had failed to do so. Finally, states were allowed to include in their calculation of a family's income the value of food stamps and housing subsidies.[41]

CONTROVERSY #3: WHO SHOULD DETERMINE BENEFIT PAYMENT RATES?

Liberals would like to see the national government provide states enough AFDC support to enable state legislators to ignore the negative economic spillover effects that result from providing welfare recipients with benefits that exceed the benefits of neighboring states. They have complained since the program's inception that this level of support has been lacking. At the present time, monthly benefit payments in all of the states fall below the national government's poverty income level ($1,000 per month for a family of four in 1988). In 1988 AFDC monthly payments in the median state (Nebraska) were only 42 percent of the income needed by those recipients to reach the national government's poverty income threshold. Moreover, AFDC monthly payments vary considerably from state to state, depending on the strength of the pro- and anti-welfare lobbying organizations, the relative fiscal capacity of the state, and the perceived negative impact that spending on welfare has on business investment.[42] As Table 3.3 indicates, in 1988 a family of four with no income would have received an AFDC monthly benefit of $823 in Alaska. That same family would have received only $144 in Mississippi.

As mentioned earlier, many conservatives are not convinced that the poor lack the economic opportunities to escape poverty. They are also

---

[41]Sar A. Levitan, *Programs in Aid of the Poor*, pp. 50–53; and "Chronology of Action on Welfare," in *Congress and the Nation, 1981–1984* (Washington, DC: Congressional Quarterly, 1985), pp. 583, 587, 588.

[42]Julie Rovner, "Welfare Reform: The Next Domestic Priority?" Congressional Quarterly, *Weekly Report* (September 27, 1986):2283.

TABLE 3.3   Maximum AFDC Benefit for a Family of Four, By State, 1988

STATE	MONTHLY BENEFIT	STATE	MONTHLY BENEFIT
1. Alaska	$823	26. Nebraska	$420
2. California	753	27. South Dakota	408
3. Vermont	676	28. Wyoming	390
4. New York	638	29. Illinois	386
5. Massachusetts	635	30. Nevada	384
6. Wisconsin	617	31. Oklahoma	384
7. Minnesota	621	32. Ohio	382
8. Connecticut	604	33. Delaware	374
9. Washington	578	34. Arizona	353
10. Hawaii	574	35. Indiana	346
11. Michigan	555	36. Virginia	347
12. Rhode Island	546	37. Idaho	344
13. New Hampshire	541	38. Missouri	330
14. Maine	509	39. Florida	324
15. Oregon	501	40. New Mexico	317
16. New Jersey	488	41. West Virginia	312
17. Pennsylvania	474	42. Georgia	310
18. North Dakota	454	43. North Carolina	291
19. D.C.	444	44. Kentucky	259
20. Kansas	444	45. South Carolina	240
21. Iowa	443	46. Arkansas	238
22. Utah	439	47. Louisiana	225
23. Montana	433	48. Texas	221
24. Maryland	432	49. Tennessee	194
25. Colorado	420	50. Alabama	147
		51. Mississippi	144

Source: U.S. Department of Health and Human Services, "Aid to Families With Dependent Children: Need and Payment Amounts," Washington, DC, April 22, 1988.

skeptical of the liberals' arguments concerning the poor's willingness to make the personal sacrifices necessary to escape poverty if they are given generous AFDC benefits. Some conservatives have argued that even if the poor genuinely desired to work, the benefits of the total welfare package (Medicaid, AFDC, Food Stamps, etc.) are so great that the poor correctly realize that it is not in their interest to give up their welfare benefits for an entry-level job. Thus, they have resisted liberals' attempts to increase the national government's contribution to the program. They also fail to see the injustice in having states offer varying levels of monthly benefit payments. Many conservatives are convinced that the citizens of each state have an inherent right to determine for themselves how much they want to spend on welfare in their state. In addition, they argue that welfare's negative spillover effects on business investment decisions deserve to be considered when a state determines its monthly benefit payments. The cure for poverty is not to increase AFDC payments beyond their logical levels, but to foster a sound fiscal environment for business investment and expansion that will provide the jobs needed by the poor to escape poverty.

CONTROVERSY #4: DOES AFDC HELP OR HURT THE POOR?

Liberals and conservatives share the objective of reducing welfare dependency. They disagree on the best way to achieve this end. Liberals generally view the expansion of welfare benefits and eligibility criteria as the best way to provide the poor with the economic security to enable them to go to school or to acquire the necessary skills to compete in the private job market. Conservatives disagree. They believe that social welfare programs reach well beyond the ranks of the truly needy and encourage the able-bodied to avoid work. As a result, they seek to restrict welfare benefits and eligibility criteria, and are generally much more critical of AFDC than are liberals.[43]

Many conservatives have argued that AFDC and other social programs, such as Medicaid and Food stamps, have largely been a waste of valuable economic resources. They point out that much of AFDC's budget is spent on a vast bureaucracy that is largely devoted to shuffling papers rather than to serving people.[44] Moreover, the bureaucracy is not only wasteful but also degrades the poor. As one author put it:

> In Los Angeles . . . AFDC applicants are advised that determining eligibility will take at least three appointments, each requiring from 5 to 12 hours of waiting and interview time. . . . Determination of eligibility requires many embarrassing personal questions . . . and possibly home inspections. Often denials of benefits are made for trivial reasons in order to keep the rolls low. The recipient is stigmatized as being poor and unable, or unwilling, to work.[45]

Many conservatives also argue that AFDC and other social programs have contributed to the perpetuation of poverty in America. They point out that the percentage of the nonelderly population with incomes beneath the poverty line fell linearly from approximately 21 percent in 1959 to 11 percent in 1969. The poverty rate stayed at the 10 to 12 percent level throughout the 1970s and rose to the 13 to 15 percent level in the 1980s. In

---

[43]Sar A. Levitan and Clifford M. Johnson, *Beyond the Safety Net: Reviving the Promise of Opportunity in America* (Cambridge, MA: Ballinger, 1984), p. 30.

[44]Milton Friedman and Rose Friedman, *Free to Choose* (New York: Avon Books, 1979), p. 98. State governments will spend an estimated $2.47 billion to administer the AFDC program in 1987, 18 percent of the $16.12 billion spent on the entire program. See U.S. Office of Management and Budget, *Budget of the United States Government, Appendix, FY 1987* (Washington, DC: U.S. Government Printing Office, 1986), p. I-K43.

[45]Clarke E. Cochran et al., *American Public Policy: An Introduction*, pp. 228, 229.

other words, just as the Great Society's welfare programs got going, progress against poverty stopped.[46]

They argue that the poverty rate stopped falling in the 1970s because AFDC and other social programs provided so much in benefits that recipients correctly reasoned that their standard of living would fall in the short term if they went to work on a full-time basis.[47] Thus, AFDC and the other social programs actually perpetuated poverty because they discouraged individuals from entering the work force, where they had at least a chance of escaping poverty. They also point out that the high cost of AFDC and other social programs inflicts unnecessarily high taxes on individuals and businesses. These taxes, in turn, restrict the availability of jobs for the poor.[48] Thus, AFDC and other social welfare programs create a vicious poverty cycle that impedes national economic growth and makes poverty a nearly permanent condition.

Liberals respond to these criticisms by pointing out that the widespread belief that once people are on welfare, they and their descendants are always on welfare, is a myth. Households frequently move in and out of poverty as economic conditions fluctuate. The typical AFDC recipient is enrolled in the program for only two years, and 85 percent of AFDC recipients are enrolled for less than eight years.[49] In addition, four out of five children escape their parents' poverty.[50] Thus, for most AFDC recipients, the program does not result in a lifelong dependency on government assistance.[51] Moreover, liberals question the conservatives' assertion that social welfare expenditures have weakened the national economy. They point out that while it is true that the national government's social welfare expenditures redistribute income within the economy, those expenditures remain in the economy. One analyst has suggested that one of the reasons the public has not demanded the wholesale dismantling of social welfare programs is that the net annual income loss to the middle and upper classes through all of these programs is only about 2 or 3 percent of personal income.[52]

Conservatives are not convinced by the liberals' statistics. They point out that while it may be true that the typical AFDC recipient leaves the program in two years, nearly one-third of these individuals are back within

[46]David T. Ellwood and Lawrence H. Summers, "Is Welfare Really the Problem?" p. 58.

[47]Martin Anderson, *Welfare: The Political Economy of Welfare Reform in the United States*, pp. 43–56; and Charles Murray, *Losing Ground*, pp. 154–166.

[48]Milton Friedman and Rose Friedman, *Free to Choose*, pp. 98–115.

[49]Clarke E. Cochran et al., *American Public Policy: An Introduction*, p. 225; and David T. Ellwood and Lawrence H. Summers, "Is Welfare Really the Problem?" p. 71.

[50]Sar A. Levitan and Clifford M. Johnson, *Beyond the Safety Net*, pp. 36, 37.

[51]Clarke E. Cochran et al., *American Public Policy: An Introduction*, pp. 71–73.

[52]Robert H. Haveman, "The War on Poverty and the Poor and Nonpoor," *Political Science Quarterly* 102:1 (Spring 1987): 65–78.

a year because of a job loss or insufficient income.[53] Moreover, 15 percent of AFDC recipients (approximately 1.6 million people, mostly unmarried mothers) stay on the program for more than eight years, and they collect more than half of the benefits paid out.[54] Finally, if AFDC and the other social welfare programs are so successful and worthwhile, why has the poverty rate stayed so high?

WORKFARE: THE COMPROMISE OF THE 1990s?

Conservatives have always advocated a work requirement (called workfare) for AFDC recipients. In their view, giving the poor a government handout without demanding something in return promotes the establishment of a permanent culture of poverty that rejects the middle-class values of thrift and hard work and does nothing to enhance the poor's job skills. A work requirement, on the other hand, would provide the poor with the basic job skills (such as how to fill out an application form, knowing to report to work on time, calling in when sick, etc.) that most middle-class Americans take for granted and that are necessary to gain employment. In this way AFDC recipients' self-esteem will be boosted because they will be receiving government wages instead of a government handout. AFDC's expense will be moderated because many of its recipients will be hired by private companies once they have mastered the basic job skills. Conservatives would prefer that this work experience take place with a private company but are willing to settle for public service jobs, such as trash pickup in public parks and along highways.[55]

Liberals have traditionally opposed mandatory work requirements for AFDC because the majority of AFDC recipients have always been single women and their children. It was their view that these women should not be expected to work, given their responsibility to care for their children. In general, they viewed mandatory work requirements as a form of punishment that did little to promote the family's economic success. What these women really needed was enough money from AFDC to survive and additional governmental assistance to pay for child care so they could attend government-subsidized education and job training centers that would provide them with the skills necessary to enter the work force once their children were old enough to go to school. In their view, the conservatives' resistance to paying for the poor's child care, adult education, and job training was the real cause of the government's lack of success in eradicating poverty during the 1970s and 1980s.

[53]Lester M. Salamon, *Welfare: The Elusive Consensus*, p. 23.

[54]David T. Ellwood and Lawrence H. Summers, "Is Welfare Really the Problem?" p. 72.

[55]Julie Rovnor, "Welfare Reform: The Next Domestic Priority?" p. 2284.

Liberals' resistance to mandatory work requirements has eased recently. Now that half of the nation's labor force is composed of women and many of them have decided to return to work while leaving their children in the care of friends, relatives, or day care centers, many liberals are beginning to soften their resistance to work requirements for AFDC recipients. In 1982 they agreed to a Reagan administration proposal to allow the states the option to create their own workfare programs. Since then, nearly every state has established at least one experimental workfare program in at least one of its counties; and eight states, including California, New York, and Massachusetts, have established statewide programs.[56]

MASSACHUSETTS' ET PROGRAM: A LOOK INTO THE FUTURE

Massachusetts' Employment and Training Choices workfare program, informally known as "ET" was established in 1983 and quickly attracted nationwide attention as a dramatic success. Convinced that the poor do not want to be on welfare and actually desire to work, the Massachusetts workfare program is voluntary. To encourage AFDC recipients to participate, the state offers them vouchers to pay for child day care while they are enrolled in the program and, for up to one year after a participant leaves AFDC rolls, transportation allowances and Medicaid coverage. Participants are allowed to choose from among four programs: job referral services for those who already have basic job skills but need help in being placed, adult education and training services for those who lack basic educational or job skills, job placement services with private companies that have agreed to provide on-the-job training for those who need to retrain for new jobs (designed primarily for older workers who lost jobs in the manufacturing and industrial sector because of technological advances or foreign imports), and career counseling services for those who are not certain what they want to do.[57] In the first two years of its operation, 44,000 AFDC recipients volunteered to participate in the program and more than 17,000 of its graduates were offered employment by the private sector. Seventy percent of those offered jobs by the private sector gained full-time employment, and the rest were hired on a part-time basis. Those with full-time employment are no longer AFDC recipients and now earn, on average, more than twice what they had received under AFDC. The program had proven to be so successful that in 1986 it had a waiting list of over

---

[56]Ibid., pp. 2281–2286; Julie Kosterlitz, "Liberals and Conservatives Share Goals, Differ on Details of Work for Welfare," *National Journal* (November 26, 1985):2419–2421; and Patrick Knudsen, "House Leaders Still Pressing Welfare Revision," Congressional Quarterly, *Weekly Report* (November 14, 1987): 2805.

[57]Neal R. Peirce and Carol Steinbach, "Massachusetts, After Going from Rags to Riches, Looks to Spread the Wealth," *National Journal* (May 25, 1985):1230.

20,000 people. Massachusetts officials claim that the program saved the state, after accounting for administrative and other support expenses, approximately $50 million during its first two years.[58]

Critics of the Massachusetts workfare program argue that many of those who volunteered to join would have left the AFDC rolls and received private employment even if they had never entered the program. Moreover, Massachusetts' relatively low unemployment rates during the early and mid-1980s may have had more to do with the program's graduates receiving offers of full-time employment than the training they received from the program.[59]

Nevertheless, the success (whether perceived or real) of a workfare program, even a voluntary one, in the politically liberal and Democratic state of Massachusetts has softened many Democrats' opposition to the idea of workfare. The debate in the 1990s over workfare, therefore, will probably not be whether it is appropriate but under what conditions it will occur.

THE NEGATIVE INCOME TAX: AN ACADEMIC ALTERNATIVE

Lacking the political strength to nationalize or to dismantle AFDC, liberals and conservatives have focused their political fighting on the program's eligibility standards and monthly benefit levels. Although political reality indicates that these battles will continue and any changes in AFDC will probably be of an incremental nature, there is a growing chorus of voices advocating the replacement of AFDC with a negative income tax. Milton Friedman, one of the country's leading conservative economists, is generally regarded as the first to propose the negative income tax as a replacement for AFDC and other social welfare programs.[60]

Instead of assisting the poor through intergovernmental financing and administrative structures, the negative income tax would have the national government provide a cash grant directly to any individual who earned less income than the amount not taxed by the national government. Under current tax law, the national government allows individuals to earn an amount equal to the sum of a standard deduction (that varies depending

---

[58]Julie Kosterlitz, "Liberals and Conservatives Share Goals, Differ on Details of Work for Welfare," p. 2420

[59]Ibid.

[60]Milton Friedman, *Capitalism and Freedom* (Chicago: University of Chicago Press, 1962), ch. 12; and Milton Friedman and Rose Friedman, *Free to Choose*, pp. 110–118. It has been estimated that the national, state, and local governments spent over $150 billion on government-sponsored welfare programs in 1987 (Medicaid, AFDC, Food Stamps, SSI, etc.). It would cost only approximately $59 billion in direct cash grants to raise all Americans' incomes above the national government's poverty income threshold. See Julie Kosterlitz, "Income Security Focus," *National Journal* (August 30, 1986): 2092; and Julie Rovner, "Welfare Reform: The Next Domestic Priority?" Congressional Quarterly, *Weekly Report* (September 27, 1986):2284.

on whether the taxpayer is single, married, or the head of a household), $2,000 for each personal exemption claimed, and a host of other deductions and exemptions allowed on specific types of earned income. For example, college tuition scholarships, AFDC benefits, and child support payments are types of income that are not taxed.

Obviously, the amount of nontaxable income varies from family to family, depending on the value of the standard deduction, the number of personal exemptions claimed, and the nature of the family's income. Under current law, the typical married couple with two children is not taxed on the first $13,000 of earned income.[61] This is a little higher than the current national poverty rate for a nonfarm family of four.[62]

Friedman proposed that the national government replace its social welfare programs and what he viewed as their wasteful, expensive, and intrusive bureaucracies with a check sent directly to every individual who failed to earn enough income to pay national income taxes. He suggested that the check equal 50 percent of the difference between the individual's actual earned income and the amount the national government exempted from its income tax. In this way, all Americans would be guaranteed a minimum income and provided an incentive to seek employment. The work incentive would be derived from the opportunity for every individual to keep half of the government subsidy for every dollar earned up to the amount exempted from the national income tax.

Under current law, individuals lose all of their AFDC benefits once they reach their state's standard-of-need income threshold. Since state income thresholds are so low, it often does not make economic sense for AFDC recipients to seek work because they will lose both their AFDC benefits and their Medicaid benefits. Moreover, as an AFDC recipient's earned income rises, states reduce AFDC benefits and the national government reduces food stamp allotments. The prospect of reducing and perhaps even losing their AFDC, Medicaid, food stamps, housing assistance, and assorted other social services benefits serves as a powerful deterrent for the poor to earn too much money.[63]

The negative income tax does not enjoy universal support. Critics point out that it lessens but does not eliminate the disincentive to work for those already on welfare. Moreover, it discourages work by low-income males, who currently are not entitled to AFDC benefits. Under a negative income tax, their incomes would remain near the poverty level whether

---

[61]This figure is based on a $5,000 standard deduction for couples filing a joint income tax return and $8,000 for the family's four personal exemptions.

[62]The national poverty rate for a nonfarm family of four was $11,614 in 1987. This figure has increased by approximately $400 a year since 1980. See U.S. Department of Commerce, *Statistical Abstract of the United States, 1988* (Washington, DC: U.S. Government Printing Office, 1987), p. 406.

[63]Christopher K. Leman, *The Collapse of Welfare Reform*, pp. 54–56.

they continued to work or quit their jobs.[64] Opponents also argue that some low-income families would receive a larger subsidy under the negative income tax format if they separated and collected benefits independently. Thus, it could cause more family breakups than the current AFDC program. A negative income tax would also need to compensate for cost-of-living differentials between urban and rural areas and among the various regions of the country.[65] In addition, the cash payment would not cover anywhere near what Medicaid currently pays toward the costs of individuals who need long-term care in either a hospital or a nursing home.[66]

Opponents also argue that the current policy of treating specific types of poor people differently under separate social welfare programs makes sense. Some groups, they argue, should be provided incentives to work, while others should be provided a "decent" level of income without a work requirement or work incentive feature. For example, AFDC may not provide much incentive to work, but most AFDC beneficiaries should not be expected to work, since they are either children or their single, divorced, or abandoned mothers who need to be at home or, at most, could be expected to work part-time because of their responsibility to take care of their children. Disabled Americans also should not be subjected to a program whose main feature is the promotion of the work incentive.[67] Finally, the U.S. Office of Economic Opportunity (OEO) experimented with the negative income tax in several cities during the 1970s. To the surprise of OEO officials, it had a negative impact on the poor's incentive to work and contributed to the breakup of marriages.[68]

President Nixon offered a variation on the negative income tax theme in his Family Assistance Plan in 1969, and President Carter offered a different version in his 1977 Program for Better Jobs and Income. Neither proposal was able to overcome the disagreement over the size of the subsidy level to be provided or the total cost to the national government.[69]

---

[64]Martin Anderson, *Welfare: The Political Economy of Welfare in the United States*, pp. 100–105, 117–127; and Robert A. Moffitt, "The Effect of a Negative Income Tax on Work Effort: A Summary of the Experimental Results," in *Welfare Reform in America: Perspectives and Prospects*, ed. Paul M. Sommers (Boston: Kluwer-Nijhoff Publishing, 1982), pp. 209–229.

[65]Sar A. Levitan, *Programs in Aid of the Poor*, p. 53.

[66]Julie Kosterlitz, "Income Security Focus," p. 2092.

[67]David T. Ellwood and Lawrence H. Summers, "Is Welfare Really the Problem?" pp. 67–78.

[68]Charles Murray, *Losing Ground*, pp. 148–153.

[69]Christopher K. Leman, *The Collapse of Welfare Reform*, pp. 70–112; Lester M. Salamon, *Welfare: The Elusive Consensus*, pp. 136–148, 175–218; and Martin Anderson, *Welfare: The Political Economy of Welfare Reform in the United States*, pp. 169–209.

CONCLUSIONS

The fundamental disagreement over poverty's cause and the purpose of social welfare programs has led to the liberal/conservative stalemate over AFDC. Although the negative income tax continues to attract support among some academics and politicians, AFDC's intergovernmental financing and administrative structure seems secure. In 1978, Martin Anderson wrote that significant welfare reform in America or the establishment of any variety of a guaranteed income was a political impossibility because no plan could be devised that simultaneously yielded a level of welfare benefits that pleased liberals, financial incentives to work that pleased conservatives, and an overall cost that pleased taxpayers.[70] These same obstacles to reform are present today.[71]

Forecasting the future of any intergovernmental program is always hazardous; but given the national government's fiscal difficulties, the widespread belief that national taxes are already too high, and the public's continuing skepticism concerning AFDC's impact on poverty, the conservatives' desire to reduce national AFDC costs by imposing more restrictive national eligibility standards and by reducing the national government's income disregard requirements will probably be fulfilled. In an era of fiscal retrenchment, funding for programs with weak political constituencies is always in jeopardy.

The national government's decisions concerning AFDC's funding and eligibility criteria will present fiscal and political problems for state and local governments during the 1990s. They will be forced to make difficult decisions concerning their own welfare policies. If, as expected, the national government continues to tighten eligibility criteria and refuses to increase expenditures to compensate for inflation, the states and localities will have to decide if they are willing to raise taxes either to supplement AFDC benefit payments or to offer state and local relief to those who are poor but ineligible for AFDC. Since state and local fiscal and political conditions vary considerably, it is reasonable to expect that the national government's efforts to reduce costs will probably result in even greater variation in the availability and level of welfare benefits across the nation than is currently the case.

It is also likely that in the early 1990s statewide workfare programs will be adopted by most of the states. State officials will push for workfare

[70]Martin Anderson, *Welfare: The Political Economy of Welfare Reform in the United States*, p. 131.

[71]For a discussion of the political obstacles facing AFDC reform, see William P. Albrecht, "Welfare Reform: An Idea Whose Time Has Come and Gone," in *Welfare Reform in America*, ed. Paul M. Sommers, pp. 15–28.

programs because they offer a convenient way to mollify a taxpaying public that is generally convinced (despite evidence to the contrary) that most of the poor are lazy bums. States with liberal or progressive traditions will probably adopt workfare programs along the lines of Massachusetts' ET program. States lacking a liberal or progressive tradition will probably adopt mandatory workfare programs that do not provide government subsidies for child care, transportation, or medical care during and after the training experience. As the workfare programs spread and diversity becomes apparent, it is likely that liberals, social welfare advocates, civil rights organizations, and some moderates will join forces to impose national workfare standards that include compensation for child care, medical care, and transportation expenses. It is also likely that conservatives and some moderates will oppose these efforts as too expensive, given the national government's budgetary problems. In either case, there is a very good chance that some form of workfare is going to become a permanent feature of the AFDC program.

CHAPTER 4

Food Stamps

The Food Stamp program was started on a temporary, pilot basis in 1961 and became a "permanent" program (subject to periodic reauthorizations) in 1964. Designed to help poor people obtain a nutritionally adequate diet, it provides individuals who have incomes and assets below levels designated by the national government with coupons that are redeemable for food at most retail food stores.[1] Food stamps cannot be used to buy alcoholic beverages, tobacco or cigarettes, household supplies, medicine, pet food, or any other nonfood item. The national government determines the value of food stamps each eligible household receives each month. It first computes the applicant's net monthly income (total income minus certain deductions). Applicants with no income receive enough food stamps to cover the cost of a nutritionally adequate diet for their household size. Applicants with income receive food stamps that are worth the difference between the cost of a nutritionally adequate diet for their household size and 30 percent of their net monthly income.[2] The national government pays the entire cost of the food coupons.

Food Stamps are an intergovernmental program because state welfare agencies certify those who are eligible to participate in the program through local welfare offices, issue identification cards, and pay for half of the program's administrative expenses. At the present time, all 50 states, the District of Columbia, Guam, and the Virgin Islands participate in the

[1]In 1987 eligible households must have gross incomes lower than 130 percent of the national goverment's poverty level and lower than 100 percent of that amount after allowable deductions are made. Households also must have assets valued at no more than $2,000. If the household includes an elderly member, it can have assets up to $3,000. Burial plots and vehicles used to produce income or to transport a disabled person are excluded from this calculation. See Robert Rothman, "Bill Expands Food Stamp Benefits, Eligibility," Congressional Quarterly, *Weekly Report* (December 21, 1985):2677, 2683; and U.S. Department of Health and Human Services, *Social Security Bulletin, Annual Statistical Supplement, 1984–85* (Washington, DC: U.S. Government Printing Office, 1985), p. 59.

[2]A nutritionally adequate diet is determined by the U.S. Department of Agriculture's Thrifty Food Plan.

Food Stamp program.[3] Over 18 million people receive food stamps (see Table 4.1), at an annual cost to the national government of nearly $13 billion and an additional $1 billion to the states.[4]

This chapter examines the evolution of the Food Stamp program, focusing on the debates over its intergovernmental structure and the role of the states and localities in determining its eligibility criteria and benefit levels. Following the rationales outlined in the chapters on Medicaid and AFDC, liberals have generally advocated the nationalization of the program as a means to ensure that the poor are treated equally across the nation. Given their belief that the nature of the American economy makes it extremely difficult for many of the poor to escape poverty, they have also advocated the establishment of relatively easy eligibility standards and generous benefit levels for the program. Conservatives, on the other hand, have opposed the nationalization of the Food Stamp program because they believe that welfare is primarily a state and local responsibility, and that the economy offers sufficient economic opportunities for most of the poor to

TABLE 4.1   Number of Food Stamp Recipients and Average Monthly Benefit: Selected FYs, 1962–1992

YEAR	RECIPIENTS (THOUSANDS)	MONTHLY BENEFIT
1992 (est.)	18,154	—
1990 (est.)	18,635	—
1988 (est.)	19,301	—
1986	19,720	$45.01
1984	20,870	42.77
1982	21,716	39.18
1980	21,077	34.34
1978	16,044	26.86
1976	18,557	23.85
1974	12,896	17.62
1972	11,103	13.47
1970	4,340	10.58
1968	2,211	6.52
1966	864	6.25
1964	367	6.50
1962	143	7.66

Sources: U.S. Office of Management and Budget, *Special Analyses, Budget of the United States Government, FY 1988* (Washington, DC: U.S. Government Printing Office, 1987), p. A-11; and U.S. Department of Health and Human Services, *Social Security Bulletin, Annual Statistical Supplement, 1984–85* (Washington, DC: U.S. Government Printing Office, 1985), p. 256.

[3]Puerto Rico has received a block grant for nutrition assistance since 1982 and no longer participates in the Food Stamp program.

[4]U.S. Office of Management and Budget, *Budget of the United States Government, FY 1988, Appendix* (Washington, DC: U.S. Government Printing Office, 1987), p. I-E84.

escape poverty. They also oppose efforts to change the program's eligibility standards to allow more people to qualify for assistance or to increase benefit levels. Instead, they advocate tight eligibility criteria to ensure that only the truly needy (those who cannot help themselves) are given governmental assistance, and relatively low benefit payments to help reduce the national deficit and to encourage those in the program to seek work.

THE EVOLUTION OF THE FOOD STAMP PROGRAM: 1935–1964

Prior to the Great Depression in the 1930s, the provision of food assistance to needy Americans was considered the responsibility of private charities and of state and local governments. As the Great Depression deepened, it became obvious that neither private charities nor state and local governments could cope with the widespread hunger that engulfed America. Despite the obvious need for food assistance, conservatives in Congress continued to strongly oppose any effort to enact a nationally financed food relief program. They argued that welfare was a state and local responsibility, and that a nationally financed program could exacerbate the hunger problem. They were convinced that the best way to get out of the Great Depression was to balance the national government's budget and to keep spending and taxes as low as possible.

In their view, a nationally financed food relief program would cause the national government to incur a deficit that, in turn, would cause a further decline in the national economy and ultimately lead to greater unemployment and hunger. They did agree, however, to a compromise offered by congressional liberals in the Potato Control Act of 1935, Section 32 of which authorized the secretary of agriculture to purchase surplus farm products and distribute them to poor families. In this way, liberals were able to provide the poor with food while conservatives, many of whom represented rural, agricultural districts, were able to stabilize and protect farm prices by expanding the farm market.[5]

Liberals were not satisfied with the surplus distribution plan. They complained that foods, including perishables, were distributed on a monthly basis. Since the poor generally did not have refrigerators, most of the food had to be eaten soon after distribution or it would spoil. Thus, many families ate relatively well at the beginning of the month but went hungry at the end of the month. In addition, only foods that were in surplus were distributed to the poor. This meant that the poor's nutritional needs often were not met. Moreover, food retailers objected to the distribu-

[5]U.S. Advisory Commission on Intergovernmental Relations, *Public Assistance: The Growth of a Federal Function* (Washington, DC: U.S. Government Printing Office, 1980), p. 74; and "Evolution of the Food Stamp Program," *Congressional Digest* (January 1981):6.

tion program because it disrupted their normal flow of customer traffic.[6]

With the backing of a strong lobbying effort by the retail food industry, the secretary of agriculture, using Section 32 of the Potato Control Act of 1935 as his authority, created the national government's first Food Stamp program in 1939. Only persons enrolled in the national government's Aid to Dependent Children (ADC) program or a state public assistance program were eligible to participate. Instead of receiving surplus farm products for free, recipients were required to purchase a certain number of orange food stamps at face value. They were then given blue food stamps worth half of the orange stamps' face value. The orange stamps could be used to purchase any food item at any retail food outlet. The blue stamps could be used only to purchase food designated as being surplus by the U.S. Department of Agriculture (USDA). In this way, food retailers were able to keep their normal flow of customer traffic, liberals were able to continue the national government's role in providing food assistance to the needy, and conservatives were able to continue the national government's role in stabilizing food prices and subsidizing agriculture.[7]

Liberals soon became disenchanted with the Food Stamp program. Many of the states had established very strict eligibility standards for qualifying for the ADC program. As a result, many of the poor who had received free food under the surplus distribution program no longer were eligible for food assistance. Moreover, the very poorest in America could not afford to buy the orange stamps. This meant that the most needy were not receiving any food assistance at all. Finally, the USDA reported that many retail outlets were allowing food stamp recipients to purchase nonfood items with their stamps, and that most retailers did not bother to make certain that the blue stamps were being used to purchase only food items that had been designated as being in surplus.[8]

Without strong support in Congress, America's first Food Stamp program ended in 1942. As the nation began to move toward entry into World War II, the food stamp issue disappeared. The liberals' concerns about hunger were dissipated as the economy moved into high gear and unemployment and hunger receded as a national political issue. The conservatives' fears about price supports were ended as demand for American agricultural products soared both within the United States and abroad.[9]

In 1954, Rep. Leonor K. Sullivan (D-MO) began a campaign to bring back food stamps. Her goal was to assist the poor, not to stabilize farm prices. For years her efforts met with stiff resistance. Many in Congress

[6]U.S. Advisory Commission on Intergovernmental Relations, *Public Assistance: The Growth of a Federal Function*, p. 74.

[7]Ibid., pp. 74, 75.

[8]Ibid., p. 75.

[9]Ibid.

believed that the main purpose of food programs was the reinforcement of the farm economy, not meeting the nutritional needs of the poor. They advocated the free distribution of surplus farm products to the poor and objected to the establishment of any Food Stamp program that would allow the poor to buy nonsurplus agricultural products. Conservatives also continued to object to food stamps because they viewed them as being counter to the principles of federalism and too costly.[10]

In 1959, Representative Sullivan finally persuaded Congress to agree to give the secretary of agriculture authority to set up an experimental Food Stamp program for two years. The authorization was attached as an amendment to a noncontroversial agricultural bill and was adopted by Congress partially to protect the noncontroversial bill and partially in the expectation that the conservative Eisenhower Administration would not exercise its authority to implement the Food Stamp program. That expectation was realized.

In 1961, President Kennedy, a Democrat, announced that he was instructing his secretary of agriculture to establish a pilot Food Stamp program that would assist approximately 300,000 persons residing in 8 areas of high, chronic unemployment. Recognizing that conservatives controlled the Agriculture Committees in Congress and probably would not approve legislation to establish the program, he claimed that Section 32 of the Potato Control Act of 1935 gave him the authority to set up the program without further congressional action. Republicans and conservatives of both political parties on the Agriculture Committees were angered by Kennedy's action, not only because he was sidestepping their authority but also because none of the areas designated for food assistance were in their congressional districts.[11]

In 1962 Michael Harrington's book *The Other America* served as a rallying point for those interested in using the resources of the national government to combat poverty (see Chapter 3 for further details). The public's growing sympathy for the poor gave Representative Sullivan new hope for the Food Stamp program. On April 22, 1963, she introduced a bill to establish a permanent, national Food Stamp program. To mollify conservatives, the bill allowed states to administer the program and to set the program's eligibility criteria (reducing the intensity of the federalism issue). Also, recipients were required to pay at least $2 per $12 worth of stamps (reducing the program's cost). Finally, the national government would pay for the entire cost of the food coupons and 62.5 percent of the travel expenses and salaries of state personnel engaged in certifying eligible households (to attract state support).[12]

10Ibid., p. 76.

11Ibid.; and "Evolution of the Food Stamp Program," p. 7.

12U.S. Advisory Commission on Intergovernmental Relations, *Public Assistance: The Growth of a Federal Function*, pp. 78–80.

The legislation was supported by the Kennedy Administration, farm organizations, labor unions, and the National Association of Counties. County officials have historically played the lead role in financing and managing public welfare programs. They have welcomed any fiscal assistance that the national government has been willing to provide. However, conservative Democrats and Republicans united in opposition to Sullivan's bill. In March 1964, the Republican members of the Agriculture Committee summed up their grievances:

> We oppose the enactment of H.R. 10222 [Sullivan's bill] because the establishment of a nationwide food stamp plan is not needed; it would be extremely expensive and inefficient; it would destroy the rights and usurp the responsibilities of state and local governments; it would aggravate the problems of commodities now held in surplus stocks by the government; it would add hundreds of new employees in the Department of Agriculture; it would give the Secretary of Argiculture new broad and sweeping powers; it would be adverse to the needy people it is designed to help; and it would be of little benefit to U.S. farmers.[13]

The Food Stamp program appeared dead. But another bill, dealing with wheat and cotton, was also facing difficulties. Northern liberals offered to trade their support for the wheat and cotton bill if conservatives from the South and West would support the Food Stamp bill. Conservatives accepted the offer in a classic example of congressional logrolling, and the Food Stamp program was enacted.[14]

THE BATTLE OVER FOOD STAMPS' ELIGIBILITY CRITERIA AND PAYMENT LEVELS

Liberals and most county officials were delighted to see the Food Stamps program enacted on a "permanent" basis. However, states retained the right to determine the program's eligibility standards, recipients were required to pay for a portion of their stamps, and states that elected to participate in the program had to withdraw from the national government's agricultural surplus distribution program.[15] These restrictions significantly impaired the Food Stamp program's ability to meet the poor's

[13]Ibid., p. 77.

[14]Ibid., p. 78; and "Surplus Disposal Programs—1945–1964," in *Congress and the Nation, 1945–1964* (Washington, DC: Congressional Quarterly Service, 1965), p. 740.

[15]The national government allowed the states to determine exactly how much recipients had to pay for their stamps. Although recipients were required to contribute at least $2 toward the value of the stamps, it was estimated that they would spend approximately $6 for each $10 food coupon. See "Evolution of the Food Stamp Program," *Congressional Digest* (January 1981):7.

nutritional needs. In this regard, many liberals complained that the program was a "flop."[16]

Although the number of states participating in Food Stamps expanded from 22 in 1964 to 44 in 1969, states that switched from the national government's free distribution of surplus agricultural products to Food Stamps experienced a 40 percent decline in the number of people receiving food assistance. This decline was primarily caused by the requirement that recipients pay for a portion of their food stamps. The very poorest in the nation could not afford the required minimum contribution of $2. Another reason for the decline in participation was the lack of effort by state welfare administrators to publicize the availability of food stamps.[17]

Convinced that the Food Stamp program was not reaching enough people (see Table 4.1 for enrollments), liberals attempted during the 1960s to change its eligibility criteria so that more people would qualify for benefits. A number of political obstacles stood in their way. First, the House and Senate Agriculture Committees and their subcommittees having jurisdiction over the Food Stamp program were chaired by conservatives. These chairmen were not convinced that expensive social welfare programs would eliminate poverty, and were more interested in stabilizing farm prices by distributing surplus agricultural products to the poor than in helping the poor attain a nutritionally balanced diet through a Food Stamp program. They also were convinced that hunger was not a widespread national problem. Thus, they questioned the need for a national program aimed at solving a national problem that did not exist.[18]

Second, Republicans were united in opposition to an increase in food assistance at the same time the war in Vietnam was threatening to "bust" the national government's budget. Third, many states' rights advocates were convinced that food assistance for the poor was a state and local responsibility. Fourth, most conservatives and even some liberals were convinced that food stamps were not the best way to help the poor obtain a nutritionally balanced diet. They advocated giving the poor cash to buy their food, either in the form of enhanced AFDC benefits or through a guaranteed annual income (see discussion of the negative income tax in chapter 3).[19]

[16]U.S. Advisory Commission on Intergovernmental Relations, *Public Assistance: The Growth of a Federal Function*, p. 79.

[17]Ibid.

[18]Ibid.; and "Feeding the Hungry," in *Congress and the Nation, 1965–1968* (Washington, DC: Congressional Quarterly Service, 1969), p. 587.

[19]Ibid. Advocates of direct cash payments argue that providing cash instead of food stamps would reduce administrative costs and enhance the recipients' dignity by enabling them to buy food with cash like everyone else. Food stamp advocates counter these arguments by stating that the poor may unwisely use the cash grant to purchase nonfood items, and since food stamps clearly benefit agriculture and the grocery industry as well as the poor, Congress is much more likely to fund a Food Stamp program than a direct cash program.

A series of events in 1968 greatly strengthened the liberal's position on food stamps. In April, a self-appointed Citizens Board of Inquiry into Hunger and Malnutrition issued a 100-page report, entitled *Hunger U.S.A.*, that strongly denounced the national government's efforts to meet the nutritional needs of the poor. Their report, which received a great deal of press coverage, argued that between 10 million and 14.5 million Americans were underfed, and that there were 256 "hunger counties" that had no public food assistance programs of any kind. It also indicated that food stamps could help alleviate the problem, but not without substantial revisions in the eligibility criteria and a much greater commitment of national funds. The report specifically cited the need to get rid of the recipient contribution requirement, and the needs to have more uniform national eligibility criteria and much higher benefit levels.[20]

Then, in May 1968, a CBS television special entitled "Hunger in America" touched off a storm of controversy.[21] The narrator of the program, Charles Kuralt, substantiated *Hunger U.S.A.*'s conclusions when he told the national television audience that "Ten million Americans don't know where their next meal is coming from" and that the programs designed to alleviate the problem of hunger in America were failures.[22]

"Hunger in America" was suddenly a hot political topic. Liberals were ecstatic, but knew that while the political environment was ripe for an expansion of the national government's role in setting eligibility standards and benefit levels, the House and Senate Agriculture Committees were still opposed to the program. House Agriculture Committee Chairman W. R. Poage (D-TX), for example, issued a public statement denouncing *Hunger U.S.A.* as "misleading."[23] He also claimed that "There seems to be little or no evidence that any substantial hunger in this country exists as the result of the refusal of assistance agencies . . . to give needed aid to those who are unable to work."[24] After several floor battles in the House and the Senate in 1969, Congress decided not to restructure the Food Stamp program. Instead, it increased its funding by only $25 million, to $340 million for FY 1970.[25]

Congress' decision in 1969 convinced many liberals that the Food Stamp program would face many difficult political battles in the 1970s. The White House was occupied by a conservative Republican, and the Agriculture Committees obviously were not interested in expanding the pro-

---

[20]"Feeding the Hungry," in *Congress and the Nation, 1965–1968*, p. 592.

[21]U.S. Advisory Commission on Intergovernmental Relations, *Public Assistance: The Growth of a Federal Function*, p. 81.

[22]Ibid.

[23]"Feeding the Hungry," in *Congress and the Nation, 1965–1968*, p. 592.

[24]Ibid.

[25]Ibid., pp. 593, 594; and "Welfare Legislation," in *Congress and the Nation, 1969–1972* (Washington DC: Congressional Quarterly, 1973), p. 629.

gram. Despite these obstacles, Food Stamps became one of the nation's most expensive intergovernmental programs during the 1970s. Although President Nixon was never a strong advocate of either food stamps or welfare legislation in general, he recognized that the Democrat-controlled Congress and the American public were committed to a major expansion in the Food Stamp program.

In a move seen by some as a means to prevent the Democrats from getting all the political credit for combating hunger, Nixon issued an executive order in 1970 that eliminated the requirement that food stamp applicants with an income below $30 a month pay for a portion of their food stamps. This requirement had prevented the very poorest in the nation from receiving food stamps. He also ordered that the Department of Agriculture's definition of the cost of an economy diet ($100 per month for a family of four at that time) be used by all states in setting their benefit levels. This increased the value of the food stamps received by most recipients. He also ordered that no recipient of food stamps was to pay more than 30 percent of total income for the stamps. Thus, with the stroke of a pen, President Nixon had circumvented the opposition of the House and Senate Agriculture Committees, thwarted the will of state rights' advocates by establishing national standards for food stamp benefits, and upstaged the Democratic party.[26]

Not to be outdone, the Democratic majorities in Congress (with the support of the National Association of Counties and other public interest groups) adopted legislation in 1971 that changed the political debate from whether the Food Stamp program would survive to how big it would get. The 1971 Food Stamp Amendments extended the Food Stamp program for three years, tripled its authorization level for FY 1971, left expenditures for 1972 and 1973 open-ended (causing funding to increase automatically if the economy weakened and more people became eligible for food stamps), and authorized the secretaries of agriculture and health, education, and welfare to jointly establish uniform national eligibility criteria. Thus, states were no longer involved in the determination of eligibility criteria or benefit levels.

The 1971 Food Stamp Amendments also adopted Nixon's standard of 30 percent of income as the upper limit for a recipient's contribution to the cost of the food stamps, provided stamps free of charge to families of four or more with an income below $30 a month, and (as a gesture to conservatives) established a work requirement. All food stamp recipients who were able-bodied adults between the ages of 18 and 65 were required to register with the county welfare agency for work and to accept suitable employment. The amendments also required county welfare agencies to advertise the Food Stamp program's availability to the poor and increased

[26]U.S. Advisory Commission on Intergovernmental Relations, *Public Assistance: The Growth of a Federal Function*, p. 83.

the national government's contribution toward state administrative costs to 50 percent.[27]

As Table 4.1 indicates, the number of food stamp recipients increased dramatically following the enactment of the 1971 Food Stamp Amendments. In 1970 there were 4.3 million recipients. In 1972 that number had increased to 11.1 million. The number continued to grow during the mid-1970s, following Congress' decision in 1973 to require all counties within states offering food stamps to participate in the program by July 1974.[28]

The dramatic increase in the number of food stamp recipients during the early 1970s led to a dramatic increase in the cost of the program and a reemergence of conservative opposition. Food stamp expenditures jumped from $579 million in 1970 to $5.5 billion in 1976. Citing the need to reduce the size of the national deficit, President Ford asked Congress on a number of occasions during the mid-1970s to reduce food stamp costs by tightening the program's eligibility standards. He was particularly opposed to the established practice of deducting certain expenses from an applicant's gross income (such as a standard amount to cover the cost of getting to and from work, and child care expenses) before determining eligibility for food stamps. He argued that these deductions allowed many people with incomes well above the national government's poverty income threshold to receive food stamps. Consistent with his conservative ideology, he complained that income disregards had to be eliminated in order to ensure that the program targeted its benefits to those who were truly needy. He also objected to the eligibility of strikers and college students with middle- or upper-income parents.

Liberals, most moderates, and the intergovernmental lobby organizations opposed Ford's efforts, but he did win some concessions. The Food and Agriculture Act of 1977 eliminated the program's open-ended budget authority, forcing Congress to vote annually on the program's funding level. If an economic recession occurred and the number of people entitled to food stamps increased dramatically, those newly eligible would not receive stamps unless Congress voted to increase the program's appropriation.[29] In addition, the program's work requirement was tightened for college students and mothers with children between the ages of 12 and 18, and, for the first time, households receiving AFDC or SSI payments were

[27]Ibid.

[28]In 1969 only about half of all the counties in America participated in the Food Stamp program; most of the counties that did not participate were poor and had a major hunger problem. See J. Fred Giertz and Dennis H. Sullivan, "Food Assistance Programs in the Reagan Administration," *Publius: The Journal of Federalism* 16 (Winter 1986):138, 139.

[29]Although Congress now has the ability to reduce food stamp expenditures whenever enrollments increase faster than anticipated, it has routinely approved increases whenever the economy has weakened and enrollments and program costs have exceeded anticipated levels. See Ibid.

no longer automatically entitled to food stamps. They were now required to meet the same asset and income limitations as others to be eligible for food assistance.

However, liberals were able to defend the use of income disregards in determining eligibility for the program. Although an applicant's family's net adjusted monthly income could not exceed national poverty levels, an applicant could deduct 20 percent of earnings (to compensate for national, state, and local taxes), $60 a month for work-related expenses (adjusted twice a year to reflect changes in the cost of living), up to $75 a month (adjusted annually to reflect changes in the cost of living), and child care expenses and any housing costs exceeding 50 percent of the applicant household's net adjusted income.[30]

Although most food stamp recipients continued to have gross monthly incomes well below the national government's poverty threshold, the income disregards did allow some families with incomes as much as 160 percent of the poverty threshold to qualify for food stamps.[31] Finally, the purchase requirement for families with monthly incomes above $30 a month was eliminated. Starting in 1979, all recipients received their food stamps free of charge.[32]

Although AFDC and SSI recipients were no longer automatically entitled to food stamps, the program continued to serve a key liberal goal of reducing interstate variations in total welfare benefits. While many states continued to restrict AFDC benefits to those with incomes well below the poverty level, the Food Stamp program's income disregards ensured that all of the nation's poor were at least provided one form of public assistance, regardless of where they lived. Also, because the amount of each household's food stamp allotment is reduced as its income increases, households in states that provide relatively low AFDC payments receive more food stamps than those who live in states that provide relatively generous AFDC payments.

In 1988, for example, a family of three with no income would have received $779 a month in AFDC payments if they lived in Alaska and only $120 a month if they lived in Mississippi (a difference of $659). Since the Food Stamp program recognizes AFDC payments as income, it would have provided this family with food stamps worth $201 a month if they lived in Alaska and $228 a month if they lived in Mississippi. As a result, total

[30]U.S. Department of Health and Human Services, *Social Security Bulletin, Annual Statistical Supplement, 1984–1985* (Washington, DC: U.S. Government Printing Office, 1985), p. 59; U.S. Advisory Commission on Intergovernmental Relations, *Public Assistance: The Growth of a Federal Function*, p. 87; Dianne D. Jenkins, "The New Food Stamp Legislation," *Food and Nutrition* 7:5 (October 1977):2–10; and Elizabeth Wehr, "Panel Expands Food Stamps, Adding $1 Billion to Program," Congressional Quarterly, *Weekly Report* (May 12, 1984):1144.

[31]J. Fred Giertz and Dennis Sullivan, "Food Assistance Programs in the Reagan Administration," p. 138.

[32]Dianne Jenkins, "The New Food Stamp Legislation." pp. 2–10.

AFDC and food stamp benefits for the family would be $980 a month if they lived in Alaska and $348 if they lived in Mississippi (a difference of $632 a month). Thus, food stamps helped narrow the difference between the amount of public assistance received by the poor in Alaska and Mississippi by $27 a month (from $659 to $632). Table 4.2 provides the state-by-state variations in the value of food stamps that a three-person family received in 1988 if it had no earned income.

MACROECONOMIC THEORIES AND FOOD STAMPS

When President Reagan entered office in 1981, he was convinced that the Food Stamp program was subject to rampant waste and fraud.[33] He also was sure that the burgeoning size of both the annual and the cumulative national deficit had dire economic implications. Since he was committed to spending more on defense, he believed that the national government had to significantly reduce expenditures on domestic programs. He therefore announced his intention to target welfare programs to the "truly needy." This translated into a number of proposals to restrict eligibility criteria for food stamps and to reduce the amount of benefits provided to those who remained eligible.

Taking advantage of the "honeymoon" period following his victory over Jimmy Carter and the capture of the Senate by the Republicans, President Reagan was able to get Congress to approve a number of changes in the Food Stamp program in the Omnibus Reconciliation Act of 1981. All households that did not contain an elderly person and had a gross income exceeding 130 percent of the national poverty level ($8,450 for a nonfarm family of four in 1981) were excluded from the program, as were households, with one or more members involved in a labor strike. The amount of the income deduction allowed for housing costs that exceeded 50 percent of adjusted net income was frozen for three years, the standard deduction for work-related expenses was reduced from 20 percent of earned income to 18 percent, and national funding of outreach programs aimed at informing eligible persons of their right to food stamps was eliminated. These changes have caused national expenditures for food stamps to level off during the 1980s at $11 to $13 billion and the number of recipients to fall from 21 million in 1981 to 18 million in 1989. If they had not been enacted, the national government's costs for food stamps would have

---

[33]Public opinion polls have indicated that most Americans support increased national expenditures on most social welfare programs. But the public is divided on food stamps. In 1985, 17 percent of the public wanted food stamp expenditures increased, 37 percent thought that its funding should remain about the same, and 26 percent wanted its funding decreased. See James Sundquist, "Has America Lost Its Social Conscience—and How Will It Get It Back?" *Political Science Quarterly* 101:4 (1986):521, 522.

TABLE 4.2   Maximum Monthly Food Stamp Benefits, Family of Three Persons, 1988

STATE	MAXIMUM BENEFIT	STATE	MAXIMUM BENEFIT
1. Hawaii	$308	26. Nebraska	$202
2. Alabama	228	27. Colorado	201
3. Arkansas	228	28. Alaska	201
4. Georgia	228	29. Virginia	201
5. Kentucky	228	30. Montana	200
6. Louisiana	228	31. Wyoming	199
7. Mississippi	228	32. South Dakota	198
8. New Mexico	228	33. North Dakota	196
9. North Carolina	228	34. Kansas	195
10. South Carolina	228	35. Rhode Island	195
11. Tennessee	228	36. Utah	195
12. Texas	228	37. D.C.	194
13. West Virginia	228	38. Iowa	193
14. Florida	225	39. New Jersey	188
15. Missouri	223	40. Pennsylvania	187
16. Indiana	221	41. Maine	183
17. Arizona	219	42. Washington	174
18. Ohio	219	43. Michigan	171
19. Oregon	219	44. New Hampshire	162
20. Maryland	217	45. New York	162
21. Idaho	216	46. Massachusetts	154
22. Oklahoma	214	47. Wisconsin	152
23. Delaware	212	48. Minnesota	148
24. Illinois	210	49. Connecticut	127
25. Nevada	210	50. Vermont	126
		51. California	117

Source: U.S. Congress, House, Ways and Means Committee, *Background Material and Data on Programs Within the Jurisdiction of the Committee on Ways and Means,* 100th Cong. 2nd sess. (Washington, DC: U.S. Government Printing Office, March 1988), p. 408.

increased to over $13 billion, and the number of people receiving food stamps would have risen to over 22 million.[34]

President Reagan proposed even larger cost-saving measures for the Food Stamp program in 1982, but the nation was in the middle of a recession, and House Democrats refused to accept most of them.[35] However, to reduce future budget growth, Congress did agree to bar from the program college students who failed to qualify for AFDC benefits and did not have children under the age of 12, to lengthen the period of ineligibility for people who quit their jobs from 60 days to 90 days, to allow states to require

[34]"Chronology of Action on Welfare," in *Congress and the Nation, 1981–1984* (Washington, DC: Congressional Quarterly, 1985), pp. 583–585.

[35]Congress restored the standard deduction for earned income (to compensate for work-related expenses) to 20 percent in 1985.

food stamp recipients to actively look for work, to increase civil penalties to $10,000 for each violation of food stamp law by stores, and to require states to reduce their error rates to 5 percent by FY 1985 or lose a portion of their administrative funds.[36]

Claiming that the Reagan administration was insensitive to the needs of the poor, Democrats in Congress have refused to make any additional major changes in the Food Stamp program since the early 1980s. The Reagan administration countered these charges of insensitivity by pointing out that the national government was already spending significantly more on food assistance than ever before. A report by the administration's Task Force on Food Assistance declared on January 9, 1984, that "allegations of rampant hunger simply cannot be documented" and that there was "no evidence that widespread malnutrition is a major health problem in the United States."[37] Since hunger was not as widespread as believed, and there was a genuine need to keep the national government's costs in line with its income, the task force recommended that the states be allowed to drop out of the Food Stamp and child nutrition programs and accept a food block grant instead, with states determining eligibility and benefit levels.[38] Although the House and Senate Agriculture Committees did consider the idea of a food block grant in 1985, the tide of public opinion was once again moving in favor of the liberals, and the food block grant died in committee.[39]

CONCLUSIONS

The unresolved debate over the seriousness of the hunger problem in America will most likely continue during the 1990s. Liberals will continue to argue that hunger is a very serious national problem, and that the Food Stamp program's eligibility criteria and benefit levels should be set by the national government. Conservatives will continues to argue that the size of the national government's deficit, coupled with the need to build up the nation's defense, requires that all domestic programs be scrutinized for cost

[36] "Chronology of Action on Welfare," pp. 594–596.

[37] Ibid.

[38] Ibid.; and Elizabeth Wehr, "Report of Task Force Draws Mixed Reaction from the Hill," Congressional Quarterly *Weekly Report* (January 14, 1984):51, 52.

[39] Robert Rothman, "Panel Would Expand Food Stamp Eligibility," Congressional Quarterly, *Weekly Report* (June 15, 1985):1180; and David Rapp, "Budget, Partisan Pressures Keep Farm Bills in Committee," Congressional Quarterly, *Weekly Report* (August 3, 1985):1530. The President's Task Force on Food Assistance indicated that two groups deserved to receive food stamps but were not eligible: the homeless and recently unemployed workers who could not meet the program's asset test but had very serious cash flow problems. See J. Fred Giertz and Dennis Sullivan, "Food Assistance Programs in the Reagan Administration," pp. 141, 142.

effectiveness and that programs, such as Food Stamps, that can be run effectively by state and local governments ought to be turned over to those governments or, at the very least, be converted into block grants.

It is always difficult to predict what national programs will look like in the future. The public's sympathy for the poor's needs is enduring, but support for their receiving food stamps is weak. Moreover, the outcomes of national political contests are always difficult to predict, especially since voters are no longer necessarily voting according to their partisan affiliation. However, regardless of which political party is in power in Washington during the 1990s, it is very likely that the national government's current fiscal difficulties will persist. As a result, it is very likely that the national government will continue to seek ways to reduce food stamp expenditures, either by tightening eligibility criteria or by reducing benefit levels. It also would not come as a complete shock if the Food Stamp program was converted into a block grant during the 1990s. Neither the House nor the Senate Agriculture Committee has a great deal of enthusiasm for the program, and that could make a big difference in the program's funding levels during the 1990s if the national government's deficit woes continue. Moreover, nationally financed programs, like food stamps, that have a relatively weak political constituency and are subject to strong ideological differences concerning their structure and operations, are always subject to change on Capitol Hill, especially during periods of fiscal retrenchment.

Finally, the president's proposal to turn food stamps over to the states in 1982 (see chapter 2 for details) serves as a reminder that the Reagan administration had firmly rejected the traditional justifications for the establishment of nationally financed intergovernmental programs. Unlike the Nixon, Ford, and Carter administrations before it, the Reagan administration rejected the traditional arguments for a national presence in income maintenance programs (the need to use the national government's superior fiscal resources to equalize welfare benefits among the states, the need to overcome the program's negative spillover effects on business investment, and the perceived need to force states and localities to treat politically weak constituencies fairly).

Instead, it took a more macroeconomic view of the intergovernmental system. By offering to nationalize Medicaid in return for turning AFDC and the Food Stamp programs over to the states, the administration was convinced that the number of bureaucrats administering the programs would be reduced and cost efficiencies would then be realized. These cost efficiencies, in turn, would contribute to the national government's efforts to move toward a balanced national budget and the economic prosperity needed to get people off AFDC, Food Stamps, and Medicaid. Thus, the need to promote economic growth overrode the need to equalize welfare benefits among the states, the need to overcome welfare's negative spillover impact on business investment, and the perceived need (not shared by the Reagan administration) to force states to treat politically weak constituencies fairly. Of course, the Reagan administration was also interested in turning Food Stamps and AFDC over to the states for a number of political and ideological reasons, but the swap was clearly consistent with its macroeconomic view of intergovernmental relations.

CHAPTER 5

Job Training Partnership Act

The Job Training Partnership Act of 1982 (JTPA) authorized the funding of three intergovernmental and six nationally administered programs that were designed to combat unemployment by providing youth and adults with job experience and training. The three intergovernmental programs are a $1.8 billion block grant that provides the hard-core unemployed with job training, counseling, and work experience; a $750 million block grant to operate a summer youth employment and training program; and a $128 million categorical grant to retrain workers who have lost their jobs because of technological advances or international trade competition. State and local governments administer the programs and the national government finances all of the cost. The six nationally financed and administered job training programs are targeted at specific population groups.[1] Together, these nine programs serve over 400,000 people at a cost of approximately $3.3 billion annually.

These programs had operated under the Comprehensive Employment and Training Act of 1973 but were subject to widespread criticism. Youth unemployment, especially for blacks, increased during the 1970s despite the expenditure of billions of CETA dollars.[2] Moreover, most of CETA's budget was spent on two public service jobs programs that were widely criticized, first by conservatives and later by many liberals as well, for providing the unemployed with temporary "dead end" government jobs instead of the skills necessary to get a permanent job in the private sector.

JTPA was created to improve these programs' performance. It significantly changed the administrative rules governing their operations. Local governments, in cooperation with local business leaders, now exercise

---

[1]The six national programs are Job Corps ($650 million), Native Americans ($60 million), migrant farmworkers ($63 million), veterans' employment ($14 million), national activities ($70 million), and trade adjustment assistance ($25 million). See U.S. Office of Management and Budget, *Budget of the United States Government, FY 1988, Appendix* (Washington, DC: U.S. Government Printing Office, 1987), p. I-P2.

[2]Charles Murray, *Losing Ground* (New York: Basic Books, 1984), pp. 69–82.

broad control over its programs' content and the states have replaced the national government as the primary governmental body responsible for administrative oversight. Thus planning, administration, and oversight responsibilities have been significantly decentralized and the private sector's role in structuring training programs has been increased dramatically.[3] In addition, while most of CETA's money was spent on enrollees' wage allowances during their training and on allowances for child care and other support services, JTPA requires each local job training plan to allocate at least 70 percent of its funds to job training activities. It also limits administrative expenses to 15 percent and support services to 15 percent of total program funding.[4]

Although the Reagan administration hailed JTPA as a huge success and proudly pointed to Department of Labor statistics indicating JTPA's programs had been far more successful at placing enrollees into permanent jobs than had CETA, many analysts, including representatives of the nation's intergovernmental lobby organizations, have raised serious questions about JTPA's performance.[5] They argue that the program ignores the needs of the hard-core unemployed and has far too little money to meet the needs of the 6 million Americans who fit the legislation's definition of economically disadvantaged or the 8 million Americans who can be expected to be out of work in any given year in the near future (see Table 5.1 for yearly unemployment figures).[6] The program's critics also argue that it often provides largely cosmetic services, such as interview training and résumé writing, instead of real job training; lacks sufficient policy direction from the national government; and is subject to wide variations in the quality of state and local administrative efforts. This chapter examines each of these accusations as well as the historical development of the national government's approach to reducing unemployment.

[3]Robert Guttman, "Job Training Partnership Act: New Help for the Unemployed," *Monthly Labor Review* (March 1983):3–6.

[4]Richard Corrigan, "Private Sector on the Spot as It Prepares to Take over Job Training," *National Journal* (April 30, 1983):896.

[5]The Department of Labor indicates that approximately 68 percent of JTPA enrollees were able to find jobs in the private sector between 1983 and 1985, whereas CETA placed only 15 percent of its enrollees in private sector jobs between 1975 and 1981. See Neal R. Peirce and Robert Guskind, "Job Training for Hard-Core Unemployed Continues to Elude the Government," *National Journal* (September 28, 1985):2197, 2198; and "Partners in Training," *Nation's Business* (November 1985):48K. CETA's placement rate for its job training block grant was approximately 30 percent in the 1975–1981 period. The 15 percent figure quoted above includes placements from CETA's public service jobs programs, which were not primarily designed to place people into private sector jobs. See Grace A. Franklin and Randall B. Ripley, *CETA: Politics and Policy, 1973–1982* (Knoxville: University of Tennessee Press, 1984), p. 196.

[6]An economically disadvantaged person has been defined as either a member of a family with an income beneath the national government's poverty threshold or a recipient of food stamps or AFDC. See Charles Bartsch, "Job Training Partnership Act," *Information Service* 28 (June 1984):2–4.

TABLE 5.1 Percent of U.S. Labor Force Unemployed Selected Years, 1931–1989

YEAR	PERCENT OF LABOR FORCE	YEAR	PERCENT OF LABOR FORCE
1989 (est.)	5.5	1959	5.5
1987	6.5	1957	4.3
1985	7.2	1955	4.4
1983	9.5	1953	2.9
1981	7.5	1951	3.3
1979	5.8	1949	5.9
1977	6.9	1947	3.9
1975	8.3	1945	1.9
1973	4.8	1943	1.9
1971	5.8	1941	9.9
1969	3.5	1939	17.2
1967	3.8	1937	14.3
1965	4.5	1935	20.1
1963	5.7	1933	24.9
1961	6.7	1931	15.9

Sources: U.S. Department of Labor, *Employment and Earnings* (April 1987):20, 21; U.S. Department of Commerce, *Statistical Abstract of the United States, 1986* (Washington, DC: U.S. Government Printing Office, 1986), p. 390; U.S. Department of Commerce, *Statistical Abstract of the United States, 1970* (Washington, DC: U.S. Government Printing Office, 1970), p. 213; and U.S. Department of Commerce, *Statistical Abstract of the United States, 1960* (Washington, DC: U.S. Government Printing Office, 1960), p. 205.

JOB TRAINING OR JOB CREATION: FROM THE DEPRESSION TO THE 1970s

Prior to the Great Depression of the 1930s, the national government addressed the issue of unemployment indirectly, by maintaining a balanced budget, adjusting the tariff on imported goods to protect domestic manufacturers, and regulating the value of the dollar. As unemployment soared to nearly 13 million during the Depression (25 percent of the labor force), the liberal, Democratic Congress abandoned the necessity of balancing the budget and began to experiment with Keynesian macroeconomics to spur the economy. It suggested that the national government should increase its level of expenditures when the economy was weak, even if the increased expenditures led to a deficit. The governmental expenditures would provide consumers with more disposable income to be spent on goods and services, leading, in turn, to greater consumer demand for those goods and services. As demand increased, business inventories would fall. Businesses would then hire additional workers to meet increased demand. This would further increase the amount of disposable income in the economy and lead to economic recovery.

As part of its new willingness to increase governmental spending, the national government adopted eight public service employment programs between 1932 and 1935 for immediate reduction of the unemployment rate.[7] Between 1933 and 1942 the Public Works Administration (PWA) spent a total of $4.5 billion to hire the unemployed to work on construction projects such as the Skyline Drive that cuts across Virginia's Blue Ridge Mountains, tunnels for Chicago's subway system, and hundreds of elementary and secondary schools. At its peak (July 1934) the PWA employed 541,000 people. The Works Progress Administration (WPA) spent a total of $13.4 billion between 1935 and 1943. It hired approximately 2 million people a year to build more than 600,000 miles of highway, 125,000 public buildings, and over 8,000 parks. WPA workers also were hired to write plays and poetry and to paint murals for public buildings. During its peak year (1938) it employed 3.3 million people.[8]

Although outnumbered in Congress during the 1930s and 1940s, conservatives vigorously opposed Keynesian macroeconomic solutions to reduce unemployment. They argued that deficit spending would lead to economic ruin. They feared inflation from an overheated economy and higher interest rates from a national deficit. They were particularly opposed to the liberals' insistence on creating short-term government jobs for the unemployed during periods of economic stagnation. Instead of offering the unemployed a "dead-end, leaf-raking" job lasting only as long as the government funds it, conservatives advocated the funding of much less expensive programs that would provide the unemployed with vocational education and job training.

By giving the unemployed the skills necessary to get a "real job" in the private sector, the national government would save billions of dollars in the long run by transforming individuals who are consumers of government tax dollars into suppliers of government tax dollars. Moreover, conservatives have argued that public sector employment programs are prone to significant operational difficulties. The WPA, for example, was criticized for being a political patronage operation and for offering jobs to supply such critically important governmental functions as tap dancing and shadow puppetry.[9]

The national government eliminated its public service employment programs during World War II as it focused its economic resources on national defense, and the unemployment rate dropped to between 2 and 4

---

[7]The eight programs were state and local work relief under the Reconstruction Finance Corporation; Civilian Conservation Corps; public works projects of the Federal Emergency Relief Administration; Civil Works Administration; Federal Work Relief Program of the Federal Emergency Relief Administration; Works Progress Administration; National Youth Administration; and the Public Works Administration. See U.S. Advisory Commission on Intergovernmental Relations, *Reducing Unemployment: Intergovernmental Dimensions of a National Problem* (Washington, DC: U.S. Government Printing Office, 1982), p. 14.

[8]Ibid., p. 14; and "Chronology of Action on Labor and Pension Policy," in *Congress and the Nation, 1981–1984* (Washington, DC: Congressional Quarterly, 1985), p. 653.

[9]U.S. Advisory Commission on Intergovernmental Relations, *Reducing Unemployment*, p. 17.

percent of the labor force (see Table 5.1). The liberals' interest in resurrecting public service employment and job training programs rekindled during the early 1960s only after the publication of Michael Harrington's book *The Other America,* which served to increase public awareness and concern about poverty in America, and the unemployment rate doubled to the 5 and 6 percent level.

Recognizing the public's growing acceptance of a national role in assisting the poor, and convinced that Keynesian economic thought was correct, the Kennedy and Johnson administrations proposed a series of large public works projects modeled after the WPA to spur economic growth and reduce unemployment rates. They also asked Congress to approve a number of smaller public service employment and job training programs that were designed to reduce youth and minority unemployment. The proposals for the enactment of job training programs for specific, targeted groups reflected a new view of the unemployment problem. Unemployment was no longer seen as just an extension of natural and unavoidable swings in the business cycle. Instead, unemployment was viewed as a by-product of a defect in the nation's economy. Although unemployment rates would increase and decrease with the swings in the economy brought about by the business cycle, many individuals employed in technologically obsolete industries and some social groups, particularly blacks, were going to have a difficult time finding work regardless of the condition of the overall economy.[10]

To help those suffering from what became known as structural unemployment, Democrats and Republicans joined in a bipartisan effort in 1962 to create the national government's first comprehensive job training program, the *Manpower Development and Training Act.*[11] Most of the conservatives in Congress viewed the legislation as a means of retraining adults who were likely to lose their jobs because of technological advancements, while most liberals and moderates viewed the legislation as a means of training blacks and other minority groups who had a difficult time finding work because of job discrimination and poor educational opportunities. Administered by the Department of Labor, it enrolled more than 1 million unemployed youths and adults in its job training centers between 1963 and 1968, with 600,000 of them completing their training. It was reported in 1968 that 75 percent of those who had completed their training had found jobs in the private sector.[12]

The bipartisan support for the Manpower Development and Train-

---

[10]For a discussion of the macroeconomic differences between the parties, see Lester C. Thurow, *The Zero-Sum Solution: Building a World-Class American Economy* (New York: Simon and Schuster, 1985); and Milton Friedman and Rose Friedman, *Free to Choose* (New York: Avon Books, 1980).

[11]U.S. Advisory Commission on Intergovernmental Relations, *Reducing Unemployment,* p. 53.

[12]"Job Training and Rehabilitation," in *Congress and the Nation, 1965–1968* (Washington, DC: Congressional Quarterly Service, 1969), p. 737.

ing Act continued throughout its existence, but conservatives and liberals fought bitterly over a number of other job training programs initiated by the Johnson administration in 1964. These programs were specifically targeted at urban youth and the poor, provided both job training and public service employment to trainees, and had an administrative structure that bypassed state governments and established strong programmatic and fiscal ties between the national government and local private and public agencies. Their purpose was clear: to stimulate the economy and to provide job experience for the young and the poor.

Conservatives were strongly opposed to the public service component of these programs, on the grounds that they were dead-end jobs, and viewed their administrative structure as an infringement on state governments' right to influence the nature and scope of the unemployment programs operating within their borders. The U.S. Conference of Mayors and the National League of Cities lobbied Congress to enact and, later, to reauthorize the programs. Some mayors viewed these programs as a way to reduce the possibility of urban unrest, some believed that public service jobs do provide necessary skills to enter the private work force, and all of them recognized that they subsidized the cost of providing a large number of local government services, particularly trash pickup and other city jobs that did not require skilled labor.[13]

Despite conservative opposition, the *Economic Opportunity Act of 1964* was adopted by the Democrat-controlled Congress. Administered by the national government's Office of Economic Opportunity, it created the Job Corps, the Neighborhood Youth Corps, the College Work-Study Programs, and a number of small programs designed to employ slum residents.[14] However, a number of interest groups wanted Congress to expand the national government's efforts to eradicate unemployment even further. Mayors of large cities and various civil rights organizations were particularly vocal in their support of a more vigorous national role in employment policy. They pointed to the National Advisory Commission on Civil Disorders' report, which indicated that at least 20 percent of the participants in the 1967 race riots were unemployed and that most of the

[13]U.S. Advisory Commission on Intergovernmental Relations, *Reducing Unemployment*, pp. 59, 60, 77, 94, 95.

[14]The Job Corps created residential camps and job training centers for high school dropouts. The program was designed to provide disadvantaged and troubled youth aged 16 to 21 with educational counseling, health services, and work experience. The Neighborhood Youth Corps provided work experience for poor youth aged 16 to 21. Most of its funds were spent on summer employment. It was designed to prevent youths from dropping out of school and to provide them with useful jobs. The College Work-Study Program subsidized the wages paid by colleges to students from low-income families for part-time work either on or off campus. It was designed to help poor students attend college. See Ibid., pp. 55–60; "Job Training and Rehabilitation," in *Congress and the Nation, 1965–1968*, p. 736; and Martin A. Levin and Barbara Ferman, *The Political Hand: Policy Implementation and Youth Employment Programs* (New York: Pergamon Press, 1985), p. 55.

other participants were underemployed in low-paying, low-status jobs beneath their ability and education level. According to the report, unemployment and underemployment were "inextricably linked to the problem of civil disorder."[15]

Congress responded to these demands by adopting several additional job training programs. By 1968 the national government was spending over $1.6 billion annually on 11 job training programs that served over 425,000 people.[16] Yet these programs were increasingly coming under attack by journalists, academics, public interest group lobbies, and conservatives. Conservatives argued that expenditures on these programs contributed to the national deficit and hurt the national economy by fostering unnecessarily high national income taxes. They were particularly critical of the public service employment programs as being a waste of the taxpayers' money. Journalists, many academics, and the public interest group lobbies joined conservatives in arguing that the proliferation of separate job training programs had created severe administrative problems that weakened the programs' effectiveness in combating unemployment. As one study put it, "The result was an administrative and intergovernmental maze of competing policy approaches, agencies, administrative networks, grant mechanisms, and program standards. Programs overlapped at some points and left gaps elsewhere."[17]

The U.S. Conference of Mayors and the National League of Cities asked Congress to give local officials more programmatic flexibility and decision-making authority. They advocated the creation of a block grant for job training that would give state and local governments more administrative responsibility and flexibility to implement the job training programs that they felt best served their needs. President Nixon, a Republican, agreed that a block grant would help reduce what he viewed as a system of categorical grants that was too rigid, uncoordinated, and subject to duplication of effort and wide gaps in services.

CETA: A POLITICAL COMPROMISE

In 1969, President Nixon announced in a nationally televised address that the national government's employment and job training programs were a "terrible tangle of confusion and waste."[18] He went on to say that national

---

[15]"Job Training and Rehabilitation," in *Congress and the Nation, 1965–1968*, p. 734.

[16]"Manpower Programs," in *Congress and the Nation, 1969–1972* (Washington, DC: Congressional Quarterly Service, 1973), p. 734.

[17]U.S. Advisory Commission on Intergovernmental Relations, *Reducing Unemployment*, p. 69.

[18]Richard Nixon, "Television Address on the New Federalism," in Richard P. Nathan, *The Administrative Presidency* (New York: John Wiley & Sons, 1983), p. 104.

. . . job training programs have grown to vast proportions . . . yet they are essentially local in character. As long as the Federal Government continues to bear the cost, they can perfectly well be run by states and local governments, and that way they can be better adapted to specific state and local needs.[19]

Congress did pass a bill in 1969 that would have decentralized administrative responsibilities for employment and job training programs in cities with populations exceeding 75,000 people. However, President Nixon vetoed it as too costly because it not only included $2 billion for job training programs but also added $2.5 billion for a public service employment program and an additional $3 billion for a number of new nationally administered job training programs.[20] Congress failed to override the veto. It did, however, expand the number of job training and employment programs to 17.

For two years the Democratic Congress and President Nixon fought over the appropriate funding levels for these 17 programs and the idea of converting them into a block grant. A breakthrough occurred in 1973 when President Nixon agreed to a compromise proposal that decentralized administrative responsibilities for nearly all existing employment and job training programs by folding them into a block grant in exchange for allowing the Democrats to establish a relatively small and inexpensive public service employment program.

Title I of the *Comprehensive Employment and Training Act of 1973* (CETA) consolidated 17 employment and job training programs into a single block grant to state and local prime sponsors. Only the Job Corps remained a separate categorical program. The block grant received an authorization of $1.55 billion for FY 1974, the amount allotted to the categorical grants that were folded into the block grant. Its planning and administrative responsibilities were divided between state and local governments. Cities and counties with populations exceeding 100,000 persons were designated "prime sponsors" and received direct grants from the national government to undertake locally planned and administered job training programs. State governments were designated "prime sponsors" for all other areas within the state. Thus, the governor's office of each state was responsible for planning and implementing job training programs in rural and suburban areas, and city and county governments were responsible for planning and implementing job training programs in urban areas. The Department of Labor's Employment and Training Administration was responsible for coordinating these disparate state and local efforts by approving or rejecting state and local training plans and for making certain that approved plans were carried out in an efficient and orderly manner.

[19]Ibid., p. 105.

[20]"Chronology of Legislation on Manpower Programs," in *Congress and the Nation, 1969–1972*, p. 735.

The department had the power to take over any job training program that it determined was not meeting appropriate standards of performance.

Funding for the block grant was allocated among the states according to a three-factor formula that was designed to target job training assistance to areas of greatest need. Prime sponsors were required to provide trainees with a weekly wage allowance that was at least equivalent to the national minimum wage and unemployed persons trained in an institutional setting were also provided a weekly allowance for dependent care.[21]

Funding for CETA's block grant was incrementally increased throughout the 1970s, reaching $1.8 billion in 1979. Although a number of studies criticized the block grant's effectiveness in combating structural unemployment, it generated relatively little political controversy. CETA's summer youth employment block grant was criticized by academics and some conservatives for providing youths with unproductive jobs that failed to give them the necessary skills to secure a permanent job in the private sector, but it enjoyed widespread political support as a means of reducing urban unrest during the summer months.[22]

CETA's Title II authorized the expenditure of $250 million in FY 1974 and $350 million in FY 1975 for a public service employment program. The secretary of labor was to allocate these funds among qualifying applicants. CETA specified that Title I prime sponsors and cities with populations of 50,000 to 100,000 with substantial unemployment (6.5 percent or higher for 3 consecutive months) could apply for funding. Recipients of these jobs had to be unemployed for 30 days prior to their hiring and were to receive wages at least equal to the national minimum wage and other benefits, such as health insurance and unemployment insurance. The goal of the program was to reduce structural unemployment by providing job skills to individuals who were considered unemployable.[23]

Unlike its block grant, CETA's public service employment programs were very controversial. As the economy slid into a recession following the Arab oil embargo in 1973, the Democratic Congress viewed CETA's public service component as a vehicle to stem the rising tide of unemployment. In 1974 liberal and moderate Democrats pushed through legislation over conservative opposition that created a temporary, one-year, $2.5 billion public service jobs program (Title VI) to operate alongside CETA's existing public

---

[21]CETA's funding was: 50 percent based on the amount of funding received under the categorical grants in the previous year relative to other states, 37.5 percent based on the number of unemployed persons in the state relative to the number of unemployed persons in other states, and 12.5 percent based on the number of adults in low-income families relative to the number in other states. See "Chronology of Action on Labor and Manpower," in *Congress and the Nation, 1973–1976* (Washington, DC: Congressional Quarterly, 1977), p. 684.

[22]U.S. Advisory Commission on Intergovernmental Relations, *Reducing Unemployment*, p. 84.

[23]"Chronology of Action on Labor and Manpower," in *Congress and the Nation, 1973–1976*, pp. 683-685.

service jobs program (Title II). Unlike the existing program, which was designed to help persons suffering from long-term structural unemployment problems, Title VI was a "countercyclical" measure that was designed to provide jobs to any unemployed person during the duration of the recession. As the recession endured, Congress reauthorized Title VI through FY 1982.[24] Funding for the two public service employment programs grew at such a rapid pace that CETA's emphasis on job training was lost. At its peak in 1978, CETA provided over 750,000 public service jobs to the unemployed at an annual cost of $5.7 billion.[25]

JOB TRAINING PARTNERSHIP ACT: REAGAN'S VICTORY

CETA's political support among moderates and even some liberals began to soften in 1980. Publicity about local abuses of job training funds and favoritism in the hiring of persons for public service jobs seriously weakened public support for the program. Although studies of CETA's performance following its elimination indicated that it had lasting and positive impacts on the lives of many of its trainees, the abuses reported by the press dominated the political debate concerning its future.[26] The perception of widespread fraud within CETA, coupled with its strong emphasis on public service employment, made CETA one of the Reagan administration's prime targets for funding reductions.

Responding to the public's outrage over CETA abuses and cognizant of the newly elected Republican Senate's willingness to sustain a Reagan veto of any job training bill that included a public service component, House Democrats reluctantly agreed to eliminate funding for CETA's two public employment programs in the Omnibus Reconciliation Act of 1981. They also agreed in 1982 to revamp the national government's entire approach to reducing unemployment. Instead of focusing on public service employment programs, CETA was to return to its original intent: to provide the unemployed with the necessary skills to obtain a job in the private sector. Reflecting this new emphasis, CETA was renamed the Job Training Partnership Act (JTPA).

JTPA decentralized oversight responsibilities from the Department of Labor to state governments, decentralized all other administrative

---

[24]"Chronology of Action on Labor and Manpower," in *Congress and the Nation, 1973–1976*, pp. 694–708; and "CETA Jobs Act Extended," Congressional Quarterly, *Almanac, 1977* (Washington, DC: Congressional Quarterly, 1978), p. 287.

[25]"Continuing Appropriations," Congressional Quarterly *Almanac, 1978* (Washington, DC: Congressional Quarterly, 1979), p. 161; and "$8.2 Billion Reconciliation Bill Cleared," Congressional Quarterly, *Almanac, 1980* (Washington, DC: Congressional Quarterly, 1981), p. 139.

[26]Grace A. Franklin and Randall B. Ripley, *CETA: Politics and Policy, 1973–1982*, p. 198.

responsibilities to local governments, and significantly increased the role of the private sector in determining the scope and nature of the local job training programs. Each local service delivery area, for example, was required to establish a Private Industry Council, composed of local business, education, and labor representatives, that was jointly responsible, with local governments, for putting together the service delivery area's job training plan and for monitoring the performance of the area's job training programs. Congressional conservatives and the Reagan administration have lauded JTPA's accomplishments under this decentralized structure, yet many analysts have raised serious questions concerning JTPA's performance. The rest of this chapter examines these questions.

ARE THE NEEDS OF THE HARD-CORE UNEMPLOYED BEING MET?

To ensure that the national government was getting the best value for its dollar, JTPA required the Department of Labor to establish performance standards for local job training programs that would lead to increased employment and earnings of JTPA participants, and to overall reductions in welfare dependency. These performance standards were to include limits on training costs and expected job placement rates. The Department of Labor, however, was initially reluctant to establish these standards because national standards of any kind were counter to the principles of New Federalism and President Reagan's strong desire to reduce the Department of Labor's oversight role. As a result, governors were forced in 1983 to approve local service delivery areas' job training programs before the Department of Labor had announced what its performance standards were going to be. Since the governors were used to a strong Department of Labor presence under CETA, many of them decided to play it safe and approve only those local service delivery plans that promised a high job placement rate at a relatively low cost. In this way, the governors were certain that the Department of Labor would not challenge their states' programs at a later date. The governors' actions were interpreted by local governments and Private Industry Councils as an indication that they should emphasize programs that promised a high job placement rate at low overall cost.

JTPA critics argue that the emphasis on placement rates and low cost led local JTPA administrators to routinely seek out applicants who require only brief training to find a job in the private sector and to screen out applicants who need substantial educational and training assistance. Nationally, JTPA training averaged only 14 weeks during the 1983–1985 period, half of CETA's average training length of 28 weeks. Although it would appear that JTPA can train people in half the time it took CETA and still place more of its trainees in private sector jobs, this "improvement" has nothing to do with the nature of the training programs or the skills of JTPA administrators. The improvement is due to the nature of the trainees.

Several studies of JTPA's performance during the 1983–1985 period indicate that the legislation's goal of targeting money to the economically disadvantaged was not accomplished.[27] One study pointed out that only 26 percent of JTPA's trainees in the 1983–1985 period were high school dropouts. Approximately 60 percent of CETA's Title I trainees were high school dropouts.[28] Another study indicated that nearly one-fourth of JTPA trainees received only job search assistance (interview training, résumé writing, and job referrals) in the 1983–1985 period.[29]

JTPA's critics called the screening out of applicants who need a lot of job training assistance "creaming" (a reference to the cream that rises naturally to the top of raw milk). In 1984 the National League of Cities and other public interest groups asked the Department of Labor to provide local governments an incentive to avoid "creaming" by issuing specific performance criteria. In this way, local governments could operate expensive job training programs that addressed the needs of the nation's most disadvantaged and least job-ready without fear of losing their funding.[30] The Department of Labor did issue performance criteria later in 1984, but they required local governments to improve on CETA's job placement record and required localities to meet relatively stringent cost thresholds per trainee.[31]

Another reason most JTPA administrators screen out the hard-core unemployed is JTPA's strict financial limitations on the amount of money that can be spent on support services, such as costs of transportation to the job training site and child care expenses. Since expenditures on support services cannot exceed 15 percent of total funding, local job training administrators have a very strong incentive to limit the number of trainees who require extensive support services. The hard-core unemployed generally require a disproportionate amount of these support services, since they tend to have few economic assets to live on while they are being trained.

Further, some administrators believe that it makes perfect sense to

[27]Neal R. Peirce and Robert Guskind, "Job Training for Hard-Core Unemployed Continues to Elude the Government," p. 2198.

[28]Ibid.; and Grace A. Franklin and Randall B. Ripley, *CETA: Politics and Policy, 1973–1982,* p. 194.

[29]Neal R. Peirce and Robert Guskind, "Job Training for Hard-Core Unemployed Continues to Elude the Government," p. 2198.

[30]William Barnes, "Human Development Unit Seeks Job Training Guides," *Nation's Cities Weekly* (September 24, 1984):4.

[31]The Department of Labor's guidelines are summarized in Charles Bartsch, "Job Training Partnership Act," *Information Service* 28 (June 1984):8, 9.

target job training assistance to the unemployed who already possess some job-related skills. They contend that many of the hard-core unemployed have social or mental problems that require a great deal of time and money to addresss, often without any real hope of success. In their view, it may be wiser to focus job training efforts on those who have a real chance at escaping poverty and admit that many of the hard-core unemployed are hard-core unemployed for reasons that cannot be addressed through a job training program.

CONSERVATIVE ALTERNATIVES
TO A SPENDING PROGRAM

Although the Reagan administration praised JTPA's performance, it repeatedly asked Congress to eliminate the $650 million Job Corps program entirely, claiming that its $15,000 annual cost per trainee was so outrageous that it nearly equaled the cost of sending a student to Harvard University for a year.[32] It also repeatedly asked Congress to reduce funding for the $750 million summer youth employment and training block grant program to approximately $650 million.[33] Although Congress refused both of these requests, it has kept JTPA's total funding at the $3.3 billion level throughout the 1980s. Many liberals, civil rights activists, and representatives of the nation's cities claim that $3.3 billion is far too little to make any significant progress against even structural unemployment. At $3.3 billion JTPA can offer training to only 4 percent of those who fit its definition of economically disadvantaged.

Conservatives counter these arguments by stressing that the private sector must take the lead in training the economically disadvantaged. To encourage the private sector to do its part, they advocate the continuation of the "targeted jobs" tax credit. One of the few tax loopholes to survive the massive rewrite of the tax laws in 1986, it provides employers a 40 percent reduction in their after-tax costs for the first $6,000 of wages earned by economically disadvantaged youths during their first year of employment. It costs the national government approximately $300 million a year in lost revenue.[34] Many conservatives also support the replacement of the summer youth employment and training block grant with a subminimum wage for workers under age 20 during the summer months. This would provide private employers an incentive to give unskilled teenagers summer jobs

[32]Janet Hook, "Labor Budget Seeks Trimmed Employment Aid," Congressional Quarterly, *Weekly Report* (February 9, 1985):258.

[33]Ibid.

[34]U.S. Office of Management and Budget, *Special Analyses: Budget of the United States Government, FY 1987* (Washington, DC: U.S. Government Printing Office, 1986), p. G-44.

and save the national government $750 million annually.[35] Finally, conservatives would replace job training programs with enterprise zones located in areas of high unemployment that are currently being avoided by private businesses. To encourage businesses to locate in these zones and to hire unemployed local residents, the national government would provide them with special tax breaks, such as exemption from capital gains taxes, a 10 percent investment tax credit for new construction and reconstruction of buildings, and a 5 percent tax credit for the first $10,500 in wages paid to each employee.[36]

One of the major reasons that conservatives advocate the tax credit and subminimum wage approaches to solving structural unemployment is that they are relatively easy and inexpensive to administer. Private employers just pay the subminimum wage or claim the tax credit on their national income tax forms. The only administration necessary on the government's part is occasionally to audit employers' national income tax forms to deter cheating. JTPA, on the other hand, has a number of administrative layers. The national government's Department of Labor establishes the program's performance criteria; 50 state job councils designate local service delivery areas, develop statewide training plans and programs, and monitor local training programs; 600 local service delivery areas have the day-to-day responsibility for running the training programs; and each local service delivery area has at least one local government and one Private Industry Council that must jointly put together a local job training plan that meets national and state guidelines.[37]

JTPA's critics were also quick to point out that the transition from CETA's centralized administrative structure to JTPA's decentralized structure was not a smooth one. The National Commission for Employment Policy discovered that while state governments lobbied Congress hard to gain greater administrative control over job training activities, there were

---

[35]Liberals and most moderates opposed the subminimum wage concept because they felt that employers would fire older workers who earned wages at or near the minimum level and replace them with subminimum wage youths. They also pointed out that economic analyses on the subminimum wage's impact on teenage unemployment were inconclusive and that the rate of teenage unemployment has not always increased when the minimum wage was increased. During the 1976–1979 period teenage unemployment fell when the minimum wage was increased. See Richard Corrigan, "Reagan's Youth Subminimum Wage Bill May Be Dead on Arrival in Congress," *National Journal* (March 12, 1983):552, 553.

[36]A Reagan administration proposal for up to 75 enterprise zones was rejected by Congress in 1986. It would have cost the national government $300 million in lost tax revenue. See U.S. Office of Management and Budget, *Special Analyses: Budget of the United States Government, FY 1986* (Washington, DC: U.S. Government Printing Office, 1985), p. G-36; Janet Hook, "Labor Budget Seeks Trimmed Employment Aid," p. 258; and "Text of Reagan Proposals on Structural Unemployment," Congressional Quarterly, *Weekly Report* (March 19, 1983):581. For a discussion of the pros and cons of a youth subminimum wage and enterprise zones, see Milton Friedman and Rose Friedman, *Free to Choose*, pp. 225–232; Martin A. Levin and Barbara Ferman, *The Political Hand*, pp. 130–146; "The Proposed Subminimum Wage for Youth," *Congressional Digest* (April 1985):99–125; and "Enterprise Zones," *Congressional Digest* (May 1985):131–160.

[37]Charles Bartsch, "Job Training Partnership Act," pp. 11–22.

wide variations in the amount and quality of state administrative activity during the program's first two years of operation. Some state job councils, such as Pennsylvania's and Colorado's, did create state job training guidelines that encouraged local governments and Private Industry Councils to undertake innovative programs that linked job training with economic development and education programs.

Most state job councils, however, were reluctant to set statewide job training guidelines that would allow local service delivery areas to run innovative and untested programs. They feared that the national government might disallow costs if they ran too high and demand refunds when national performance guidelines were finally established. An indication of this conservative approach to administration was that most states used the office to administer JTPA and existing state CETA activities.[38] State job councils also suffered from high turnover rates and poor attendance, particularly among the public sector representatives on the councils.[39]

Local service delivery areas also had administrative problems. Because state job councils' guidelines stressed high job placement rates and low cost per trainee, most local governments and Private Industry Councils decided to avoid new and untested job training programs in favor of programs with a proven track record. As a result, they tended to keep programs that were conducted under CETA. The only major difference between JTPA's programs and CETA's programs was the nature of the trainees who participated. A General Accounting Office report issued in March 1985 revealed that nearly every organization providing services under JTPA had performed similar services under CETA and that many of the administrators of JTPA's job training programs were holdovers from CETA programs.[40] Innovation in local service delivery area administration also was hampered by a wide variation in the quality of leadership from the Private Industry Councils. Turnover and a lack of attendance at PIC meetings was a problem in many areas.[41]

CONCLUSIONS

The ideological differences over the proper role of the national government in reducing unemployment, especially for the hard-core unemployed, led to JTPA's creation. No one is particularly enamored with it.

[38]Ibid., pp. 11, 12; and Neal R. Peirce and Robert Guskind, "Job Training for Hard-Core Unemployed Continues to Elude the Government," p. 2200.

[39]Westat, Inc., "Transition Year Implementation of the Job Training Partnership Act" (Rockville, MD: January 1985), submitted to U.S. Congress, House, Committee on Education and Labor, *Oversight Hearing on the Job Training Partnership Act*, 99th Cong., 1st sess. (Washington, DC: U.S. Government Printing Office, 1985), p. 38.

[40]Neal R. Peirce and Robert Guskind, "Job Training for Hard-Core Unemployed Continues to Elude the Government," p. 2201.

[41]Ibid.

Liberals, moderates, and representatives of the nation's cities would like to see its funding expanded and its job performance guidelines revised to enable state job councils to discourage applicant "creaming." Although Congress agreed, under the threat of a presidential veto, to eliminate CETA's beleaguered public service employment programs, liberals and moderates are likely to try to reinstate them if the unemployment rate increases beyond what they deem to be a tolerable level. Reflecting their advocacy of monetarism and supply-side economics, conservatives will continue to offer tax credits, enterprise zones, and the subminimum wage as cost-effective alternative approaches to solving the unemployment problem. They also will continue to vigorously oppose any effort to reinstate public service employment programs or to relax JTPA's cost-conscious performance guidelines.

JTPA's future will be determined in large part by the future ideological composition of Congress and the White House, and the status of the national economy. It appears that neither liberals or conservatives will dominate both houses of the Congress and the White House at the same time in the near future. It is also unlikely that the national government's deficit woes will disappear during the 1990s. As a result, the national government will probably continue to follow its current policy of stressing macroeconomic solutions to combat structural unemployment. Thus, JTPA and the targeted jobs tax credit will continue to function as relatively minor supplements to that macroeconomic program.

CHAPTER 6

Compensatory Education for the Disadvantaged

For over two decades the Compensatory Education for the Disadvantaged program has been the primary vehicle for providing remedial educational assistance to economically disadvantaged children. Created in 1965 as Title I of the Elementary and Secondary Education Act, it was a key component of the Johnson administration's war on poverty. Based on the assumption that poverty cannot be overcome without a good education, it provides $4 billion annually to local educational agencies (LEAs) to enable them to provide remedial educational services to the economically disadvantaged.[1] Approximately 14,000 school districts and 4.7 million poor children participate in the program.[2]

Over the first 15 years of the program's existence, LEAs were required to submit their programs to periodic reviews conducted by the U.S. Office of Education. That office established a long list of administrative requirements that were designed to ensure that LEAs were using the national government's funds in ways that were in compliance with the law's intent to assist the economically disadvantaged in achieving academic success. In 1981, the Reagan administration asked Congress to repeal many of these regulations, claiming that they were unnecessary and burdensome impediments that retarded the efforts of LEAs to combat illiteracy and other educational problems of the poor. It also asked Congress to convert Title I into a block grant. Although Congress subsequently refused to do so, it did agree to eliminate a large number of the program's nationally imposed administrative regulations, shifted the focus of administrative oversight responsibilities from the U.S. Office of Education to the

[1] U.S. Office of Management and Budget, *Budget of the United States Government, FY1988, Supplement* (Washington, DC: U.S. Government Printing Office, 1987), p. 5–89.

[2] U.S. Congress, House, Committee on Appropriations, *Departments of Labor, Health and Human Services, Education, and Related Agencies Appropriations for 1986, Hearings Before a Subcommittee of the House Committee on Appropriations*, 99th Cong., 1st sess. (Washington, DC: U.S. Government Printing Office, 1985), p. 288. In 1983, 74 percent of Chapter 1 participants were in kindergarten through grade 6, 13 percent were in grades 7 and 8, and 9 percent were in grades 9 through 12.

states, and, in recognition of the program's new decentralized format, changed the program's name from Title I to Chapter 1.[3]

Under the new administrative guidelines, Chapter 1's funds can be .sed by LEAs in any way that fosters the educational achievement of economically disadvantaged children. However, LEAs are urged to give priority to programs that promote basic cognitive skills in reading and mathematics.[4] They also must get their state educational agency to approve their programs and are subject to audit by the U.S. Office of Education.

This chapter examines the legislative history of Chapter 1 and three controversies that arise whenever the program's future is debated. The first controversy involves the program's administrative red tape. Liberals and many moderates view nationally imposed administrative regulations as necessary safeguards against intentional corruption and unintentional misuse of the program's funds. Most conservatives and state and local officials view national regulations as administrative straitjackets that prevent local officials from developing innovative and effective programs that best suit local educational needs.

The second controversy concerns the program's effectiveness. Nearly all of the studies concerning the program's impact on the academic achievement of the poor indicate that most students who participate in a Chapter 1 program do show improvement on standardized tests. However, their academic abilities continue to lag far behind national averages. Liberals view any kind of progress by these students as a justification for continued program funding. Conservatives disagree, arguing that the program's cost exceeds its benefits. Given the national government's deficit woes, programs with questionable cost-benefit ratios should be eliminated or at least converted into a block grant to see if state and local governments can improve on the programs' performance.

Finally the regional battle over the allocation of the program's funds is examined.

THE NATIONAL ROLE IN EDUCATION: STATES' RIGHTS AND OTHER ISSUES

Although local governments have always played the lead role in dealing with education issues, the national government has always been at least indirectly involved in educational policy. The Survey Ordinance in 1785

[3]Ibid., p. 282.

[4]U.S. Department of Health, Education, and Welfare, *Annual Evaluation Report on Programs Administered by the U.S. Office of Education, FY 1979* (Washington, DC: U.S. Government Printing Office, 1980), p. 99. Approximately 74 percent of Chapter 1 participants received compensatory reading instruction in 1983 (the latest available data) and 42 percent received remedial mathematics instruction. Another 20 percent of participants received

required that the proceeds from the rental of at least one section of land in every township developed out of the western territories be set aside to provide for the endowment of schools within that township.[5] In 1862 the Morrill Act provided land grants to the states to establish colleges specializing in agriculture and mechanical arts, and in 1867 the national government formed the Department of Education to monitor the condition and progress of state educational efforts, particularly in the South during Reconstruction. Although there were a few bills introduced in Congress during the late 1800s that would have given the U.S. Department of Education the authority to require states to operate their educational programs according to national standards, none of these bills was adopted. Most congressmen at that time were convinced that the Tenth Amendment reserved the responsibility for educational policy to the states.[6]

In 1917 the Smith-Hughes Act established the national government's first grants-in-aid program for education. It provided states $1.7 million, on a matching basis, to pay for teachers' salaries and other academic expenses related to vocational education in secondary schools.[7] During the Great Depression the national government provided loans and grants to states for school construction and the employment of teachers. In 1940 the Lanham Act authorized national funding for the construction, maintenance, and operation of schools in communities with populations swelled by increased military personnel and defense workers, and in 1944 the Servicemen's Readjustment Act (GI Bill of Rights) established a program of educational benefits for World War II veterans.[8]

Despite the enactment of these national programs, state and local governments continued to provide nearly all of the financing for education in the United States. Most Americans wanted it that way. They considered education a local issue that ought to be dealt with by state and local governments in cooperation with parents and teachers. Many Americans, particularly conservatives, also worried that the enactment of any additional

---

remedial instruction in language arts, 17 percent in guidance counseling, 15 percent in health and nutrition services, and 11 percent in English. Programmatic use percentages total to more than 100 percent because some students receive assistance in more than one area. See U.S. Congress, House, Committee on Appropriations, *Departments of Labor, Health and Human Services, Education, and Related Agencies Appropriations for 1986*, pp. 218, 286.

[5]Carl F. Kaestle and Marshall S. Smith, "The Federal Role in Elementary and Secondary Education, 1940–1980," *Harvard Educational Review* 52:4 (November 1982):387. This article argues that the impact of the 1785 Survey Ordinance and the 1787 Northwest Ordinance on common schooling was almost nil because unimproved land was plentiful and almost worthless as rental property.

[6]U.S. Advisory Commission on Intergovernmental Relations, *Intergovernmentalizing the Classroom: Federal Involvement in Elementary and Secondary Education* (Washington, DC: U.S. Government Printing Office, 1981), p. 14.

[7]Ibid., p. 17.

[8]"Federal Aid to Education," in *Congress and the Nation, 1945–1964* (Washington, DC: Congressional Quarterly Service, 1965), p. 1196.

nationally financed education programs would lead to the national government's control of educational content, a certain predecessor, in their view, of governmental tyranny. Many conservatives at that time also opposed a greater national role in education because they feared that additional expenditures in this area would lead to higher national taxes, which would hurt the national economy. In their view, so long as state and local governments met the objectives of providing students with basic skills, preparing them for entry into the work force, giving them knowledge of political institutions and processes, and instilling in them patriotic values, then the national government should not get involved.[9]

Two other factors contributed to the national government's relatively small role in educational policy prior to 1965. Southern Democrats were more than willing to join conservative Republicans in opposing national educational assistance because Northern liberal Democrats insisted school districts that segregated the races should be denied access to the funds. Until the race issue was resolved or the composition of Congress changed, there were not going to be any major national spending programs for education.

Another political barrier to a greater national role in education policy was the constitutional issue concerning the separation of church and state. During the 1940s and 1950s most of the proposed spending programs for education allowed states to spend the money in the same way that they spent their own tax revenues. This upset representatives of the Roman Catholic Church because many states prohibited the spending of their tax revenues on parochial schools. Congressmen from districts with many Roman Catholic constituents supported efforts to require states to provide a share of the national revenue to parochial schools. Congressmen from districts with few Catholics in them, particularly Southern districts composed primarily of Protestant fundamentalists, opposed these efforts on the grounds that they violated the First Amendment's provision concerning the relationship between government and religion.[10]

Although facing seemingly hopeless odds, liberals in Congress continued to advocate a larger national role in education policy during the 1940s and 1950s. They argued that the states and localities were not doing a very good job of educating the nation's children, especially the children of poor parents and minority groups who lacked political clout.[11] As late as 1965 only three states had their own compensatory education programs for the poor, and total expenditures on those programs were minuscule.[12] Liberals and some moderates also cited evidence compiled by the military

---

[9]Henry M. Levin, "Federal Grants and Educational Equity," *Harvard Educational Review* 52:4 (November 1982):424.

[10]"Federal Aid to Education," in *Congress and the Nation, 1945–1964*, p. 1195.

[11]Henry M. Levin, "Federal Grants and Educational Equity," p. 424.

[12]Mary E. Vogel, "Education Grant Consolidation: Its Potential Fiscal and Distributive Effects," *Harvard Educational Review* 52:2 (May 1982):179.

that revealed a very high level of illiteracy among World War I and World War II draftees. In addition, they pointed to state education department figures that revealed crowded classroom conditions in nearly all the states following World War II as clear evidence that the states were either unwilling or financially unable to cope with the educational needs of the unexpectedly large number of children entering the schools as a result of the baby boom. They also argued that teachers were underpaid relative to what they could earn in other professions. Thus, the best teachers were leaving the teaching profession for other fields, leaving only the loyal, the mediocre, and the worst teachers to educate the nation's children.

Since the states and localities were not meeting the challenge of providing a first-class education to the nation's children, liberals argued, the national government had to act. In their view, education was a national concern because a person's education affects not only that individual's social development and economic future, but also the social and economic development of the nation as a whole. A poorly educated work force, they argued, directly weakens the national economy and indirectly weakens national security.[13]

THE ELEMENTARY AND SECONDARY EDUCATION ACT OF 1965

The 1964 elections marked a turning point in the national government's role in education. Viewing ignorance as one of the main causes of poverty, the Johnson administration held a series of meetings with representatives of the National Education Association (NEA) and the U.S. Catholic Conference. The goal of the meetings was to develop a general aid-to-education bill that was acceptable to both groups. In the past the NEA had vigorously opposed any nationally financed education bill that included aid to private schools.

As these negotiations took place, a major political breakthrough was provided by the newly elected liberal, Democratic majorities in the U.S. House and the U.S. Senate. They erased the race issue as an impediment to the adoption of a general aid-education bill by adopting the Civil Rights Act of 1964. It authorized the withholding of national funds from institutions, including public and private schools, that practiced segregation.[14]

In the meantime, the church-state issue was resolved by the Johnson administration as the NEA and the U.S. Catholic Conference agreed to support a $1.4 billion national aid-to-education bill that targeted its funds to needy, disadvantaged children no matter what kind of school they

[13]"Federal Aid to Education," in *Congress and the Nation, 1945–1964*, p. 1195; and Henry M. Levin, "Federal Grants and Educational Equity," p. 423.

[14]"Federal Education Programs," in *Congress and the Nation, 1965–1968* (Washington, DC: Congressional Quarterly Service, 1969), p. 709.

attended. By shifting the proposal's focus away from helping particular types of schools to helping economically disadvantaged students (most of whom are educated in public schools), the concern over the separation of church and state was dissipated. To further ease the tensions surrounding the religious issue, the bill prohibited parochial schools from using the program's funds to purchase religious textbooks and library materials or to increase teacher's salaries. Moreover, political support for the bill was heightened by the Johnson administration's proposed formula for allocating the program's funds. Approximately 95 percent of all school districts in America, including at least one in every congressional district, would receive funding under the proposal's formula.[15]

The Elementary and Secondary Education Act of 1965 authorized the funding of programs for Compensatory Education for the Disadvantaged (Title I), library and textbook acquisitions, innovative educational programs, the construction of research centers at universities, education of the mentally and physically handicapped, bilingual education, the prevention of school dropouts, and administrative training and data preparation by state departments of education. Each of these programs has its own political dynamics and controversies. Bilingual educational requirements, for example, fostered strong intergovernmental tensions during the Carter administration's tenure in office.[16]

The Title I program, however, was, and continues to be, the heart of the act. It accounted for $1 billion of the act's total $1.3 billion authorization in FY 1966. It was one of the largest intergovernmental programs of its day and continues to rank as one of the ten most expensive intergovernmental programs. Although it has endured for over two decades, it has its critics. Educators have complained about its administrative red tape, Congress has continually battled over its allocation formula, academics have questioned its effectiveness, and the Nixon and Reagan administrations have proposed that it be turned into a block grant. The rest of this chapter examines these issues.

CONTROVERSY #1: IS ALL THAT ADMINISTRATIVE RED TAPE REALLY NEEDED?

Soon after the program went into operation, state and local officials began to complain about Title I's administrative requirements. The first administrative issue was school desegregation. The Civil Rights Act of 1964 prohibited discrimination in public accommodations, employment, and education. It also prohibited discrimination in any program financed by the national government. Following the guidelines of the new civil rights

---

[15]U.S. Advisory Commission on Intergovernmental Relations, *Intergovernmentalizing the Classroom*, pp. 32–34.

[16]David R. Beam, "From Law to Rule: Exploring the Maze of Intergovernmental Regulation," *Intergovernmental Perspective* 9:2 (Spring 1983):13.

legislation, the U.S. Department of Health, Education and Welfare required school districts to show evidence that they were making progress in desegregating their schools before they would be given their allotment of compensatory education funds. Many state and local officials, and congressmen representing rural areas in the South, opposed this practice as a form of intergovernmental blackmail. Nevertheless, most school districts decided to accept the program's funds and its requirement concerning desegregation. As a result, the Compensatory Education for the Disadvantaged program became one of the national government's most effective means of implementing the U.S. Supreme Court's 1954 decision in *Brown v. Board of Education of Topeka, Kansas*, which determined that racial segregation in the schools was unconstitutional.[17]

Although Title I's impact on school desegregation made the headlines, local program administrators were equally concerned about its administrative requirements that were designed to ensure that local education administrators used Title I funds to supplement local funding for compensatory educational efforts for the economically disadvantaged. Liberals and education groups feared that some school districts might use Title I funds to replace existing funding for local compensatory educational programs already in existence. School districts could then either rebate local compensatory education dollars to taxpayers by reducing local taxes, and continue to offer the same level of educational services in the district, or shift their own compensatory education dollars to other programs.

In either case, the educational services offered to the poor would not be significantly improved. To prevent this from happening, the national government required LEAs to continue to spend a least as much on educational services as they did prior to the enactment of Title I, to spend a proportionate share of state and local compensatory education money in schools served by the national government's compensatory education program, to use national government funds only for costs exceeding the average per-pupil expenditure of state and local funds, and annually to put together a comparability report to demonstrate that school districts provide educational services to students enrolled in Title I programs that are comparable with those offered other students. LEAs that failed to comply with these requirements could lose all of their Title I funds.[18]

[17]U.S. Advisory Commission on Intergovernmental Relations, *Intergovernmentalizing the Classroom*, pp. 38–40.

[18]U.S. Congress, House, Committee on Appropriations, *Departments of Labor, Health and Human Services, Education, and Related Agencies Appropriations for 1986*, p. 253; Rochelle L. Stanfield, "'If It Ain't Broke, Don't Fix It,' Say Defenders of Compensatory Aid," *National Journal* (January 30, 1982):202; Joel S. Berke and Mary T. Moore, "A Developmental View of the Current Federal Government Role in Elementary and Secondary Education," *Phi Delta Kappan* (January 1982):335; and Chrys Dougherty, *Report on Changes Under Chapter One of ECIA to the Subcommittee on Elementary, Secondary, and Vocational Education of the Education and Labor Committee*, 99th. Cong., 1st sess. (Washington, DC: U.S. Government Printing Office, 1985), p. 21.

State and local officials also objected to rules adopted in the 1970s that forced them to target Title I's funds to specific types of students and educational services. The Elementary and Secondary Education Act had declared that it was Congress' intention

> to provide financial assistance to local educational agencies serving areas with concentrations of children from low-income families to expand and improve their educational programs by various means which contribute particularly to meeting the special needs of educationally deprived children.[19]

The problem with this declaration of congressional intent was that it could be interpreted to justify the expenditure of funds on just about anything having to do with education. Were local school districts supposed to use the funds to build more schools to reduce class sizes, increase teachers' salaries to attract better teachers and to retain good teachers, build libraries or expand existing library stocks to enhance students' reading skills, buy special equipment such as overhead projectors and pianos to facilitate learning, serve free breakfast at school so poor students can concentrate on their studies, hire additional guidance counselors to deal with emotional and social as well as academic problems, or simply hire more remedial education teachers?

Moreover, although the law's allocation formula did indicate how much money each county was going to receive and how state educational agencies were to allocate each county's funds among its school districts, it did not provide any guidance concerning how much money individual schools within the school district were to receive or exactly which students should be selected to participate in the program. Were Title I funds to be spent solely on programs that met the educational needs of disadvantaged children (such as the creation of special education classes for the disadvantaged), or could they be spent as general assistance on programs that benefited all the students in a particular school (such as building more classrooms and buying books for the school's library)?[20]

Finally, state and local officials wanted to know exactly what the specific criteria for evaluating LEAs' Title I programs were. Under the law, each LEA was required to have its Title I programs approved by its state department of education and the U.S. Office of Education. Congress, however, did not establish any programmatic guidelines for the state departments of education or the U.S. Office of Education to use in evaluating LEAs' plans and programs. Among the many questions state and local education officials wanted answered were whether they should focus their resources on helping elementary school children or high school students,

---

[19]Joel S. Berke and Mary T. Moore, "A Developmental View of the Current Federal Role in Elementary and Secondary Education," p. 334.
[20]Ibid.

and whether they were expected to target their remedial education efforts on reading, math, or language skills.

These ambiguities led to a lot of confusion during the 1960s. Lacking any clear policy guidelines from Washington and having little previous experience with compensatory education, most local school districts submitted plans to the state department of education that experimented with a number of different approaches to meeting the educational needs of the poor. Since they were not provided any clear guidelines for either accepting or rejecting specific approaches, the U.S. Office of Education and most state departments of education generally let the local school districts do whatever they wanted with the money. Audits of local compensatory education programs during the 1960s revealed that most school districts decided to spend most of their Title I money to reduce class sizes by building more schools in 1966 and 1967, then in 1968 began to shift their focus to guidance counseling for high school students and remedial educational instruction for elementary and junior high school students.[21]

The emphasis on school construction during the first two years of the program, tendencies of LEAs to use the program's funds as general aid, and evidence that many LEAs were substituting Title I funds for local monies led to considerable criticism of Title I by academics and educational reformers who wanted LEAs to place a greater emphasis on special tutoring for the disadvantaged.[22] Throughout the 1970s these reformers lobbied Congress to pass laws, and the U.S. Office of Education to issue regulations, that would force state and local officials to focus their programs on remedial education for the economically disadvantaged. Their efforts were helped by the inconclusiveness of a number of studies concerning Title I's impact on the educational achievement of economically disadvantaged students.[23] In general, these studies indicated that the scores on educational achievement tests by children participating in the program were not significantly greater than those of disadvantaged children who did not participate in the program. When improvements were discovered, they usually turned out to be temporary.[24]

Responding to these criticisms, Congress adopted amendments to the Elementary and Secondary Education Act, and the U.S. Office of Education issued a number of administrative requirements during the 1970s that were designed to ensure that LEAs implemented "effective" compensatory education programs. By 1980 LEAs were required to give priority to pro-

[21]"Federal Education Programs," in *Congress and the Nation, 1969–1972* (Washington, DC: Congressional Quarterly Service, 1973), p. 584.

[22]Mary E. Vogel, "Education Grant Consolidation," p. 178.

[23]Rochelle L. Stanfield, " 'If It Ain't Broke, Don't Fix It,' " p. 201; and "Title 1: Has It Helped Educate the Children of the Poor?" *National Journal* (July 9, 1983):1445.

[24]U.S. Advisory Commission on Intergovernmental Relations, *Intergovernmentalizing the Classroom*, p. 44.

grams that promoted basic cognitive skills in reading and mathematics, to conduct educational needs assessments of their students based on objective measures of educational achievement in basic skills, to establish quantifiable objectives for their Title I programs (such as improvements in standardized test scores), to conduct their own program evaluations, to concentrate their Title I funds on disadvantaged children, to involve parents in the planning process by creating parent advisory councils, and to limit the use of funds to educational activities.[25] These rules made it abundantly clear that the national government was the ultimate standard setter for determining whether local programs were or were not in compliance with the law.[26]

State and local education officials argued throughout the 1970s that Title I's rules and regulations were burying them in a mountain of unnecessary and expensive administrative red tape. They argued that they knew how to respond to the educational needs of their communities and that all these requirements were inhibiting their ability to get the job done in a cost-efficient manner. Conservatives in Congress generally agreed. To reduce the national government's influence over educational policy, they continually advocated the conversion of all the programs in the Elementary and Secondary Education Act into a block grant that was run by the state departments of education. The first education block grant proposal was introduced by Rep. Albert H. Quie (R-MN) in 1967, and the most recent one was sponsored by President Reagan in 1981.[27]

CONTROVERSY #2: WILL BLOCK GRANTS IMPROVE THE PROGRAM'S PERFORMANCE?

Conservatives' efforts to put Title I into a block grant during the early 1980s failed for a number of interrelated reasons. First, the Democratic party, composed primarily of liberals and moderates, held the majority of seats in the U.S. House of Representatives. Second, liberals and moderates have never shared the conservatives' fear of governmental tyranny resulting from the involvement of the U.S. Office of Education in educational policy. In fact, many liberals have argued that the increased number and scope of national rules and regulations have improved local educational efforts to help the poor. In 1981, for example, they pointed to a number of

[25]Joel S. Berke and Mary T. Moore, "A Developmental View of the Current Government Role in Elementary and Secondary Education," p. 334; and U.S. Department of Health, Education, and Welfare, *Annual Evaluation Report on Programs Administered by the U.S. Office of Education, FY 1979*, p. 99.

[26]Chrys Dougherty, *Report on Changes Under Chapter One of ECIA*, p. 47.

[27]"Federal Education Programs," in *Congress and the Nation, 1965–1968*, p. 725; "Chronology of Action on Education," in *Congress and the Nation, 1981–1984* (Washington, DC: Congressional Quarterly, 1985), pp. 559–561.

academic studies indicating that LEAs were no longer substituting Title I money for local money and were doing a very good job of targeting Title I money to the economically disadvantaged.[28]

They also pointed to a number of studies conducted in the late 1970s indicating that Title I's programs had a beneficial impact on the educational achievement of the economically disadvantaged. A 1977 National Institute of Education study indicated that Title I first graders gained 12 months in reading and 11 months in mathematics, while Title I third graders gained 8 months in reading and 12 months in math over a 7-month period.[29] Moreover, required annual self-evaluations conducted by LEAs indicated throughout the 1970s that Title I children do make modest gains in mathematics and reading achievement scores on standardized tests after their enrollment in Title I programs.[30]

Liberals also pointed to academic studies arguing that categorical aid is a much more efficient means than block grants of addressing educational equity issues. These studies suggest that categorical grants are more efficient than block grants in stimulating state and local spending on compensatory education for the economically disadvantaged, in promoting uniformity of treatment of the poor nationwide, and in targeting resources to the poor.[31] They also argued that states would give a very low priority to Compensatory Education for the Disadvantaged if it were folded into an education block grant. They were convinced that the state legislatures and governors are more responsive to the educational needs of the children of middle- and upper-class parents because those parents make up the majority of voters and taxpayers.[32] Civil rights groups, representatives of the Roman Catholic church, and representatives of large cities joined the liberals in opposing block grants because they feared that their state education departments would shift the program's funding away from their constituencies and toward groups with more political power in their state legislature.[33]

Conservatives countered the liberals' arguments for continuing Title I as a categorical grant in 1981 by arguing that educational achievement gains by the poor enrolled in Title I programs may be more of a function of the return to basics (emphasis on reading, writing, and arithmetic) in the classrooms across the nation than to the rules and regulations tied to the Title I program. They also argued that these modest gains in educational achievement were not worth the program's $3 to $3.5 billion annual cost,

[28]Mary E. Vogel, "Education Grant Consolidation," p. 178.

[29]Rochelle L. Stanfield, " 'If It Ain't Broke, Don't Fix It,' " p. 201.

[30]U.S. Congress, House, Committee on Appropriations, *Departments of Labor, Health and Human Services, Education, and Related Agencies Appropriations for 1986*, p. 217.

[31]Henry M. Levin, "Federal Grants and Educational Equity," pp. 428–434.

[32]Mary E. Vogel, "Education Grant Consolidation," p. 177.

[33]"Federal Education Programs," in *Congress and the Nation, 1965–1968*, pp. 724–726.

especially given the size of the national deficit and the dangers inherent in allowing the national government to influence the education of the nation's children. They also pointed out that the educational achievement gains by the poor were both modest and very uneven across the country. State evaluations completed for the 1981 school year, for example, indicated that Title I students gained anywhere from 3 to 44 percent in standardized educational achievement tests over those who did not participate in the program. Title I's critics argued that this spotty performance record proves that if the program were eliminated, the whole educational system for the economically disadvantaged would not collapse.[34]

Some of Title I's critics even suggested that its administrative requirements may have contributed to the overall decline in educational achievement by all students since the 1960s. They argued that most school systems decided the easiest way to be certain that their Title I programs met all of the national government's regulations was to create an administrative structure for its Title I programs that was independent of the regular school program. Title I personnel were hired and paid for with Title I funds and were required to work only with Title I students, who were pulled out of the regular school classrooms and segregated from other children. In this way, the regular school system was relieved of the responsibility of responding to the educational needs of their lowest-scoring students and were placed under little additional pressure to improve their teaching effectiveness. Thus, conservatives argued that Title I programs are primarily symbolic gestures of national concern that placate liberals but do not represent a viable response to the educational needs of either the poor or the nonpoor.[35]

Under pressure from the Reagan administration and the newly elected Republican majority in the Senate to reduce administrative red tape in all intergovernmental programs, the Democratic House agreed, in the *Education Consolidation and Improvement Act of 1981* (ECIA), to reduce the scope of the U.S. Office of Education's administrative oversight responsibilities for the Compensatory Education for the Disadvantaged program and to reduce the number of national administrative requirements that LEAs have to meet. As part of these changes, Title I was renamed Chapter 1, and state departments of education were given the dual responsibilities of approving or disapproving proposed LEA Chapter 1 programs and monitoring their performance to assure that the national government's intent of educating economically disadvantaged children was being met. The U.S. Office of Education was empowered to conduct audits of LEAs' Chapter 1 programs to ensure that state monitoring, enforcement, and

---

[34]Rochelle L. Stanfield, " 'If It Ain't Broke, Don't Fix It,' " pp. 201, 202.

[35]Carl F. Kaestle and Marshall S. Smith, "The Federal Role in Elementary and Secondary Education, 1940–1980," p. 400.

technical assistance efforts were adequate to meet the national government's intent of assisting the economically disadvantaged.[36]

As part of the new emphasis on reduced paperwork and administrative requirements, Chapter 1 reduced the requirement that state and local governments maintain 100 percent of their spending on education from year to year to 90 percent of the previous year's expenditure. It also softened the penalty for noncompliance with the expenditure-maintenance requirement from a loss of all Title I funds to a reduction of Chapter 1 funds proportionate to the reduction in state or local expenditures on education.[37] The requirements to use Title I funds only for costs exceeding the average per-pupil expenditure of state and local funds and to form parent advisory councils in districts and individual school buildings were eliminated.[38]

Studies of state education departments' behavior under Chapter 1 indicate that they assumed their new oversight functions with varying degrees of enthusiasm, expertise, and commitment.[39] A major factor explaining this variability was the varying nature of state political cultures and traditions. State education departments located in states with strong traditions of local control (such as Kansas, Oregon, and Maine) were reluctant to police LEAs, while state education departments in states with strong traditions of state control (such as New York) exercised their new oversight responsibilities with great vigor.[40]

Another factor accounting for the varying enthusiasm of state education departments for engaging in effective oversight activities was the ambiguity of the law's section that dealt with the states' and the national government's oversight responsibilities. The law clearly gave the states the primary responsibility for approving LEAs' Chapter 1 plans. However, since the U.S. Office of Education had the right to audit LEAs' plans and overrule state education departments' decisions, many state education departments were reluctant to establish their own criteria for evaluating LEAs' plans until the national government established its criteria. The U.S. Office of Education was reluctant to establish those compliance criteria

[36]Chrys Dougherty, *Report on Changes Under Chapter One of ECIA*, p. 19.

[37]Joel S. Berke and Mary T. Moore, "A Developmental View of the Current Federal Role in Elementary and Secondary Education," p. 335.

[38]Chrys Dougherty, *Report on Changes Under Chapter One of ECIA*, pp. 20, 21; and Joel S. Berke and Mary T. Moore, "A Developmental View of the Current Federal Government Role in Elementary and Secondary Education," p. 335.

[39]Milbrey Wallin McLaughlin, "States and the New Federalism," *Harvard Educational Review* 52:4 (November 1982):566.

[40]Ibid., p. 567. Eighty percent of LEAs reported in 1983 that they had experienced no increase in the frequency of state monitoring visits since 1978, and 30 percent reported that they had not been audited by either the national or the state government in three years. See U.S. Congress, House, Committee on Appropriations, *Departments of Labor, Health and Human Services, Education, and Related Agencies Appropriations for 1986*, p. 254.

because of President Reagan's strong desire to reduce administrative red tape and to allow states to exercise their own judgment on these matters. It not only refused to issue compliance criteria but also did not conduct any state reviews for two years following enactment of the ECIA.

By 1984 the U.S. Office of Education was offering written opinions on questions submitted to it by state education departments concerning compliance with the law's legislative intent and was conducting audits of LEAs, but these audits were primarily focused on discovering and publicizing successful Chapter 1 programs, not uncovering Chapter 1 programs that were in noncompliance with the law.[41] A survey of state Chapter 1 administrative directors in 1985 revealed that most of them would prefer more guidance and technical assistance from the national government, especially since the national government has the right to withhold future Chapter 1 funds and to demand refunds of monies spent illegally.[42]

Studies of LEAs' behavior under Chapter 1's relaxed administrative requirements indicate that there have been some abuses. An audit of one LEA, for example, revealed that Chapter 1 funds were used to pay for a junior high school prom.[43] For the most part, however, LEAs have not made significant changes in their local programs. One reason for this continuance of past efforts was that many state departments of education used Title I compliance criteria in evaluating LEA programs to ensure that the national government did not challenge their allotment of funds.

Another important factor explaining this continuation of ongoing efforts was that many of these programs had been in place for a decade or longer, and LEAs were reluctant to make radical changes in either personnel or program emphasis. One new trend was the increasing suspicion by academics that LEAs were beginning to "juggle the accounting books" to substitute Chapter 1 funds for local education funds. Academics have noted that the temptation to substitute national funds for local funds is growing as inflation continues to erode the value of Chapter 1 funding, which has remained at the $3 to $3.5 billion level since 1979.[44] Another new trend is that the number of poor students served under the program has fallen in recent years because the cost of providing compensatory education has increased and funding for the program has remained stable.[45]

---

[41]Chrys Dougherty, *Report on Changes Under Chapter One of ECIA*, pp. 52, 53.

[42]Ibid., pp. 196–199.

[43]Ibid., p. 197.

[44]Ibid., pp. 195–197.

[45]The program served 5.4 million children in 1979, 5.3 million children in 1980, 4.8 million children in 1981, and approximately 4.7 million children each year since 1981. See U.S. Congress, House, Committee on Appropriations, *Departments of Labor, Health and Human Services, Education and Related Agencies Appropriations for 1986*, pp. 200, 201.

CONTROVERSY #3: CONGRESSIONAL FORMULAMANSHIP BATTLES

The members of the House Education and Labor Committee and the Senate Human Resources Committee have spent as much time and energy fighting over the Compensatory Education for the Disadvantaged program's allocation formula as they have in determining its structure and regulations. The formula is designed to target available resources to states with high concentrations of economically disadvantaged children.[46] The U.S. Office of Education then uses the formula's criteria to determine Chapter 1 allocations for each of the state's counties. State educational agencies distribute this amount among the counties' school districts according to the number of low-income children in each school district (as indicated by the Census Bureau) or according to the number of children in each school district that participates in the National School Free Lunch program. In this way, funds are targeted to school districts with the largest concentrations of economically disadvantaged students.[47]

Chapter 1's formula has been a bone of contention in Congress ever since the program's creation in 1965. At that time, the payment rate per eligible child was set at 50 percent of the state's average education expenditure per pupil.[48] Congressman from relatively poor states, particularly from the Southeast, argued that setting the payment rate as a percentage of average state education expenditures discriminates against states that cannot afford to spend a lot of money on education. They argued that the payment rate should be a straight dollar amount for each eligible child in that state. That exact amount would be determined by dividing the total amount of available money in the program by the total number of eligible children in the country. In this way, each state would be treated equally.

---

[46]Each state's allotment of funds is determined by multiplying the number of children from low-income families in the state by 40 percent of the state's average per-pupil expenditure (but not less than 80 percent nor more than 120 percent of the national average per-pupil expenditure). The number of children in low-income families is determined by adding the number of children in that state who are (1) in families with income below the poverty level according to the 1980 census, (2) in families receiving Aid to Families with Dependent Children (AFDC) payments that exceed the poverty level for a nonfarm family (updated annually), (3) neglected or delinquent and residing in institutions that are not state operated, and (4) foster children supported by state funds. See ibid., pp. 228, 289; and Chrys Dougherty, *Report on Changes Under Chapter One of ECIA*, p. 17.

[47]Ibid. The U.S. Office of Education does not determine the exact allotments for each school district because AFDC and foster children data are not available according to school district boundaries. Also, most state educational agencies use the number of students participating in the National School Free Lunch program to determine funding allocations among school districts because Census Bureau data concerning low-income children are not updated annually.

[48]Robert Jay Dilger, *The Sunbelt/Snowbelt Controversy: The War over Federal Funds* (New York: New York University Press, 1982), pp. 70–71.

Opponents of the straight dollar payment approach argued that the percentage payment rate method encouraged states unwilling to spend "enough" on education to do so. They also argued that while it is true that this portion of the formula benefited states located in the Northeast, the definition of economically disadvantaged children benefited states located in the Southeast. Since the cost of living was generally lower in the Southeast, people living there tended to need and to receive lower wages than people living in the Northeast. Since wages were lower in the Southeast, the number of people considered economically disadvantaged was artificially inflated in that region because wages were not adjusted to account for cost-of-living differences across the country. Moreover, states in the Southeast experienced larger percentage increases in education spending than states in the Northeast following enactment of the formula.[49]

Southern and rural congressmen have won some concessions from northeastern and urban congressmen over the years concerning the payment rate portion of the program's allocation formula. In 1968 states were allowed to use the national average education expenditure per pupil figure instead of their own if the national average was greater than the state's average education expenditure per pupil. This increased the South's share of the program's funds. Mississippi, for example, saw its funding increase from $23.5 million in FY 1967 to $44.8 million in FY 1968 because of this formula change. One of the major factors explaining why Congress approved the new formula was that the program's total authorization level was increased to ensure that no state would lose funds after the formula was changed.[50]

The current payment rate method was adopted in 1974 (see footnote 46). It also benefited the South's school districts because it treats states with educational expenditures that are less than 80 percent of the national average educational expenditure per pupil as if they had spent 80 percent of the average. Moreover, states with average educational expenditures per pupil exceeding 120 percent of the national average are treated as if they spend only 120 percent of the average. This provision reduces the share of the program's funds that go to states located in the Northeast.[51]

Congress also has battled over the formula's definition of an economically disadvantaged child. Since most states established very strict eligibility criteria for the AFDC program in the early 1960s and the median income of residents in the southern states was generally lower than those living in the Northeast, the use of AFDC enrollments in determining who qualified as an economically disadvantaged child benefited the South. By the late 1960s, however, AFDC enrollments had increased dramatically in the

---

[49]"Federal Education Programs," in *Congress and the Nation, 1965–1968*, pp. 720, 721.
[50]Ibid., pp. 710, 726.
[51]"Chronology of Action on Education," in *Congress and the Nation, 1973–1976* (Washington DC: Congressional Quarterly, 1977), p. 385.

Northeast. Between 1966 and 1974 the proportion of children eligible for compensatory education funding under the AFDC portion of its formula had increased from 10.5 percent of the total eligible population of children to 53.4 percent. As a result, the total share of the program's funds began to shift away from the South and Southwest toward the Northeast.[52]

The House Education and Labor Committee was chaired in the 1970s by Carl Perkins (D-KY). He wanted to stop this shift toward the Northeast. His committee voted in 1974 to change the way the allocation formula counts children enrolled in the AFDC program. Instead of counting all children who receive at least $2,000 annually in AFDC payments as disadvantaged children, the new allocation formula counted only two-thirds of them as disadvantaged. Perkins argued that this change made certain that Title I funds were targeted to the poorest states. Since the purpose of the program is to assist the poor, he suggested that the change was consistent with the law's central purpose.

The Senate Labor and Public Welfare Committee, on the other hand, was chaired at that time by Harrison Williams, Jr. (D-NJ). His committee decided to count all AFDC children with payments exceeding $2,000 annually as economically disadvantaged. He argued that the relatively high number of children receiving AFDC payments in excess of $2,000 annually in the Northeast reflected that region's higher costs of living rather than its wealth. However, an amendment sponsored by Sen. John McClellan (D-AK), to use the House's two-thirds count of these children, was adopted on the Senate floor over the protests of the Senate committee's leadership. The final version of the allocation formula approved in 1974 reduced the count of these children to two-thirds.[53]

Reflecting the intense regional battle over the program's funds in 1974, Congress commissioned the National Institute of Education to study the regional distribution of Title I funds and the impact of counting AFDC children in the formula. The study was completed in 1978. It indicated that in FY 1977 the northeastern states received 23 percent of Title I's funds, the north central states received 22 percent, the southeastern states received 40 percent, and the western states received 15 percent. If AFDC eligible children had not been included in the formula, the study noted, the regional distribution of funds would have been more heavily skewed toward the Southeast. The study also indicated that approximately 75 percent of the children who were classified as economically disadvantaged because they received AFDC payments exceeding $2,000 annually lived in five states: New York, Michigan, California, Illinois, and Pennsylvania.[54]

Another major formula fight ensued in the House when the Elemen-

[52]Robert Jay Dilger, *The Sunbelt/Snowbelt Controversy*, p. 71.

[53]Ibid.; and "Chronology of Action on Education," in *Congress and the Nation, 1973–1976*, pp. 383, 384.

[54]Robert Jay Dilger, *The Sunbelt/Snowbelt Controversy*, p. 73.

tary and Secondary Education Act came up for reauthorization in 1978. Using the National Institute of Education's study as a departure point, members of the House Education and Labor Committee from the Northeast and Great Lakes states, particularly from New York, Michigan, Illinois, and Pennsylvania, supported the reinstatement of the full count of AFDC children in the formula, while members from the Southeast wanted to retain the two-thirds count. Northeastern representatives also supported the use of more recent poverty counts in the formula. At that time children were considered eligible to be counted as economically disadvantaged if their families earned no more than $4,000.[55] Representatives from the Northeast wanted to drop the formula's reliance on what they considered to be outdated information from the 1970 Census of Population. Instead, they advocated the use of poverty counts in the more recent 1975 Survey of Income and Education (SIE). Congressmen from the South argued that the SIE data overstated the Northeast's poverty because the survey was taken during the height of the 1975 recession.

Changing the AFDC count to 100 percent would have increased Title I funding in the Northeast and Great Lakes states by approximately $60 million annually. Updating the poverty data base would have increased Title I funding in the Northeast and Great Lakes by $600 million annually if applied to all Title I funds and by $200 million annually if applied only to proposed funding that exceeded 1979 appropriations.[56]

Representatives from the Northeast and Great Lakes states outnumbered representatives from the Southeast on the House Education and Labor Committee, but the committee's chairman, Carl Perkins, used a number of brilliant parliamentary moves and made a number of promises on other legislation to sway enough votes to force the northeasterners to accept less than they had hoped for. After the northern members' proposal to use SIE poverty data for all Title I funds was rejected on a tie vote, they were able to get the committee to agree to use SIE poverty data for funds that were appropriated in excess of 1979 levels. In addition, on a close 18–17 vote, the House committee also approved the reinstatement of the full counting of AFDC children.[57]

At the same time the House Education and Labor Committee was battling over the formula, the Senate Labor and Human Resources Committee agreed rather quietly to reinstate the full AFDC count but not the use of SIE poverty data.[58] Harrison Williams, Jr., was still the Senate com-

---

[55]The 1965 Elementary and Secondary Act had established $2,000 as the maximum earnings amount. This was increased to $3,000 in 1966 but was never implemented because the change was made contingent on appropriations levels that were not realized. The $4,000 earnings figure was adopted in 1970. See "Federal Education Programs," in *Congress and the Nation, 1969–1972*, pp. 582–584.

[56]Robert Jay Dilger, *The Sunbelt/Snowbelt Controversy*, p. 85.

[57]Ibid., pp. 88, 89.

[58]The Senate Labor and Human Resources Committee was called the Senate Labor and Public Welfare Committee in 1974.

mittee's chairman and wanted to avoid another formula fight like the one that had divided his committee in 1974 and resulted in an embarrassing reversal of its decision on the Senate floor.[59] In the House-Senate Conference Committee, the House delegation was weakened in its bargaining with the Senate because the leader of the House delegation was Carl Perkins. He wanted the Senate's version of the formula to prevail. The final compromise that became law (and is still in force today) was to postpone the implementation of the full count of AFDC eligible children until FY 1980 and, until the 1980 Census was completed to use the 1975 SIE poverty data to allocate half of all funds appropriated above 1979 funding levels.[60]

CONCLUSIONS

The Compensatory Aid for Education program is a survivor. All attempts to collapse it under a block grant have failed and will probably continue to fail as long as Democrats control at least one house of Congress. However, it is likely that the national government's fiscal difficulties will prevent liberals from increasing the program's funding beyond the $4 billion range for the foreseeable future. Thus, the total number of disadvantaged students served by the program will continue to decrease because the costs of providing those services continue to increase. As a result, state and local governments will be forced to address the issue of which level of government, if any, is going to pay for compensatory education for those economically disadvantaged students who would have been served by Chapter 1 programs if funding had kept pace with increased costs.

Given the fiscal pressures faced by many states and localities, the most likely outcome of this debate is that most of these students will not receive any compensatory education. Moreover, given the uneven distribution of fiscal capacities among states and localities, the availability of compensatory educational services will increasingly be determined not by the needs of the students eligible for compensatory education but by the fiscal capacity and the political will of the state and locality in which the students reside to provide these services. Whether this constitutes a problem depends on how one interprets the results of all of the evaluative studies that have been conducted on the program's impact on children's scores on educational achievement tests. Liberals generally argue that even marginal improvements by the disadvantaged are worth the expense, while conservatives argue that the cost of the program far exceeds its benefits.

Finally, conservatives' efforts to collapse Chapter I into a block grant and their efforts to reduce its funding level are consistent with their macroeconomic theory of intergovernmental relations. Their desire to balance the national budget through domestic spending restraints supersedes their desire to use national funds to equalize educational opportunities.

[59]Robert Jay Dilger, *The Sunbelt/Snowbelt Controversy*, p. 91.
[60]Ibid., pp. 92–94.

CHAPTER 7

Federal Aid for Highways

Federal Aid for Highways is the national government's second most expensive intergovernmental program (only Medicaid is more expensive). Its $13 billion annual budget is used to provide states 90 percent of the cost to construct the nation's 42,500-mile interstate highway system and 75 percent of the cost to construct primary, secondary, and urban highways (called the ABC program). It also provides funding for road and bridge reconstruction, repair, resurfacing, and rehabilitation. States own the highways and bridges after they are built or repaired, but must build them according to national standards and are primarily responsible for their operation and maintenance.

Unlike most national intergovernmental programs, the national government has established a trust fund to help finance the Federal Aid for Highways program activities. The trust fund collects approximately $12 billion annually from a 9-cents-per-gallon excise tax on gasoline, a 15-cents-per-gallon excise tax on diesel fuel, and a number of other excise taxes on motor vehicle products.[1] This puts the Federal Aid for Highways program in an enviable political position. It competes with other national programs for general treasury funding only to the extent that highway needs exceed the $12 billion threshold.

This chapter examines four major controversies currently surrounding national highway assistance.[2] First, the cost of building the interstate

---

[1]In FY 1986 the trust fund netted $11.9 billion and is expected to grow at an annual rate of 2.2 percent. The excise tax on gasoline accounted for 76 percent, the excise tax on diesel fuels (and gasohol) accounted for 22 percent, and excise taxes on motor vehicle products accounted for 2 percent of the trust fund's net receipts in FY 1986. See U.S. Advisory Commission on Intergovernmental Relations, *A Critical Appraisal of Devolving Selected Federal-Aid Highway Programs and Revenue Bases: Research in Progress*, staff report (Washington, DC: U.S. Government Printing Office, November 6, 1986), pp. 7 and 8.

[2]Due to space limitations, this chapter does not attempt to analyze the many controversies concerning the ABC program. These controversies include the relative priority of intrastate versus interstate highways, the adequacy of the Highway Trust Fund to fund both intrastate and interstate highway construction and repairs, and the formula used to allocate primary, secondary, and urban road construction funds among states.

highway system has far exceeded initial predictions and the resources of the Highway Trust Fund. Most liberals, moderates, and state governors argue that the national government should either add general treasury dollars to the resources of the Highway Trust Fund or increase its excise taxes to levels necessary to complete and maintain the interstate highway system. Conservatives have questioned the need to take either of these actions. They argue that funds saved by not completing the interstate highway system could be used to reduce the national government's deficit and, by avoiding higher taxes, help the national economy.

The second controversy concerns the debate over which level of government ought to be in charge of ground transportation programs. The U.S. Advisory Commission on Intergovernmental Relations and the National Governors' Association have suggested that the Highway Trust Fund, or portions of it, and the responsibility for highway construction should be turned back to the states.[3] In this way the national government could save up to $13 billion a year and states could make their own determinations concerning the future of the interstate highway system and other nationally financed highway construction projects. Others view highway expenditures as a legitimate concern for the national government and question the fiscal ability of many states to meet the transportation needs of their residents if national assistance is withdrawn.

The third controversy involves the national government's decision to focus its resources on highway construction rather than on mass transit. Some analysts argue that the emphasis on highway construction is a desirable means to encourage economic expansion in suburban and rural areas. Others are convinced that the national government's emphasis on highway construction has contributed to the economic and environmental difficulties faced by many of the nation's largest cities.

The fourth controversy deals with the national government's use of highway crossover sanctions. Many national legislators view the Federal Aid for Highways program as a convenient vehicle to force states to take certain actions in areas of domestic public policy normally considered to be state prerogatives.[4] If states refuse to take these actions, they lose all or a portion of their national highway funds. These penalties, called crossover sanctions, are greatly resented by many state and local officials as being counter to the principles of federalism. Four crossover sanctions are examined in this chapter: highway billboard removal, highway safety standards,

[3]U.S. Advisory Commission on Intergovernmental Relations, *A Critical Appraisal of Devolving Selected Federal-Aid Highway Programs and Revenue Bases*, pp. 40–45. In 1986 the National Governors' Association considered but did not adopt a proposal to turn back the national government's 9-cents-per-gallon excise tax on gasoline and 9 cents of the 15-cents-per-gallon excise tax on diesel fuel. In return for revenues, the proposal wou ˙ ˙ .ve given the states responsibility for all noninterstate highway programs.

[4]All 50 states, the District of Columbia, and the territories participate in the Federal Aid to Highways program.

the 55-mile-per-hour speed limit, and the mandatory minimum drinking age of 21 years.

THE NATIONAL COMMITMENT TO HIGHWAY CONSTRUCTION

The national government has always been interested in promoting highway construction. It established postal roads during the early 1800s to meet its constitutional obligation to create a national postal service. To promote the general welfare and to facilitate the flow of interstate commerce, it appropriated funds in 1806 to construct the Cumberland Road from Cumberland, Maryland, to the Ohio River.[5] Congressional efforts to provide further direct cash assistance for transportation projects during the 1800s were prevented by presidents who vetoed such legislation as unconstitutional infringements on states' rights. Instead, laws that provided states with millions of acres of the national domain were enacted. Recognizing that many states lacked the fiscal resources to build enough wagon roads to facilitate economic growth, these land grants were made in the expectation that the revenue from their sale would be used for the construction of wagon roads.[6]

The first large-scale national intergovernmental grants-in-aid program was for highway construction. Adopted in 1916, the Federal Road Act was by far the most fiscally significant national intergovernmental grants-in-aid program prior to the New Deal. During the 1920s, its $90 million to $190 million annual budgets accounted for more than three-quarters of all national intergovernmental expenditures.[7] It provided states with grants on a 50–50 matching basis to help them pave rural, dirt roads used by the U.S. Postal Service. States did not object strongly to this intrusion into one of their domestic policy areas because the funds were directed to rural areas. At that time, the majority of representatives and senators in most state legislatures were from rural areas. Moreover, rural roads were the primary means for farmers to get their products to market. It would have been politically foolish for state politicians to turn down a national subsidy for agriculture when most constituents were farmers.[8]

The Federal Road Act of 1916 did, however, have a number of

[5]"Postwar Highway Program," in *Congress and the Nation, 1945–1964* (Washington, DC: Congressional Quarterly Service, 1965), p. 524.

[6]W. Brook Graves, *American Intergovernmental Relations* (New York: Scribner's, 1964), pp. 520, 521.

[7]U.S. Advisory Commission on Intergovernmental Relations, *Categorical Grants: Their Role and Design* (Washington, DC: U.S. Government Printing Office, 1978), pp. 16, 17.

[8]"Postwar Highway Program," in *Congress and the Nation, 1945–1964*, pp. 525–527.

administrative requirements that foreshadowed the conditions that would be routinely attached to many contemporary categorical grants-in-aid programs. Expenditures were prohibited in communities with populations exceeding 2,500, and states were required to establish a highway department or commission to oversee program operations and to set priorities and detailed plans. In addition, advance examination of projects, detailed progress reports, audits of expenditures, and examination of finished work were required.[9]

During the 1930s and 1940s, national funding for highway construction continued to increase incrementally, but its dominant position as the national government's number one intergovernmental grants-in-aid priority was usurped by social welfare programs. Highway funding fell to approximately 33 percent of total national intergovernmental assistance during the 1930s and to 18 percent during the 1940s and early 1950s.[10]

Although no state refused the national government's highway assistance during the 1930s and 1940s, the National Governors' Association repeatedly called for the national government to give the states the national tax dollars used to fund the national government's highway construction program and to let the states build the highways without national interference.[11] Instead, the national government decided, in the Federal-Aid Highway Act of 1956, to dramatically increase the national government's role in financing highway construction by authorizing the construction of a 41,000-mile interstate highway system. The cost of completing the entire system was estimated at $41 billion. To encourage state governments to participate in the program, the national government provided 90 percent of total costs, or $37 billion.[12] The project's targeted completion date was 1972.[13]

The law created the Highway Trust Fund to assist in the financing of what President Eisenhower called the "greatest public works program in history."[14] The trust fund was to collect an estimated $14.8 billion from excise taxes on gasoline and other transportation-related products over the program's 16 year construction period.

[9]U.S. Advisory Commission on Intergovernmental Relations, *Categorical Grants: Their Role and Design*, p. 17.

[10]Ibid., pp. 19, 22. During the 1930s, highway construction funding ranged from a low of $76 million in 1930 to a high of $341 million in 1937. During the 1940s, funding ranged from a low of $75 million in 1945 to a high of $410 million in 1949.

[11]W. Brook Graves, *American Intergovernmental Relations*, p. 520.

[12]"Postwar Highway Program," in *Congress and the Nation, 1945–1964*, p. 524. The interstate highway system was subsequently expanded to 42,500 miles.

[13]Each state was to receive a maximum allotment of funds equal to the ratio of the cost of completing the system within that state to the cost of completing the system in all the states. See Ibid., p. 531.

[14]Ibid., p. 524.

The idea was to establish a funding mechanism that targeted the cost of building the highways onto those who used them. The money would be spent on both interstate and intrastate highway construction.[15] Congress planned to appropriate revenue from the general treasury to make up the difference between the program's anticipated cost and the revenue in the Highway Trust Fund. Congress also authorized the establishment of toll roads, bridges, and tunnels within the interstate highway system as an additional revenue resource to be used if needed.

The creation of an interstate highway system had been debated in Congress since the early 1940s. In 1944, Congress included in its highway legislation a provision authorizing the construction of a 40,000-mile interstate highway system at an estimated cost of $20 billion. There was nearly unanimous congressional support for the construction of the interstate highway system at that time. The increased use of the private automobile, the rise of the truck as the principal mode of transporting goods, and the need to establish a means of transporting military equipment in a national emergency combined to make the construction of an interstate highway system politically attractive. However, the need to fund the war effort, combined with a record national deficit, led Congress to the conclusion that it could not afford to finance the construction of the interstate highway system at that time.[16] Instead, it broadened funding from a focus on rural highways (called the secondary system) by authorizing increased national funding for highways that connected the nation's principal cities (called the primary system) and for urban highways.[17]

The military's interest in the interstate highway system proved to be a decisive factor in the political debate over the interstate highway program during the 1950s. Many conservative Democrats who would normally be expected to oppose a long-term, costly national program finally decided to support it as a means to improve national defense. Liberal Democrats wisely entitled the interstate highway program the National System of Interstate and Defense Highways.[18]

[15]The trust fund collected revenue from a 3-cent-a-gallon excise tax on gasoline, diesel, and special motor fuels; a 9-cents-a-pound excise tax on inner tubes; an 8-cents-a-pound excise tax on automobile tubes; a 3-cents-a-pound excise tax on tire retreads; half of the 10 percent manufacturer's tax on trucks, buses, and truck trailers; and a $1.50-a-pound weight fee on trucks and buses, excluding local transit vehicles, weighing over 26,000 pounds. See ibid., p. 531.

[16]In 1952 Congress appropriated $25 million out of a total highway construction budget of $652 million for interstate highway construction. In 1954 it increased funding for interstate highway construction to $175 million (out of a total highway construction budget of $956 million). See ibid., pp. 529, 530.

[17]Primary highways were given 45 percent of available national highway assistance funds, secondary highways were given 30 percent, and urban highways were given 25 percent. See Donald H. Haider, *When Governments Come to Washington* (New York: The Free Press, 1974), p. 154.

[18]"Postwar Highway Program," in *Congress and the Nation, 1945–1964*, p. 524.

CONTROVERSY #1: THE COST PROBLEM

Escalating highway construction costs arose as an issue almost from the very start of the interstate highway project. National highway administrators reported to Congress at the end of 1957 that the initial cost estimate and targeted completion date for the interstate highway system were unrealistic. Based on the construction experiences of 1957, the administrators estimated that if Congress wanted to complete the system in 1972, it would have to appropriate $1 billion annually from the general treasury to supplement the Highway Trust Fund.[19]

Most of the expenses that produced the cost overrun were legitimate costs associated with the buying of land for the interstate highway system and other construction costs. Some conservatives, however, claimed that a good portion of the cost overrun was caused by the inclusion of the Davis-Bacon Act's prevailing wage rule in the Federal Aid to Highways law. This rule requires construction companies working on the interstate highway system to pay their employees at least the equivalent of the locally prevailing wage as determined by the secretary of labor. Liberal Democrats and organized labor were, and still are, among the prevailing wage rule's strongest advocates.

Both conservatives and liberals agreed that another major, and totally unexpected, source of the interstate highway system's unanticipated cost was corruption among state highway department officials. Investigations in 1957 revealed that state highway officials in Indiana used their insiders' knowledge of where the interstate highway system would be constructed to purchase land along the right-of-way. After the route was publicly announced, those officials sold the land to the state highway department, making a 500 percent profit in the process. Similar practices were discovered by national investigators in Oklahoma and Florida in 1961.[20] Massachusetts' land acquisition practices were described in 1962 by a congressional subcommittee chairman as "a miserable mess . . . honeycombed by gross incompetence and downright collusion and fraud."[21]

To prevent the interstate highway system from falling hopelessly behind schedule, Congress authorized an additional $3.2 billion over FYs 1959–1961 from the general treasury to augment the resources of the Highway Trust Fund. It also authorized a one-year, temporary increase in the national government's gasoline excise tax to 4 cents a gallon in 1959.[22] It was generally recognized that these actions were stopgap measures that would not solve the long-term financing problems facing the program.

[19]Ibid., pp. 531, 532.
[20]Ibid., pp. 531–534.
[21]Ibid., p. 535.
[22]Ibid., p. 533.

Congress purposely decided not to undertake any major decisions concerning the future of the interstate highway system until the 1960 presidential and congressional elections were decided.

President Kennedy and his successor, President Johnson, were strongly in favor of finishing the interstate highway system by 1972. President Kennedy's proposal to supplement the Highway Trust Fund's revenue with an additional $900 million annually from the general treasury until the system was completed in 1972 was approved by Congress in 1961. His request that a temporary 1-cent increase in the national government's gasoline excise tax be made permanent through 1972 and that excise taxes on inner tubes, tire retreads, and other automobile-related products be increased to bolster the resources of the Highway Trust Fund also was approved by Congress.[23]

It was assumed by most analysts that the interstate highway system's financing problem had been solved when Congress approved the expenditure of an additional $10 billion for the program in 1961. But throughout the 1960s, the cost of constructing the system continued to skyrocket. In 1965, the Commerce Department estimated that the program would cost $46.8 billion to complete. In 1968, the Department of Transportation (established in 1967) upped that estimate to $56.5 billion, with the national government's share of costs topping $50 billion.[24] Most of this added expense was attributed to unanticipated increases in the cost of highway materials and to improved, and more expensive, highway safety and design requirements.

To pay for the unexpected cost of completing the interstate highway system, President Johnson repeatedly asked Congress in the mid-1960s to increase the flow of revenue into the Highway Trust Fund. Congress, however, was reluctant to increase taxes. Moreover, the intergovernmental public interest groups were lobbying Congress at that time to increase funding for noninterstate highway construction. The National League of Cities and the U.S. Conference of Mayors were particularly vocal in their demands for increased funding for urban highways. Recognizing the need to increase expenditures for both interstate and noninterstate highways and lacking the funds to do so from the general treasury, Congress decided to limit existing interstate highway construction appropriations to the funds available in the Highway Trust Fund and to appropriate additional revenue from the general treasury for noninterstate highways. Since highway construction costs continued to rise, the pace of interstate highway construction slowed. Thus, the system's targeted completion date of 1972 was not going to be met. In 1966, Congress extended the system's completion deadline to 1973, and two years later extended it to 1974.[25]

---

[23]Ibid., p. 534.

[24]"Chronology of Legislation on Transportation," in *Congress and the Nation, 1965–1968* (Washington, DC: Congressional Quarterly Service, 1969), p. 229.

[25]Ibid.

Highway construction costs continued to increase during the 1970s. In 1972, the Department of Transportation estimated that the cost of constructing the interstate highway system, which was 70 percent complete at that time, had risen to $76.3 billion. Despite the escalating costs, Congress continued to refuse to increase the Highway Trust Fund's excise taxes or to appropriate additional revenues for interstate construction from the general treasury. As a result, interstate highway construction continued to fall behind schedule. In 1976 Congress extended the system's completion deadline to 1990.[26]

When President Reagan entered the White House in 1981, 95 percent of the interstate highway system was complete (40,438 of the proposed 42,500 miles). However, of these 40,438 miles of completed highways, only 7,915 miles were considered to be completed to final construction standards.[27] As a result, despite the expenditure of more than $63 billion by the national government and an additional $7 billion by the states, the program was far from being finished. President Reagan indicated that he was interested in completing the interstate highway system by 1990 because he shared the widely accepted view that it enhanced American economic competitiveness.[28] He was troubled, however, by the Department of Transportation's (DOT) estimate that the national government would have to spend another $48 billion to do the job.[29]

DOT also reported that the nation's infrastructure (roads, bridges, sewers, and other basic foundations of community living) had deteriorated to a dangerous level. More than 10,000 miles, or 25 percent, of the interstate highways already constructed were in immediate need of major repair or replacement, and an additional 26,000 miles would require major repairs by 1995. Moreover, 20 percent of bridges in the nation were in need of immediate major repair or replacement, and over 40 percent of all bridges would require major repair or replacement by 1990. DOT estimated that it would cost between $275 billion and $363 billion to repair all the deficiencies in roads supported by national grants and an additional $60 billion to repair the nation's bridges by 1995.[30]

Faced with the competing needs to move toward a balanced national budget and to address the infrastructure crisis, Congress decided in 1981 to support (with some modifications) a proposal by the Reagan administration to reduce anticipated total interstate highway construction expenses by approximately $15 billion (saving the national government $13.5 billion).

[26]Ibid., pp. 150; and "Chronology of Legislation on Transportation," in *Congress and the Nation, 1973–1976* (Washington, DC: Congressional Quarterly, 1977), p. 550.

[27]William J. Lanouette, "Critics Seek Big Bucks from Big Trucks to Repair Damage to Interstate Roads," *National Journal* (November 28, 1981):2122.

[28]U.S. Advisory Commission on Intergovernmental Relations, "A Critical Appraisal of Devolving Selected Federal-Aid Highway Programs and Revenue Bases," p. 12.

[29]"Transportation Policy," in *Congress and the Nation, 1981–1984* (Washington, DC: Congressional Quarterly, 1985), p. 297.

[30]Ibid., p. 302.

This was accomplished by reducing noise abatement and landscaping requirements, and disallowing funding for highways with more than six lanes in rural areas and more than eight lanes in densely populated, urban areas.

In an attempt to address the infrastructure problem, Congress dramatically increased funding for the "4R" repair program, which is used to resurface, restore, rehabilitate, and reconstruct previously completed segments of the interstate highway system, from $500 million annually to over $2 billion annually, starting in 1983.[31] Congressional leaders also suggested that the national government's 4-cents-per-gallon excise tax on gasoline be increased to give the Highway Trust Fund enough resources to complete the interstate highway system by 1990 and to continue the increased funding for the "4R" repair program. Representatives of the U.S. Conference of Mayors, the National League of Cities, and the National Association of Counties all testified in favor of higher Highway Trust Fund excise taxes at congressional hearings.[32] An alliance of railroads, motorists, and environmentalists also testified in favor of increased excise taxes, especially on diesel fuel. They argued that since diesel-fueled trucks cause a substantial amount of wear and tear on the interstate highway system, they ought to pay a greater share of the costs associated with its repair and maintenance.[33]

President Reagan voiced his strong opposition to any tax increases. He had been elected in 1980 on the promise to reduce national taxation and to scale back the size and intrusiveness of the national government. Instead of increasing the Highway Trust Fund's taxes to meet the 1990 deadline, he proposed that those segments of the interstate highway system where actual construction was not already under way be eliminated from the program.[34] If the states affected believed that the highways were

---

[31]U.S. Office of Management and Budget, *The Budget of the United States Government, FY 1988, Appendix* (Washington, DC: U.S. Government Printing Office, 1987), p. I-R3; and U.S. Office of Management and Budget, *The Budget of the United States Government, FY 1984, Appendix* (Washington, DC: U.S. Government Printing Office, 1983), p. I-Q1.

[32]U.S. Senate, Committee on Environment and Public Works, Subcommitee on Transportation, *Federal-Aid Highway Act of 1982*, 97th Cong., 2nd sess. (Washington, DC: U.S. Government Printing Office, April 21, 1982). The National Governors' Association did not take a position on the higher user fees because it was advocating the turnback of noninterstate highway and other intergovernmental programs to the states in exchange for the national government's assuming responsibility for Medicaid. See Timothy J. Conlan and David B. Walker, "Reagan's New Federalism: Design, Debate, and Discord," in *American Intergovernmental Relations Today*, ed. Robert Jay Dilger (Englewood Cliffs, NJ: Prentice-Hall, Inc., 1986), pp. 198, 199.

[33]William J. Lanouette, "Critics Seek Big Bucks from Big Trucks to Repair Damage to Interstate Roads," p. 2122. The American Trucking Association argued that weather and chemicals damage highways the most.

[34]Ibid., pp. 2122–2125; Judy Sarasohn, "Highway Plan Would Drop Aid to Some Major Programs," Congressional Quarterly, *Weekly Report* (April 25, 1981):699, 700; and "Transportation Policy," in *Congress and the Nation, 1981–1984*, pp. 289, 297, 298.

needed, they should pay for them. Representatives from the affected states (primarily Louisiana and Florida) were outraged. They organized opposition to the administration's proposal and it failed.

In 1982, congressional leaders pushed through legislation that raised the excise tax on gasoline from 4 cents to 9 cents a gallon. The legislation succeeded this time because liberals and moderates were distressed at the rising unemployment rate, which stood at 10.7 percent at that time. They now viewed the increased tax on gasoline not only as a means to ensure the completion of the interstate highway system by 1990 but also as a way to create 300,000 additional construction jobs. While conservatives were reluctant to view the legislation as a jobs bill, many of them were willing to support it because they recognized that infrastructure has a profound impact on economic development and had become convinced that the national government had to do something about the impending infrastructure crisis. It was estimated that the proposed increase in the gasoline excise tax, along with increases in several other excise taxes, would raise an additional $5.5 billion annually for the Highway Trust Fund (approximately $78 billion by 1995).[35] Although this figure fell far short of the revenue needed to meet the infrastructure crisis, it was the most revenue that could be achieved, given the concerns about the size of the national deficit, the president's threat of a veto of any new taxes, and a continuing emphasis on the need to increase defense expenditures.

Facing strong bipartisan support for the gasoline excise tax increase, President Reagan decided not to veto the measure. To fend off any possible political problems concerning his pledge not to increase national taxes, he carefully avoided using the words "tax increase" when referring to the measure. Instead, he called it an acceptable increase in highway "user fees" that would be used to repair the nation's highways and bridges.[36]

The 1982 gasoline excise tax increase and the scaling back of national construction requirements in 1981 convinced most highway analysts that the interstate highway system would be completed in 1990. However, that completion date was threatened in 1984 and in 1985. In each of those years members of the House Public Works and Transportation Committee and the Senate Environment and Public Works Committee attempted to add a number of pet "demonstration" highway projects to the interstate system.[37]

---

[35]"Transportation Policy," in *Congress and the Nation, 1981–1984*, p. 301.

[36]Ibid.

[37]Robert Rothman, "Scramble on to Add Pork to Road Bill," Congressional Quarterly, *Weekly Report* (May 5, 1984):1070; Stephen Gettinger, "Dual Battle Set over Highway Funding Bills," Congressional Quarterly, *Weekly Report* (August 18, 1984):2047, 2048; Robert Rothman, "Hill Politics Delay Repair of America in Ruins," Congressional Quarterly, *Weekly Report* (September 8, 1984):2193–2197; Stephen Gettinger, "Senate Clears Bill Freeing States' Road Funds," Congressional Quarterly, *Weekly Report* (March 9, 1985):463; and Stephen Gettinger, "Hill, Administration Return to Highway Funding Impasse," Congressional Quarterly, *Weekly Report* (January 26, 1985):153.

Funding allotments to the states for 1985 and 1986 were delayed as the bill's conferees could not decide whose pet projects would be added to the interstate system. The funding problem was finally resolved in 1987 when Congress approved a five-year reauthorization of all transportation programs (FYs 1987–1991). The $88 billion reauthorization bill contained nearly $1 billion for 120 highway demonstration projects. President Reagan vetoed the bill on the grounds that the demonstration projects were unnecessary and unwise, given the size of the national deficit, but Congress overrode the veto. As a result, the interstate highway system and the 120 additional highway demonstration projects are now expected to be finished by the end of FY 1991.

CONTROVERSY #2: TURNBACKS AND THE HIGHWAY TRUST FUND

Barring any further efforts to expand the 42,500-mile interstate highway system, most analysts agree that it will be completed in FY 1991. Construction is under way on the last two major gaps in the system, 173 miles on I-49 in Louisiana and 112 miles on I-75 in Florida.[38] Some analysts have suggested that the Highway Trust Fund and its excise taxes should be terminated once the system is completed. They point out that its primary purpose was to finance the construction of the interstate highway system and that the states were supposed to finance the maintenance of the system once it was completed.[39]

President Reagan agreed. In his 1982 New Federalism proposal he asked Congress to turn over to state governments total responsibility for all future financing, administration, and programmatic decisions concerning all highways built with national assistance. Half of the revenue generated by the gasoline excise tax was to be given to the states to help them finance the maintenance of the interstate highway system, the 260,000 miles of primary roads (U.S. highways), and the 523,500 miles of secondary and urban roads that were constructed with assistance from the Highway Trust Fund.[40] Although these roads constitute only 21 percent of all roads in the nation, they carry over 80 percent of the vehicle traffic.[41]

Congress refused to approve President Reagan's 1982 New

[38]Stephen Gettinger, "Hill, Administration Return to Highway Funding Impasse," p. 153.

[39]Rochelle L. Stanfield, "Hard Times for the Highway Trust Fund May Mean Trouble for Highway Repair," *National Journal* (August 16, 1980): 1362–1364. The Highway Trust Fund was also designed to finance the construction of primary, secondary, and urban highways.

[40]Rochelle L. Stanfield, "The New Federalism is Reagan's Answer to Decaying Highways, Transit Systems," *National Journal* (June 12, 1982):1040–1044.

[41]Ibid., p. 1041.

Federalism proposal.[42] National lobby organizations representing the trucking, manufacturing, and construction industries strongly opposed the plan. They argued that it would cost at least $404 billion between 1981 and 1990 to finish and repair the 825,000 miles of roads constructed with the assistance of national funds.[43] They were convinced that the states lacked the fiscal capacity to raise that much revenue even with continued national assistance. In their view, enactment of the proposal would lead to a further deterioration of the nation's highways, greater costs for truckers who would have to detour around bridges and roads that could not be traveled safely, greater costs for manufacturers who would be charged more by truckers for carrying goods from city to city, and fewer construction jobs.

Representatives of the nation's cities and counties also opposed the highway turnback proposal. They also were convinced that the states lacked the fiscal capacity to handle transportation expenses without national assistance. As highways deteriorated, local officials worried that constituents would place the blame for increasing traffic congestion and bumpy rides on them. City officials also feared that state officials would shift available funding away from urban highways and mass transit toward primary and secondary highways because those highways serve politically powerful suburban areas. Moreover, state officials have always played a role in maintaining primary and secondary roads. City officials feared that state officials would have a bias toward those highways' needs.

State officials, on the other hand, were willing to consider taking over sole responsibility for constructing and maintaining secondary roads, but opposed any move to give them total financial responsibility for primary and interstate highways. They believed that the national government should help finance primary and interstate highways because those highways have a profound impact on interstate commerce and the condition of the national economy. State officials also argued that they could not finance the construction and maintenance of primary and interstate highways without national assistance. The National Governors' Association pointed out that the average state excise tax on gasoline (9.2 cents at that time) was already higher than the national government's tax. They argued that it would be politically impossible for them to raise state excise taxes to the levels necessary to maintain the nation's highways. Citing the fiscal problems facing the states, even President Reagan's secretary of transportation, Drew Lewis, broke ranks with the president and joined the chorus of voices opposing the turnback proposal.[44]

The U.S. Advisory Commission on Intergovernmental Relations

[42]See Timothy J. Conlan and David B. Walker, "Reagan's New Federalism," pp. 189–200.

[43]Rochelle L. Stanfield, "The New Federalism is Reagan's Answer to Decaying Highways, Transit Systems," p. 1041.

[44]Ibid., p. 1040.

(ACIR) reopened the highway turnback debate in 1986. An ACIR staff report at that time was very critical of the national government's role in the Federal Aid to Highways program. It argued that highways should reflect state as well as national priorities.[45] It suggested that the national government had seriously undermined the cooperative national-state intergovernmental relationship that has existed since the formation of the Federal Aid to Highways program in 1956:

> Congressional inaction on program reauthorization, increased funding for "special" projects, unnecessary nationwide construction standards, sanctions, Gramm-Rudman-Hollings, and a large undistributed balance in the Highway Trust fund have all worked to erode the ability of the states to best use the funds that have been dedicated specifically for highway programs.[46]

The report suggested that turning back the responsibility for noninterstate highway programs to the states would prevent many of these problems from occurring in the future. It argued that "there is no compelling reason" for national government responsibility or involvement in noninterstate highway programs.[47] In 1987, ACIR's Commissioners voted in favor of a resolution asking Congress to set the turning back of nearly all noninterstate highway programs as a long-term goal of the national government. The Commission also recommended that the national government relinquish a portion of the national excise tax revenue to the states to help them finance noninterstate highway construction and maintenance. Although Congress did not take any action on the proposal, ACIR's recommendation set off a feud within the intergovernmental lobbies as the U.S. Conference of Mayors and National League of Cities continued to lobby against highway and mass transit turnback proposals.[48]

CONTROVERSY #3: HIGHWAYS VERSUS MASS TRANSIT

Prior to the 1960s, conventional forms of mass transit (bus, subway, ferryboat, and commuter railroad) were provided primarily by private firms.[49] Competition from government-subsidized highways and the preference to

---

[45]U.S. Advisory Commission on Intergovernmental Relations, "A Critical Appraisal of Devolving Selected Federal-Aid Highway Programs and Revenue Bases," p. 36.

[46]Ibid., p. 61. The Federal Aid to Highways programs are included in the Gramm-Rudman-Hollings deficit reduction requirements even though they do not contribute to the national deficit and are financed by a dedicated trust fund.

[47]Ibid., p. 62.

[48]U.S. Advisory Commission on Intergovernmental Relations, *Devolving Selected Federal-Aid Highway Programs and Revenue Bases: A Critical Appraisal* (Washington, DC: U.S. Advisory Commission on Intergovernmental Relations, 1987), p. 2.

[49]Bruce D. McDowell, "Governmental Actors and Factors in Mass Transit," *Intergovernmental Perspective* 10:3 (Summer 1984):7. Nonconventional forms of mass transit (paratransit) include organized car and van pool, minibus, taxi, jitney, subscription bus, shuttle, and courtesy car.

drive to work caused many of these private firms either to go out of business or to reduce service to selected, profitable routes. As private firms withdrew from the mass transit field, their stranded customers lobbied state and local governments either to subsidize specific routes or to offer mass transit as a public service. Moreover, as population densities increased in urban centers, environmentalists lobbied state and local governments to enter the mass transit field as a means to reduce automobile traffic congestion, noise, and air pollution.

At the same time that mass transit was making a transition from private to public ownership, many analysts and politicians were beginning to question the national government's focus on highway construction. City planners objected to the highways' role in promoting "white flight" to the suburbs. Environmentalists objected to the automobile's impact on air quality. Automobile owners complained about increasingly congested highways and the expansion in many large cities of the morning and afternoon rush hours into the rush morning and the rush afternoon. Traffic congestion was so bad in some cities that new terms, such as "gridlock," became a part of our language. Community activists objected to highway construction that divided established neighborhoods and business districts, and led to increased noise and air pollution.

Lobbyists for these groups advocated what they called a "balanced transportation system," a phrase that generally meant less national assistance for highway construction and more for mass transit (especially for buses, trains, and subways).[50] They also wanted the national government to use some of the revenue from the Highway Trust Fund for mass transit. In this way, mass transit would be guaranteed an annual budget and would be freed, as highways are, from the political battles that accompany the annual budgetary approval process.

A number of influential lobby organizations that benefited from highway construction projects opposed these efforts. The automobile and trucking industries and unions, road builder associations, oil companies, gasoline retailers, real estate developers, and construction unions all joined forces to protect "their" trust fund.[51] Their economic arguments were augmented by the ideological arguments of conservatives. They viewed mass transit as a state and local responsibility. Although mass transit projects may be subject to underfunding by cities because the benefits of mass transit tend to spill over into neighboring jurisdictions, these spillovers almost always occur within a single state's or county's geographic boundaries. In their view, the responsibility for correcting any negative economic spillovers in mass transit was primarily a state or county responsibility. The only exceptions were in those rare instances, such as Washington, D.C., and

[50]"Transportation Policy," in *Congress and the Nation, 1969–1972* (Washington, DC: Congressional Quarterly Service, 1973, p. 147.
[51]Ibid.

Cincinnati, Ohio, where a mass transit system's customers reside in several states.

Many liberals in Congress hold a different view of mass transit. Instead of focusing on who benefits from the service and where they live, they focus on mass transit's role in reducing air pollution. Since air pollutants are carried by the prevailing winds and often cross state boundaries, liberals argue that the national government has the right and the obligation to subsidize mass transit.

The intergovernmental lobbies agreed that the national government should provide more money for mass transit programs. However, they were divided over the best strategy for promoting mass transit. The U.S. Conference of Mayors, consisting of the nation's larger cities, wanted a portion of the Highway Trust Fund's revenue dedicated for mass transit. The National League of Cities, consisting of the nation's smaller cities, was supportive of the U.S. Conference of Mayors' efforts, but generally let them take lead on the Highway Trust Fund issue and focused their resources on getting more aid for mass transit from general treasury dollars. The National Association of Counties also was reluctant to push hard for dedicating Highway Trust Fund revenue for mass transit purposes. Its highest priority was to convince Congress to increase funding for secondary highways. The National Governors' Association took no official position on the mass transit/Highway Trust Fund issue. It wanted to end the separate allocations for the various highway and mass transit systems altogether. It advocated a unified transportation budget with all national funding allocations determined by the states.[52]

The National Government's Role in Mass Transit

Despite increasing traffic congestion during the 1940–1970 period, Americans increasingly avoided mass transit. The number of automobiles in the United States increased from 25.8 million in 1945 to 80 million in 1967. At the same time, the number of passenger trips on buses, subways, and elevated trains decreased from 23 billion in 1945 to 7.7 billion in 1967.[53] The public's reluctance to use available mass transit, coupled with the highway lobbies' opposition to mass transit aid, kept the national government's mass transit assistance at relatively minuscule levels throughout the 1960s and early 1970s. In 1961 the Housing Act authorized the token expenditure of $25 million in grants and $50 million in low-interest loans for experimental or demonstration mass transit projects. The grants and loans were administered by the Housing and Home Finance Agency (DOT was not formed until 1967). Indicating the automobile lobby's strength, the law came from the congressional banking committees, not from the con-

---

[52]Donald H. Haider, *When Governments Come to Washington*, pp. 176–181.
[53]Ibid., p. 149.

gressional transportation committees. Nevertheless, the national government had entered the mass transit area.[54]

In 1964 the Urban Mass Transportation Act (UMTA) was adopted to reduce traffic congestion and air pollution; to provide increased mobility for the poor, the young, and the elderly; and to create an incentive for cities to create compact, transit-oriented transportation systems.[55] It provided states with $375 million over a three-year period to cover up to two-thirds of the cost of planning, engineering, and designing urban mass transportation systems; 100 percent of the cost of relocating families displaced by mass transit; and half of the cost of mass transit projects that showed urgent need but lacked required planning reports. Cities used the funds primarily to purchase private mass transit companies near bankruptcy and to expand public bus service.[56] UMTA was subsequently renewed, and national mass transit aid reached an annual authorization level of $175 million in 1970.[57]

Advocates of mass transit, led by the U.S. Conference of Mayors, attempted throughout the 1970s to convince Congress to increase funding for mass transit and to create a mass transit trust fund so that UMTA would no longer have to compete with all other national programs for general treasury revenues every time it came up for renewal. The mass transit trust fund would have received revenue from the existing excise tax on gasoline.

Congress rejected the trust fund proposals, primarily because the highway lobbies were so strongly opposed to them, and Presidents Nixon and Ford indicated that they would veto them because the new trust fund would eventually lead to larger domestic expenditures and higher national taxes. However, funding for mass transit was increased to $3.1 billion over FYs 1971–1975 and to $7.8 billion over FYs 1975–1980. Funding covered two-thirds of the cost of planning, designing, and constructing mass transit systems.[58] In an effort to further appease the disappointed mayors, Congress increased funding for noninterstate highway construction and, in 1970, raised the matching grant for noninterstate highways from 50 percent of costs to 70 percent.[59]

[54]Milton Pikarsky and Daphne Christensen, *Urban Transportation Policy and Management* (Lexington, MA: Lexington Books, 1976), p. 96.

[55]George W. Hilton, "The Urban Mass Transportation Assistance Program," in *Perspectives on Federal Transportation Policy*, ed. James C. Miller (Washington DC: American Enterprise Institute for Public Policy Research, 1975), p. 133.

[56]Daphne Christensen, "Autos and Mass Transit," in *Transportation in America*, ed. Donald Altschiller (New York: H. W. Wilson, 1982), p. 112.

[57]"Mass Transit Aid Program," in *Congress and the Nation, 1945–1964*, p. 560; and "Transportation Policy," in *Congress and the Nation, 1965–1968*, p. 241. Urban mass transportation grant outlays for FY 1970 were $104 million.

[58]"Chronology of Legislation on Transportation," in *Congress and the Nation, 1969–1972*, p. 156.

[59]Donald H. Haider, *When Governments Come to Washington*, p. 179.

In 1975, Congress also authorized the expenditure of $3.9 billion for mass transit operating expenditures over FYs 1975–1980. Opponents of operating subsidies argued that they encouraged local mass transit inefficiency by guaranteeing subsidies for bus or rail routes that service relatively few people. Congressional representatives of rural districts and states complained that the subsidies would be a windfall for the nation's nine largest cities. Advocates of operating subsidies, particularly the U.S. Conference of Mayors, argued that all major mass transit systems were losing money. In their view, it did not make sense to encourage cities to expand their mass transit systems by giving them larger capital, construction grants and then deny them operating assistance when existing systems were already draining city budgets despite recent fare increases.[60]

In 1981, the Reagan administration announced its strong opposition to mass transit operating subsidies as being inefficient, a state and local government responsibility, and too costly, given the size of the national deficit. The administration proposed a phaseout of all operating subsidies by FY 1985. It also announced its strong opposition to any funding increases for mass transit capital grants. It acknowledged studies by mass transit advocates that indicated it would cost approximately $50 billion over a ten-year period to replace or to repair inadequate buses and subway cars.[61] It was not convinced, however, that the national government should play the primary role in paying these costs. Under the threat of a presidential veto, Congress agreed in 1981 to reduce mass transit operating grants from $1.8 billion to $1.5 billion for FY 1982 but refused to kill the subsidy altogether. Congress also agreed to cut capital grants from $1.6 billion to $1.5 billion.[62]

In 1982 the U.S. Conference of Mayors and other mass transit advocates were elated when Secretary of Transportation Drew Lewis announced that the Reagan administration had decided to support congressional efforts to increase the resources of the Highway Trust Fund by raising the gasoline excise tax from 4 cents to 9 cents a gallon. Congress' plan included a provision that set aside revenues collected from 1 cent of the gasoline excise tax, approximately $1.1 billion annually, for mass transit capital grants. The highway lobbies did not oppose this provision because highway and bridge construction got 80 percent of the new tax revenue (4 cents of the additional 5 cents per gallon). The Reagan administration did not oppose the mass transit provision because the funds were to be used only for capital, construction projects and Congress agreed to convert the mass transit program into a block grant.

[60]"Chronology of Action on Transportation and Communications," in *Congress and the Nation, 1973–1976*, pp. 510, 522–524.

[61]Ibid., p. 302.

[62]Ibid., pp. 299, 300.

Although President Reagan thought that Congress' request for $3.5 billion for the mass transit block grant was too expensive, he did not veto it because the program's conversion into a block grant significantly reduced administrative red tape by eliminating the need for cities to apply to DOT for mass transit assistance. Instead, funds were allocated directly to localities according to a formula based on service factors (such as total miles of existing mass transit routes) and population. Moreover, the block grant restricted expenditures for operating expenses.[63]

Throughout the remainder of the 1980s, the Reagan administration asked Congress to cut the block grant's funds to help balance the national budget and the intergovernmental lobbies asked Congress to increase its funds. The program is currently funded at approximately $2 billion annually.[64]

CONTROVERSY #4: CROSSOVER SANCTIONS

The national government has always imposed a number of strict administrative conditions on its highway assistance programs. Among these requirements are guidelines to assure fair competitive bidding practices, auditing requirements to prevent embezzlement and fraud, and specific design requirements, such as those concerning noise abatement, traffic interchanges, width of traffic lanes (12 feet), and width of median areas (36 feet), to foster uniform safety and health standards.

State government officials have always been concerned over the amount of administrative red tape tied to categorical grants. Highway assistance, however, is viewed as a particularly burdensome intergovernmental program because of its crossover sanctions. These sanctions impose a penalty on a recipient of a particular program, usually in the form of reduced funding, who fails to comply with the requirements of another, totally independent program.[65] The following examination of the first crossover sanction attached to national highway assistance, the Highway Beautification Act of 1965, provides a good idea of how crossover sanctions work, and the politics and rationales that lead to their creation and continuation. This section is followed by brief descriptions of three additional highway crossover sanctions that are generally considered to be among the most important ones affecting the states.

[63]Ibid., pp. 301–307.

[64]U.S. Office of Management and Budget, *Budget of the United States Government, FY 1988* (Washington, DC: U.S. Government Printing Office, 1987), p. 4-143.

[65]David R. Beam, "Washington's Regulation of States and Localities: Origins and Issues," in *American Intergovernmental Relations Today*, ed. Robert Jay Dilger, pp. 232, 233; and Cynthia Cates Colella, "The United States Supreme Court and Intergovernmental Relations," in ibid., pp. 62–64.

Highway Beautification

To improve the appearance of the interstate highway system, the national government began in 1958 to offer states an extra half of a percent reimbursement for their interstate construction expense (90.5 percent instead of 90 percent) if they agreed to ban advertising billboards within 660 feet of interstate highways. By 1965, 25 states had signed agreements to participate in the program, but only 10 actually implemented the controls and their programs covered only 209.2 miles of the entire interstate system.[66]

A number of civic and environmental groups, such as the National Wildlife Federation and the Garden Club of America, lobbied Congress and the Johnson administration to impose strict national controls and penalties to get rid of all billboards and junkyards along the nation's highways. President Johnson's wife, Lady Bird, made this issue a personal crusade and convinced her husband to support highway beautification. In February 1965, he asked Congress to enact legislation that would ban advertising billboards and junkyards within 1,000 feet of all highways receiving financial assistance from the national government. A national survey completed in May 1965 indicated that there were 17,726 automobile graveyards, junkyards, and scrap metal heaps, and over a million billboards, that would be affected by the ban.[67] States that refused to comply with these bans would be punished by forfeiture of 100 percent of their national highway assistance.

A number of lobby organizations, led by the Roadside Business Association and the Outdoor Advertising Association of America, opposed the bans as being contrary to the basic tenets of federalism. They insisted that highway beautification was clearly a state and local issue. Opposition to the president's proposal also came from the National Association of Counties, the American Road Builders Association, and other lobby organizations representing the construction industry. These groups objected to the way the proposal would compensate billboard and junkyard owners who were going to be forced out of business by the bans. Instead of allocating funds from the general treasury for this purpose, the proposal would use revenue from the Highway Trust Fund. This meant that highway beautification efforts would reduce the availability of highway construction funds.[68]

Faced with such a wide array of interests that opposed the bill, Congress was reluctant to approve it. President Johnson, however, intervened personally on behalf of the bill. One member of the House Committee on Public Works and Transportation commented that he had "never before

---

[66]"Chronology of Legislation on Conservation," in *Congress and the Nation, 1965–1968* (Washington, DC: Congressional Quarterly Service, 1969), p. 478.

[67]Ibid., pp. 481, 487.

[68]Ibid., p. 477.

seen such pressures and arm twisting from the Executive Branch . . . as I have seen with respect to the highway beautification bill."[69]

The Highway Beautification Act of 1965 placed strict controls on outdoor advertising billboards within 660 feet of all interstate and primary highways in the United States. Only billboards that met size and spacing criteria established by the secretary of transportation or were within areas zoned for industrial or commercial use were allowed. Junkyards within 1,000 feet of interstate and primary highways must be removed, or natural or artificial barriers must be erected to make them invisible to highway traffic. States that failed to comply with the new controls would lose 10 percent of their national highway construction assistance. The national government would provide states 75 percent of the cost of compensating billboard and junkyard owners who were forced to relocate their businesses because of the law. The funds were to be allocated from the general treasury.[70]

All 50 states announced that they would participate in this "voluntary" highway beautification program. Financing the program, however, soon became a major problem. The House and Senate Public Works Committees authorized the expenditure of $12 million for billboard and $40 million for junkyard compensation for FY 1966, but the House and Senate Appropriations Committees cut that request to $10 million for billboard and junkyard compensation combined.[71]

In 1966, Congress failed to authorize any new funds for the program. Some press reports suggested that its failure to fund the program was the result of an intensive lobbying effort by the outdoor advertising industry, but congressional observers interviewed by *Congressional Quarterly* reporters suggested that the lobbying efforts of conservation groups had alienated many of the program's supporters. These groups advocated the use of state police powers to remove all billboards in violation of the law without compensation to the owners. Another reason Congress failed to fund the program was the growing consensus on Capitol Hill that President Johnson's FY 1968 budget had to be trimmed. The Bureau of Public Roads, which administered the beautification program, reported that it would cost $558 million to remove the 1 million billboards that violated the law and another $121 million to screen or relocate 17,726 junkyards that violated the law.[72]

The national government's failure to appropriate additional money for the program in 1967 did not exempt the states from the billboard and junkyard controls. Legally, they were still required to remove the offend-

[69]Ibid.
[70]Ibid., pp. 476–479.
[71]Ibid., p. 479.
[72]Ibid., p. 487.

ing billboards and junkyards. The states, however, were not willing to pay the full cost of removing the offending billboards and junkyards. It was their collective judgment, which proved to be correct, that Congress' lack of enthusiastic support for the program would prevent the Bureau of Public Roads from withholding 10 percent of their highway assistance funds if they refused to obey the law. Recognizing that the highway beautification program would probably be killed by Congress if it withheld 10 percent of the states' highway funds, the Bureau of Public Roads tried to negotiate with the states to get them to agree voluntarily to revise their laws to conform to the national standards. In this way, the Bureau's administrators hoped to build political support for the program among the states and to prevent the spread of additional billboards and junkyards along nationally funded highways. By the end of 1967, eight states and the District of Columbia had revised their laws to conform to the national standards.[73] By 1970, 32 states had agreed to the standards.[74]

The Bureau of Public Roads' effort to build state support for the highway beautification program was successful. The states supported Congress' creation of the Highway Beautification Commission in 1973 to study the program's financing problem and Congress' decision in 1974 to prohibit "jumbo" outdoor advertising signs that can be read from interstate highways in rural areas even if erected beyond the 660-foot limit.[75] The states also supported the House and Senate Public Works Committees' efforts during the 1970s to fund the program at $75 million annually. The House and Senate Appropriations Committees, however, reduced funding for the program to approximately $1 million a year throughout the 1970s. This was enough funding to keep the Highway Beautification Commission operating and to pay the salaries of administrators within the Bureau of Public Roads.

In 1980, the House and Senate Appropriations Committees approved the expenditure of $8 million for billboard and junkyard removal in FY 1981. For the first time since the program's inception, it looked like Congress had finally decided to take billboard and junkyard removal seriously. The incoming Reagan administration, however, announced its opposition to any expenditures for this purpose. In 1982, funding was reduced to $400,000. House Public Works and Transportation Committee Chairman James J. Howard (D-NJ) commented that with funding at the $400,000 level, it would take over 1,600 years to remove all the billboards that were

[73]Ibid.

[74]"Congress Extends Interstate Highway System," Congressional Quarterly, *Almanac, 1970* (Washington, DC: Congressional Quarterly, 1971), p. 797.

[75]"Highway Beautification," Congressional Quarterly, *Almanac, 1973* (Washington, DC: Congressional Quarterly, 1974), p. 455; and "55 MPH Speed Limit, Higher Truck Weights Voted," Congressional Quarterly, *Almanac, 1974* (Washington, DC: Congressional Quarterly, 1975), p. 704.

in violation of the law.[76] Despite his protests, funding continued at this nominal level in 1983 and 1984 and, at the urging of the Reagan administration, was eliminated entirely in 1985.

The Highway Beautification Act's standards concerning billboards and junkyards are still in force. The states continue to refuse to remove the offending billboards and junkyards until the national government is willing to live up to its promise to pay 75 percent of the cost of removing them and providing their owners with just compensation. The Bureau of Public Roads continues to refuse to impose its 10 percent funding penalty on the states fearing that Congress will respond to the states' anticipated outcry and kill the program entirely. It is also continuing its efforts to convince all of the states to voluntarily restrict the proliferation of billboards and junkyards along the nation's highways. Congress, in the meantime, continues to give highway beautification a low priority and is content to leave the issue as it stands.

Highway Safety

The national government's interest in fostering highway safety legislation first appeared in an amendment to the Federal Aid to Highways Act of 1956. The amendment directed the secretary of commerce to study the relative merits of highway safety measures and to report his findings to Congress. In 1958 Congress approved an interstate compact that sought to seek ways to protect the public from unsafe or poor-risk drivers (adopted by nine states by 1966). It also established the Vehicle Equipment Safety Commission to formulate uniform standards for new or improved automobile safety equipment.

In 1965 Congress moved closer to a mandatory safety program when it specified that each state should have a highway safety program approved by the secretary of commerce.[77] In 1966 the Highway Safety Act used both the carrot and the stick to encourage states to implement an acceptable highway safety program. First, it established a grants program that reimbursed states half the cost of safety projects approved by the national government. The national government currently spends approximately $127 million annually on the program.[78] The act also mandated that any state failing to establish an approved highway safety program would lose 10 percent of its national highway grants.

The carrot-and-stick approach worked. All 50 states decided to par-

[76]"Taxes Hiked to Finance Roads, Mass Transit," Congressional Quarterly, *Almanac, 1982* (Washington, DC: Congressional Quarterly, 1983), p. 324.

[77]"Chronology of Legislation on Consumer Issues," in *Congress and the Nation, 1965–1968*, p. 790.

[78]U.S. Office of Management and Budget, *Historical Tables: Budget of the United States Government, FY 1986* (Washington, DC: U.S. Government Printing Office, 1985), Table 12.3.

ticipate in the program. The national government established national standards for, among other things, driver education courses, the training and certification of driver education instructors, testing procedures for obtaining a driver's license, recordkeeping systems for accidents and vehicle registration, highway design and maintenance, traffic control, vehicle codes and inspections, and surveillance of traffic for detection of potential, high-accident locations.[79] It also requires states to establish uniform traffic laws and highway markers throughout the state and to prohibit persons from driving if the alcohol concentration in their blood equals or exceeds 0.10 percent.[80]

55-Mile-Per-Hour Speed Limit

The Emergency Highway Energy Conservation Act of 1973 established the 55-mile-per-hour (mph) national speed limit on a one-year basis, effective January 1974, to save fuel following the Arab oil embargo. Prior to that time most states had established a 70 mph speed limit on major highways. Advocates of the law claimed that lowering the speed limit to 55 mph would save between 130,000 and 165,000 barrels of oil a day.[81] States that did not reduce their speed limit to 55 mph would lose all of their national highway assistance. All 50 states "voluntarily" reduced their speed limits to 55 mph.

The national government's one-year, temporary 55 mph speed limit was extended in the Federal Aid to Highways Amendments of 1974. To ensure compliance with the new mandate, states were required to certify annually that they were enforcing the 55 mph speed limit. Advocates of the national speed limit argued that the nation's need to reduce dependence on imported oil outweighed the states' right to determine speed limits. They also argued that the lowered speed limit would reduce the number and severity of traffic accidents. The National Academy of Sciences reported in 1975 that the number of automobile-related traffic deaths had dropped to the lowest level in 11 years following the imposition of the 55 mph speed limit. The number of highway fatalities declined from 55,511 in 1973 to 46,402 in 1974. A study completed by the Academy in 1983 indicated that the 55 mph speed limit had saved between 2,000 and 4,000 lives and had prevented between 2,500 and 4,500 serious injuries annually since 1974.[82]

Although the 55 mph limit had lived up to its sponsors' expectations,

---

[79]"Chronology of Legislation on Consumer Issues," in *Congress and the Nation, 1965–1968*, p. 790.

[80]Ibid., p. 805.

[81]"Chronology of Action on Energy," *Congress and the Nation, 1973–1976* (Washington, DC: Congressional Quarterly Service, 1977), p. 211. Gasoline is a derivative of crude oil.

[82]James J. Howard, "Limiting Speed Has Saved Lives," *San Bernardino County, The Sun*, July 13, 1986, p. F3.

the National Governors' Association and congressional members from the West, where major cities are generally separated by hundreds of miles of highways, continued to express concern that the limit infringed on states' rights and added considerably to travel time. The National Academy of Sciences' 1983 report indicated that the 55 mph speed limit's chief cost was that it added approximately 1 billion hours per year to the time traveled on the nation's highways. This meant that the typical highway user spent an average of seven additional hours annually on the road because of the lowered speed limit.[83]

Viewing the 55 mph speed limit as an infringement on states' rights, President Reagan sponsored legislation, adopted as part of the Omnibus Budget Reconciliation Act of 1981, that reduced the states' penalty for failing to comply with the 55 mph speed limit to 10 percent of noninterstate national highway assistance. The criteria for determining noncompliance with the speed limit were relaxed as well. At least 50 percent of traffic on the highways would have to exceed the speed limit before the national government would penalize a state by withholding national highway assistance funds.[84]

According to a poll conducted in 1986 by NBC News and the *Wall Street Journal*, 70 percent of the American public support the 55 mph speed limit.[85] Yet a poll conducted by the Associated Press at about the same time indicated that 85 percent of Americans admitted that they regularly exceeded the 55 mph speed limit.[86] The Federal Highway Administration (FHA) reported in 1985 that speed sensors embedded in the pavement on various highways across the country indicated that 43 percent of all motorists ignored the 55 mph speed limit.[87]

Responding to the charge that her department was not enforcing the law, Secretary of Transportation Elizabeth Dole announced in 1986 that she intended to withhold 10 percent of Arizona's and Vermont's noninterstate highway funds because FHA studies indicated that their motorists exceeded the 50 percent compliance figure. She also announced that Maryland, New Hampshire, and Rhode Island would lose 10 percent of their noninterstate funds unless they took more aggressive steps to enforce the speed limit. In January 1987 she withheld 1 percent of Arizona's noninterstate highway funds and announced that no further action would be taken pending state efforts to comply with the speed limit law. Her message to the states was clear: enforce the law or suffer the consequences.[88]

83"National 55 MPH Speed Limit," *Congressional Digest* (December 1986):289.
84Ibid., p. 290.
85"Life in the Slow Lane," *Washington Post*, weekly edition June 9, 1986, p. 37.
86"55 Limit Has Support—in Theory," *USA Today*, September 2, 1986, 1A.
87"Federal Agencies Involved," *Congressional Digest* (December 1986):314.
88"California Could Lose Highway Funds," *San Bernardino County, The Sun*, May 30, 1986, p. A3.

Opponents of the 55 mph speed limit agreed that it probably has saved some lives and injuries in large, congested metropolitan areas. They argued, however, that it did not make sense for highways designed to accommodate 70 mph traffic and located in rural areas. They also argued that the 55 mph speed limit was an unjust intrusion upon states' rights, given the relatively abundant supply of oil available to the country since the early 1980s.

In 1986, 20 senators, calling themselves the States' Rights Coalition, sponsored legislation to allow states to raise the speed limit to 65 mph on interstate highways outside urban areas with populations exceeding 50,000.[89] Approximately 34,000 of the interstate highway system's 43,000 miles would be affected. The Senate Transportation Committee rejected their bill, but the Coalition refused to give up.[90] They received President Reagan's support and introduced their bill on the Senate floor as an amendment to legislation reauthorizing expenditures for transportation programs. One of the amendment's cosponsors, Sen. Steven Symms (R-ID), claimed on the Senate floor, "I know of no law in the country, particularly west of the Mississippi, that causes more skepticism of Big Brother in Washington than [this] seemingly unenforceable law."[91] Another sponsor, Senator Russell B. Long (D-LA), argued that the 55 mph speed limit "breeds contempt for the law" and was a "joke."[92]

Despite a report by the National Academy of Sciences that the bill could cause at least 500 additional highway deaths annually, the Senate approved the Coalition's bill by a wide margin, 56–36.[93] The House, however, had rejected an amendment containing similar language when it considered the transportation reauthorization bill earlier in the year. The House continued to oppose any changes in the 55 mph speed limit law; and the Coalition's amendment, as well as the transportation reauthorization bill, died in the House-Senate conference.

The 55 mph speed limit issue refused to die. The States' Rights Coalition reintroduced the 65 mph proposal as an amendment to the Senate's five-year (FY 1987–1991) transportation reauthorization bill. The 65 mph amendment was approved by the Senate, 65 to 33, on February 3, 1987. The House's five-year reauthorization bill, however, had already been adopted and retained the 55 mph speed limit on all highways receiving national assistance. James Howard, chairman of the House Public Works and Transportation Committee, vowed to lead the fight to preserve the 55 mph speed limit during the conference committee meetings.

[89]Chic Hecht, "Law Should Adjust to Realities," ibid., July 13, 1986, p. F3.
[90]Paul Starobin, "Chambers Go Separate Ways on Omnibus Highway Bill," Congressional Quarterly, *Weekly Report* (July 19, 1986):1625, 1628.
[91]Karen Tumulty, "65-M.P.H. Road Speed Backed in Senate Vote," *Los Angeles Times*, September 24, 1986, p.1.
[92]Ibid., p. 23.
[93]Ibid., p. 1.

Given Howard's remarks, it looked like the transportation reauthorization bill was once again headed for trouble. Most of the House conferees, however, were more interested in passing a reauthorization bill than in preserving the 55 mph speed limit. Congress' failure to adopt a reauthorization bill the previous year had forced the Federal Highway Administration to dip into the Highway Trust Fund's reserves to keep highway and mass transit construction going in many states. Unless a reauthorization bill was adopted soon, all construction would end, thousands of construction workers would be laid off, and any hope of completing the interstate highway system by 1991 would be lost. Worried about the political backlash of not approving a highway bill, House conferees convinced Howard to separate the speed limit from the rest of the transportation bill. In an unusual legislative move, the full House was asked to vote twice on the conference committee's transportation reauthorization bill. The first vote was to decide whether to accept the Senate's 65 mph proposal, and the second vote was to decide whether to accept the conference committee's $88 billion, five-year reauthorization bill for transportation programs.

Howard led the floor fight against the Senate's 65 mph proposal. He insisted that at least 3,500 people would die in the ensuing five years if the speed limit was raised to 65 mph on rural stretches of the interstate highway system. Nevertheless, the House approved the Senate's amendment, 217–206, on March 18, 1987. It then approved the five-year, $88 billion transportation reauthorization bill. The Senate quickly followed the House's action by approving both the 65 mph speed limit amendment, 60–21, and the reauthorization bill, 79–21.

It finally looked like the flow of highway and mass transit funds to the states would resume and the states would have the opportunity to increase the 55 mph speed limit on most of the interstate highway system. President Reagan, however, vetoed the bill. He announced that the $88 billion cost of the reauthorization bill was too high and a prime example of political pork barrel at its worst. The president's veto, his first following the Iran-Contra scandal, and his ability to prevent it from being overridden by Congress attracted extensive coverage from the national news media. The heavily Democratic House easily overrode the veto, 350–73. The Senate, on the other hand, initially upheld the veto by a single vote, 66–34, on April 1, 1987. It appeared that the president had triumphed and that his political strength had returned.

However, Sen. Terry Sanford (D-NC) then announced his intention to switch his vote. The Democratic leadership quickly requested that another vote on the bill take place the following day. Recognizing the symbolic importance of the issue, President Reagan went to the Capitol and personally lobbied 13 Republican senators who had voted to override his veto. He reportedly begged just one of them to switch his vote so that the veto would be sustained and his reputation restored. The following day

Senator Sanford switched his vote, but none of the 13 Republican senators switched. The president's veto was overridden, 67–33.

Within 24 hours of the Senate's action, New Mexico and Arizona became the first states to lift the 55 mph speed limit on the interstate highway system. Most of the western states quickly followed suit. By the end of the year, 38 states had raised the 55 mph speed limit on at least some portions of their highways. In the meantime, opponents of the higher speed limits announced that if the number of fatalities and injuries on the interstate highways increase, they will attempt to reinstate the 55 mph speed limit on all of the nation's highways.

The Drinking Age

In 1982, Congress authorized the expenditure of an extra $125 million in highway safety funds in FYs 1983–1985 for states that voluntarily enacted tough drunk-driving laws. One of the many ways to qualify for the bonus money was to adopt 21 as the minimum age for drinking alcoholic beverages. Mothers Against Drunk Drivers (MADD), a grass-roots organization composed largely of victims of drunk drivers and their relatives, were disappointed that only four states had decided to increase their minimum drinking age to 21 to receive the extra funds. They argued that 50 percent of the 45,000 annual traffic deaths were caused by drunk drivers, with over 5,000 of those fatalities being under 21. They also argued that alcohol-related accidents were the leading cause of death among youths 15–24 years old and pointed to a National Transportation Safety Board study indicating that at least 1,250 lives could be saved if the 28 states that allowed drinking by those 18 to 21 years old were to switch to the 21-year-old standard.[94]

MADD launched an intensive Capitol Hill lobbying effort in 1984 to use national highway assistance as a lever to force the states to adopt 21 as the minimum drinking age. MADD members were regularly interviewed on national and regional television talk shows and flooded Washington with telegrams and phone calls demanding legislation to make 21 the minimum drinking age. Several college organizations, the Distilled Spirits Council of the United States, and some retail sellers of alcohol opposed MADD's effort, but MADD's tragic stories won the nation's sympathy.[95] President Reagan, who had opposed the imposition of a national minimum drinking age as an unwarranted infringement on states' rights, announced that he had changed his mind and would support the 21-year-old standard.[96]

---

[94]Brian Nutting, "Panel Approves Bill Seeking National Drinking Age of 21," *Congressional Quarterly, Weekly Report* (February 11, 1984):276; and "Chronology of Action on Transportation," in *Congress and the Nation, 1981–1985*, p. 323.

[95]Brian Nutting, "Panel Approves Bill Seeking National Drinking Age of 21," p. 276.

[96]Stephen Gettinger, "Congress Clears Drunk Driving Legislation," *Congressional Quarterly, Weekly Report* (June 30, 1984):1558.

On June 28, 1984, Congress approved legislation authorizing the withholding of 5 percent of national highway assistance in FY 1987 and 10 percent in FY 1988 from states that do not raise their minimum drinking age to 21. Those funds will be restored if a state subsequently raises its drinking age to 21. President Reagan signed the legislation into law on July 17, 1984.[97] By the end of 1988, all 50 states and the District of Columbia had a minimum drinking age of 21.

CONCLUSIONS

Now that the interstate highway system is nearing completion, the national government is going to have to make some very important decisions concerning the future of highway grants. Should they continue to be focused on highway construction, or should the Highway Trust Fund be used to repair existing highways? Should the national government get out of the highway business altogether, repeal the Highway Trust Fund's taxes, and let the states and cities decide what to do about excise taxes on gasoline and the construction and maintenance of highways? Should mass transit be a national responsibility? If so, what share of the Highway Trust Fund's money should be given to mass transit? Should there be a national transportation block grant that allows states and cities to continue to receive national funds but permits them to make their own choices concerning the highway/mass transit emphasis?

The answers to these questions depend on your values. Liberals tend to see highway construction, highway repair, and mass transit as national responsibilities. They point to the constitution's interstate commerce and general welfare clauses as justifications for national action. They argue that many state and local governments, particularly large cities, lack the fiscal resources to keep up with transportation expenses. Moreover, states and localities lack an incentive to fully fund transportation programs because their benefits are often shared with neighboring cities, counties, or states. As you might expect, liberals from large cities tend to favor mass transit over highways, and highway repairs over new highway construction.

Conservatives, on the other hand, argue that the national government cannot afford to pay for transportation programs, especially ones, like mass transit, that primarily benefit relatively small geographic areas. Why should someone in Illinois help pay for the New York City subway system? If the people in New York City want a subway system, they should pay for it through city, county, or state taxes, or through fares that realistically reflect

[97]"Chronology of Action on Transportation," in *Congress and the Nation, 1981–1985*, p. 323. South Dakota sued Transportation Secretary Dole in 1984, claiming that the fiscal sanction for noncompliance with the 21-year-old drinking age infringed on state constitutional powers to set drinking ages. The U.S. Supreme Court ruled against South Dakota in June 1987, claiming that the power to set drinking ages was a valid use of congressional spending power to promote public safety by discouraging drunken driving by teenagers.

costs. This same argument holds for highways. If the residents in a state, county, or city want to have an excellent highway system that is free of potholes and has state-of-the-art safety and noise abatement features, they can vote for politicians or initiatives that will increase taxes or tolls to pay for it.

CHAPTER 8

Community Development Block Grants

The Community Devolopment Block Grant program (CDBG) was created by the Housing and Community Development Act of 1974. It consolidated seven preexisting categorical grants that were distributed to cities and counties to assist in their community development efforts. The consolidated programs were urban renewal (grants to local public agencies to help acquire land for slum clearance), model cities (grants to selected cities to improve social and public services and to rehabilitate neighborhood buildings), water and sewer facilities (grants to finance construction of water and sewer facilities), open space (grants for acquistition of land for recreational and other uses), neighborhood facilities (grants for development of multi-purpose neighborhood centers), rehabilitation loans (to rehabilitate housing), and public facilities loans (to support public works projects).[1] The national government currently spends approximately $3 billion on the program.[2]

The CDBG program marked a radical departure in the way the national government assisted local community development efforts. The block grant provided national community development funding to cities and, for the first time, urban counties. It also gave recipients much greater programmatic choice. Before the 1974 act, each of the seven community development categorical grant programs was handled by a different office in HUD and implemented separately by city officials. This administrative fragmentation gave rise to serious coordination problems. Moreover, projects sometimes duplicated efforts or worked at cross-purposes with other projects. Under the block grant approach, cities and urban counties were allowed to put together their own mix of projects from among the seven

[1]Assistant Secretary for Community Planning and Development, *1975 Annual Report of the U.S. Department of Housing and Urban Development* (Washington, DC: U.S. Government Printing Office, 1976), p. 31; and "First Major Housing Bill Since 1968 Enacted," Congressional Quarterly, *Almanac, 1974* (Washington, DC: Congressional Quarterly Service, 1975), p. 350.

[2]U.S. Office of Management and Budget, *The Budget of the United States Government, FY 1988, Supplement* (Washington, DC: U.S. Government Printing Office, 1987), pp. 5–81.

eligible programs.[3] Theoretically, the block grant approach was supposed to promote more efficient and coordinated local community development efforts.

The new grant also reduced the number and intrusiveness of the national government's administrative regulations and the role of Housing and Urban Development (HUD) officials in determining which city or county received funding. Instead of applying to HUD for approval of proposed projects, the 1974 act provided that all but 12 percent of CDBG's funds were automatically allocated to eligible communities by a needs formula.[4]

This chapter examines the political battle to enact CDBG during the early 1970s, the ongoing struggle to change its administrative requirements and its allocation formula, and, to a lesser extent, research concerning its effectiveness in improving urban community development efforts. The political battle over its enactment in the early 1970s reveals the theoretical and political arguments of both those who advocate the categorical approach and those who advocate the block grant approach for assisting urban community development. The ongoing political battles over the program's administrative requirements reveal the uneasiness of many national policymakers concerning the intentions and abilities of locally elected officials to make "good" public policy decisions.

The successful efforts of congressmen from the Northeast-Great Lakes region of the country to change the program's needs formula in 1977 reveals the influence of political considerations in determining grant formulas. Finally, since the programs that make up CDBG were initially a collection of independent categorical grant programs, several studies, particularly the five-part study of the Brookings Institution's Monitoring Studies Group, have examined and compared how cities have used national community development funds both before and after the move away from categorical grants. Thus, the CDBG program offers an excellent opportunity to gain insight into the ongoing debate over which grant type is better: categorical or block.

THE NATIONAL GOVERNMENT'S ROLE IN COMMUNITY DEVELOPMENT

The national government first became involved in local community development efforts in 1892, when Congress appropriated $20,000 to study urban slum clearance. In 1908 President Theodore Roosevelt cre-

---

[3]Michael D. Reagan and John G. Sanzone, *The New Federalism*, 2nd ed. (New York: Oxford University Press, 1981), pp. 140–146.

[4]The needs formula divided CDBG funds among cities with populations exceeding 50,000 and urban couties with populations exceeding 200,000 by comparing the ratio of each city's and county's population, extent of housing overcrowding, and poverty (weighted twice in the formula) with the average figures of all other eligible cities and counties. See "First Major Housing Bill Since 1968 Enacted," p. 346.

ated a commission to study slum conditions. But for most of our history, local community development efforts (the process by which government, through physical development projects and social programs, improves the surroundings and living conditions of the people) have been viewed as state and local governmental responsibilities. The first direct national programs to address local community development problems were not created until the Great Depression. In 1935 the U.S. Supreme Court ruled that one of them (dealing with slum clearance) was an unconstitutional infringement on states' rights. Since then, the national government has assisted state and local community development efforts only through voluntary intergovernmental programs.[5]

Following the Supreme Court's decision in 1935, the national government did not reenter the community development area until 1949. The Housing Act of 1949 created the urban renewal program that was designed to clear slums for other uses. It also provided, in its preamble, the national government's rationale for aiding local community development efforts. The preamble stated that the national government has the responsibility to promote housing and local community development efforts because the general welfare and security of the nation (two national responsibilities) are dependent on the health and living standards of its people, which are, in turn, dependent on the availability and condition of the nation's housing stock and the suitability of the nation's living environment.[6] Since the cities' fiscal resources are unable to handle these community development responsibilities without outside help, the national government has the right to make that financial help available through intergovernmental grants-in-aid programs.

During the 1960s the national government added six major community development programs to address what it viewed as the "urban crisis."[7] Although there were many differing views concerning the extent of the urban crisis and the proper role of the national government in addressing essentially local problems, national intergovernmental programs for community development had become an accepted practice in Washington, DC. These programs were to improve the physical appearance of cities, the social aspects of city life, the performance of local governments in addressing the needs of city residents, and the participation of local residents in the local political decision-making process.[8]

By the late 1960s, many analysts were convinced that the national

[5]Richard P. Nathan, Paul R. Dommel, Sarah F. Liebschutz, and Milton D. Morris, *Block Grants for Community Development* (Washington, DC: U.S. Government Printing Office, 1977), pp. 18–21.

[6]Ibid., pp. 20, 21.

[7]The open space land grant and the public facility loan programs were created in 1961, the water and sewer facilities and neighborhood facilities programs were created in 1965, the model cities program was created in 1966, and the neighborhood development program was created in 1968. See ibid., p. 22.

[8]Ibid., pp. 17–19.

government's efforts to combat urban decay and poverty through categorical grants had failed. Several major research organizations, including the U.S. General Accounting Office, the U.S. Advisory Commission on Intergovernmental Relations, and a presidential commission, concluded that the administrative process for funneling community development funds to cities was, in the words of a contemporary scholar, "clogged by gross inefficiencies."[9] These studies documented instances of fragmentation of effort, lack of programmatic coordination, serious inequities concerning funding allocations based on grantsmanship skills instead of need, and a general sense of confusion and delay brought about by excessive regulations and unnecessarily complicated application procedures.[10]

Many analysts and local officials were also worried about the categorical grants' impact on local decision making. In many instances, grant administrators at the national and local levels were making important community development decisions without the input of locally elected officials. These officials argued that since the public held them accountable for the success or failure of these projects at election time, they should have a major role in deciding what the projects would be and where they would be located.[11]

Advocates of the categorical approach were convinced that since the national government was providing the money to finance these community development projects, it had the obligation to make certain, through the categorical grant approach, that the money was being spent on national, as well as local, goals. They were also skeptical of the intentions and abilities of local officials to adequately meet community development needs, particularly the needs of low- and moderate-income families.[12]

The most important advocate for change in the national government's approach to assisting community development during the 1970s was President Nixon. In 1969 he had launched his bold New Federalism program that would have completely revised the welfare system, created a comprehensive new job training program, revamped the U.S. Office of Economic Opportunity, and created a modest general revenue-sharing program.[13] The New Federalism program met with stiff resistance from the Democratic Congress. Frustrated by Congress' lack of action, President

---

[9]Donald F. Kettl, *Managing Community Development in the New Federalism* (New York: Praeger Publishers, 1980), p. 5.

[10]Ibid.

[11]Ibid., pp. 5, 6.

[12]"First Major Housing Bill Since 1968 Enacted," pp. 352, 361, 362; and Henry S. Reuss, *Revenue-Sharing: Crutch or Catalyst for State and Local Governments?* (New York: Praeger Publishers, 1970), pp. 37–70, cited in Kettl, *Managing Community Development in the New Federalism*, p. 9.

[13]Richard Nathan, *The Administrative Presidency* (New York: John Wiley & Sons, 1983), pp. 99–109.

Nixon again rejected during his 1971 State of the Union Address "the patronizing idea that government in Washington, D.C. is inevitably more wise, more honest and more efficient than government at the local or state level."[14] He went on to propose the creation of a $5 billion general revenue-sharing program and an additional $11 billion to convert categorical grants in the community development, education, transportation, job training, and law enforcement areas into separate special revenue-sharing programs. He claimed that "under this plan, the national government will provide the states and localities with more money and less interference— and by cutting down the interference the same amount of money will go a lot further."[15] He added that "whenever it makes the best sense for us to act as a whole nation, the Federal Government should and will lead the way. But where States or local governments can better do what needs to be done, let us see that they have the resources to do it there."[16]

President Nixon's special revenue-sharing program for community development would have consolidated the urban renewal, model cities, and neighborhood facilities programs; eliminated the need for cities to apply for funding for these programs by allocating the funds according to a needs formula; reduced administrative and procedural requirements associated with the three categorical grants-in-aid programs; assigned all decision-making responsibility to general-purpose local governments instead of the special independent authorities (as allowed under the model cities and urban renewal programs); and eliminated the programs' requirements to match a percentage of the approved projects' costs. The Democratic Congress rejected the proposal.[17]

Frustrated by the lack of action in Congress, President Nixon declared a moratorium on all new commitments for housing and urban development programs on January 8, 1973, and asked Congress to eliminate all funding for community development categorical grants.[18] He also wanted Congress to approve a new community development program that folded the existing programs into a single grant, designated urban counties with populations exceeding 200,000 as well as cities with populations exceeding 50,000 as entitlement communities, and provided a "hold harmless" provision to protect communities already receiving funding from the categorical programs against losing any revenue.

The addition of urban counties and the "hold harmless" provisions was designed to attract political support for the proposal by spreading available funds to more congressional districts and to appease selected

[14]Ibid., p. 115.
[15]Ibid., p. 114.
[16]Ibid.
[17]Richard P. Nathan et al., *Block Grants for Community Development*, p. 36.
[18]"First Major Housing Bill Since 1968 Enacted," pp. 345, 346.

jurisdictions that would lose funding under a proposed needs formula.[19] The U.S. Conference of Mayors, the National League of Cities, and the National Association of Counties announced that they supported the president's proposal because it continued the national government's commitment to helping cities and counties cope with community development problems, and enhanced the role of city and county elected officials in determining the use of the program's funds.

Some members of Congress charged that the president's community development spending moratorium was unconstitutional, but they were unable to convince him to lift it. As the funding stalemate dragged on into 1974, and Nixon's preoccupation with his impeachment hearings after the Watergate scandal seemed destined to preclude any presidential action concerning the suspended community development programs, Congress decided that it was better to compromise with the president than to have no funding whatsoever for community development. It agreed to consolidate the seven existing categorical grants into a community development block grant, but objected to the large degree of recipient choice offered by the president's special revenue-sharing approach.

Instead, HUD would administer the block grant and be given authority to deny funding to any city or urban county that failed to agree to limit use of the funds to one of the following: (1) general acquisition of land for public purposes; (2) construction or improvement of public works facilities, neighborhood facilities, senior centers, water and sewer facilities, parks and recreation facilities, flood and drainage facilities, street lights, parking facilities, solid waste disposal facilities, and fire protection facilities; (3) housing code enforcement; (4) slum clearance and renewal; (5) historic preservation; (6) relocation payments to individuals displaced by slum clearance; and (7) planning and other activities, including health, social, welfare, education, or other community services if they were not available under other national programs.

To further ensure that the funds would be used to serve national goals, communities were required to give "maximum feasible priority" to programs designed to assist low- and moderate-income families or to improve blighted areas. Localities also were required to submit an annual application to HUD that included a general summary of planned activities and a detailed plan for meeting the program's national objectives. HUD was authorized to refuse funding to any community that failed to meet those objectives.

On a more conciliatory note, Congress accepted the Nixon administration's three-part allocation needs formula. It determined each eligible

---

[19]Richard P. Nathan et al., *Block Grants for Community Development*, p. 37. The National Association of Counties' lobbying efforts were largely responsible for the inclusion of counties in the program. HUD originally indicated that only about a dozen counties would participate in the program, but 73 did in 1975 and over 100 participate today. See Paul R. Dommel and Michael J. Rich, "The Rich Get Richer: The Attenuation of Targeting Effects of the Community Development Block Grant Program," *Urban Affairs Quarterly* 22 (June 1987): 552-579.

city's and county's allotment of funds by considering its population, poverty (counted twice), and overcrowded housing.[20] The population criterion was included to ensure that all cities got their "fair share" of the program's funds. The poverty and overcrowding criteria were included to target available funding to cities that lacked the fiscal resources to meet identifiable housing needs.[21]

Recognizing that the population criterion would cause previous funding levels to fall in many large cities, Congress enacted a "hold harmless" clause that guaranteed all cities and urban counties that received funding from the categorical grants an amount at least equal to the average amount of funding that they received over the 1968–1972 period. This "hold harmless" provision would be retained throughout the proposed three-year authorization for the program, FYs 1975–1977. If, as anticipated, the program was renewed at the end of the three-year funding cycle, the "hold harmless" provision would be phased out by thirds during FYs 1978–1980. After FY 1980, all funding would be based solely on the needs formula.[22]

President Ford signed the three-year, $8.6 billion CDBG program into law on August 22, 1974. It was a product of political compromise. Recipient choice had been enlarged, grantsmanship weakened, and administrative red tape reduced, but not to the extend promised by special revenue sharing. Communities had to submit an annual application and a three-year community development plan to meet the national objective of giving priority to programs that assisted the poor, promised to eradicate urban blight, or met other urgent community development needs. Citizens were to be given "adequate" opportunity to participate in the development of the three-year plan. At least two public hearings on the plan were mandated by the law.[23]

DECENTRALIZATION: PROGRAMMATIC IMPACTS

The CDBG program's new emphasis on local discretion attracted a lot of research attention both from academe and from interested lobby organizations during its first three operating years. The studies, especially a series

---

[20]In 1975, 521 cities and 73 urban counties were granted approximately $1.8 billion by CDBG's formula. In addition, 740 smaller cities were awarded approximately $400 million by CDBG's formula and 1,272 cities were awarded grants totaling $300 million by HUD officials. In 1984, 691 cities and 104 urban counties were given approximately $2.2 billion by CDBG's formula. Moreover, approximately 2,000 small cities received grants totaling $1 billion from a separate, state-administered block grant for small cities that was created in 1982. U.S. Department of Housing and Urban Development, *Community Development Block Grant Program: Directory of Allocations, FY 1978* (Washington, DC: U.S. Government Printing Office, 1978), p. vii; and U.S. Department of Housing and Urban Development, *Programs of HUD, 1984/85* (Washington, DC: U.S. Government Printing Office, 1985), p. 7.

[21]Paul R. Dommel and Michael Rich, "The Rich Get Richer," p. 554.

[22]"First Major Housing Bill Since 1968 Enacted," p. 359.

[23]Donald F. Kettl, *Managing Community Development in the New Federalism*, pp. 19–21.

conducted by the Brookings Institution's Monitoring Studies Group, revealed that there was, as anticipated, a significant decentralization of substantive decision making, with locally elected officials exercising more control over community development policy than under the categorical grants. Moreover, these officials were using their discretion to fund smaller-scale, more diversified programs. Large urban renewal projects started under the categorical programs were completed, but few new ones were started. Instead, funding for housing rehabilitation in selected neighborhoods and small-scale public improvement projects (streets, sidewalks, parks, water and sewer lines) increased and social services, the primary focus of the model cities program, declined sharply. In 1976 approximately 34 percent of CDBG funds was used for housing rehabilitation and 31 percent for small-scale public improvements.[24]

Most of the studies that examined local government's actions under CDBG during the 1970s were generally critical of their funding decisions. For example, in 1980 Donald Kettl wrote:

> Critics focused on two alleged shortcomings: first, that cities engaged in almost no real planning for the use of the money; and second, that CDBG funds were dispersed throughout communities, diminishing the program's opportunity to accomplish any real good, especially in easing the plight of the poor.[25]

Kettl pointed out that some communities had used their newly acquired discretion in a highly questionable manner. One city used its CDBG funds to construct a marina, another built a tennis complex in an affluent neighborhood, and another widened a road that led to the local country club.[26] The Brookings Institution's Monitoring Studies Group revealed that these "horror stories" were not isolated instances of evading the law's required emphasis on programs assisting the poor. The typical CDBG recipient was spending a majority of its funds in middle- and upper-class neighborhoods.[27] These findings led to inevitable questions concerning locally elected officials' capacity to make "good" public policy decisions.

Scholars were (and still are) divided on the subject. Donald Kettl's exceptional study of four Connecticut cities' experiences under CBDG suggest that cities had a difficult time adjusting to their new responsibilities.

---

[24]Paul R. Dommel, Richard P. Nathan, Sarah F. Liebschutz, and Margaret Wrightson, *Decentralizing Community Development* (Washington, DC: U.S. Government Printing Office, 1978), pp. 11, 12, 60–79, 166–192.

[25]Donald F. Kettl, *Managing Community Development in the New Federalism*, p. 25.

[26]Ibid.

[27]Ibid., pp. 25, 26; Richard P. Nathan et al., *Block Grants for Community Development*, p. 499; and Richard LeGates and Dennis Keating, "Selected Legal Cases and Complaints Involving the Community Development Block Grant Program," in Paul R. Dommel et al., *Decentralizing Community Development*, Appendix IV.

He points out that city officials were subjected to a political overload as many agencies and neighborhood groups sought funding for their favorite projects. It was politically easier to provide a little funding to several of the agencies and neighborhood groups requesting money than to fund just one group or to concentrate all projects in a single neighborhood. Cities also faced an administrative overload as they were asked to administer a relatively large program from scratch. New staff had to be hired and procedures established. This caused delays that led to what Kettl believes are erroneous impressions that cities could not handle their new responsibilities.[28]

Although the academic community was still debating whether cities could run the CDBG program responsibly, the reported abuses of the program had a powerful political impact in Washington, DC. Under pressure from liberal congressmen and several major lobby organizations, such as the National Association for the Advancement of Colored People, HUD began to make more extensive reviews of local applications and three-year plans to ensure that recipients complied with the law's required "maximum feasible priority" to projects that assist persons of low or moderate income.[29]

When the Carter administration took office in 1977, HUD accelerated its regulatory efforts. The new secretary of HUD, Patricia Roberts Harris, told a congressional subcommittee in February 1977 that she expected:

. . . communities to direct development and housing programs toward low and moderate income citizens. I do not consider this to be just an objective of the block grant program—it is the highest priority of the program, and we in the federal government must see to it that the thrust of the program serves that objective.[30]

On April 15, 1977, Secretary Harris announced that HUD was changing its focus from reviewing applications for technical or procedural violations of the law to reviewing applicants' substantive efforts to assist low- and moderate-income persons. Under the new administrative ruling, field staff were instructed to scrutinize all information bearing on an applicant's efforts to implement projects that directly benefit low- or moderate-income persons.[31] The Carter administration, however, failed to convince Congress to rewrite the law so that it clearly indicated that the targeting of

---

[28]Donald F. Kettl, *Managing Community Development in the New Federalism*, pp. 131–143.

[29]Ibid., p. 133.

[30]*Housing and Community Development Act of 1977*, Hearings Before the Subcommittee on Banking, Finance, and Urban Affairs, U.S. House of Representatives, 95th Cong., 1st sess., pt. 1 (Washington, DC: U.S. Government Printing Office, February 1977), p. 9, cited in Paul R. Dommel, Victor Bach, Sarah Liebschutz, and Leonard S. Rubinowitz, *Targeting Community Development* (Washington, DC: U.S. Government Printing Office, 1980), pp. 14, 15.

[31]U.S. Department of Housing and Urban Development, *1977 Annual Report* (Washington, DC: U.S. Government Printing Office, 1978), p. 25.

funding to low-income persons was the program's highest priority. When Congress renewed CDBG for an additional three years on October 12, 1977, it included the eradication of slums and urban blight and other urgent community needs as equal priorities along with projects benefiting low- and moderate-income persons. Nevertheless, on October 25, 1977, HUD announced that communities receiving CDBG funds should target at least 75 percent of those funds to low- and moderate-income neighborhoods. HUD also "encouraged" applicants to concentrate funds in residential neighborhoods needing revitalization.[32]

HUD's actions resulted in a loss of local discretion concerning program use. Instead of a two-step decision-making process where local governments created their plans and HUD reviewed those plans for obviously inappropriate or illegal uses, local governments were now subjected to a three-step decision-making process in which HUD defined program objectives, local decision makers created their plans within the HUD guidelines, and HUD determined whether those plans appropriately interpreted the national program's goals.[33] As Kettl put it:

> Slowly, the same disease that had afflicted other block grant programs attacked CDBG: "creeping categorization," a term coined by the U.S. Advisory Commission on Intergovernmental Relations to describe the efforts of federal grant agencies, interest groups, and congressional committees to concentrate the attention of state and local governments on specific national priorities.[34]

HUD's new regulations did lead to an increase in the percentage of CDBG's funds targeted to low- and moderate-income groups in central cities, from 57 percent in 1975 to 62 percent in 1977 and 1978, and to 63 percent in 1979. When targeting efforts in smaller satellite cities were included, the percentage of CDBG's funds targeted to low- and moderate-income groups increased from 54 percent in 1975 to 60 percent in 1977 and to 61 percent in 1979.[35]

HUD attributed most of the increase in assistance to low- and moderate-income areas to changes in the location of projects in suburban and smaller, relatively affluent cities. Large cities, particularly ones located in the industrial Northeast and Great Lakes regions, had such widespread economic problems in the late 1970s that they had little difficulty meeting

[32]Paul R. Dommel et al., *Targeting Community Development*, pp. 13–21.

[33]Ibid., p. 36.

[34]Donald F. Kettl, *Managing Community Development in the New Federalism*, p. 134.

[35]Paul R. Dommel, James C. Musselwhite, and Sarah F. Liebschutz, *Implementing Community Development* (Washington, DC: U.S. Government Printing Office, 1982), p. 100. HUD claimed that the percentage of CDBG's funds targeted to low- and moderate-income persons had increased to 61 percent in 1977 and to 66 percent in 1978. See U.S. Department of Housing and Urban Development, *1978 Annual Report* (Washington, DC: U.S. Government Printing Office, 1979), p. 10.

the social targeting criteria.[36] HUD's emphasis on programs targeted to low- and moderate-income persons also resulted in a shift in the types of activities funded by CDBG. Urban renewal efforts continued to decline, and added emphasis was placed on housing rehabilitation and social services, such as job training, child care, and rodent control.[37]

After the Reagan administration entered office in 1981, HUD dropped the requirement that applicants attempt to target a set percentage of a project's funds to assist low- and moderate-income persons. Instead, HUD suggested, and Congress subsequently enacted, changes in the law to eliminate both the requirement for a detailed, comprehensive, annual application for funds and HUD's power to veto recipients' use of the funds. As HUD's *1981 Annual Report* indicated, "These actions will serve to substantially increase local discretion and lessen the extent of Federal involvement in determining how and where entitlement funds are used."[38]

Some analysts and most liberals were concerned that cities could not be trusted with this new degree of freedom. They feared that locally elected officials would target nearly all the funds to middle- and upper-income neighborhoods because those neighborhoods have a proportionately larger number of voters, campaign volunteers, and campaign contributors than poor neighborhoods. Studies of how cities actually used their funds in the early 1980s, however, indicated that they did not radically alter either their administrative operating procedures or the distribution of projects among neighborhoods. Housing rehabilitation, for example, continued to be the cities' dominant program choice, representing over one-third of total budgetary expenditures; and expenditures on public works projects, such as improvement or construction of playgrounds, parks, streets, sidewalks, and water and sewer lines, continued to be the second largest expenditure item for CDBG, representing approximately one-quarter of total budgetary expenditures during the 1980–1983 period.[39]

However, HUD's lack of enforcement of the low-income priority criterion did allow communities to increase expenditures for projects designed to assist local economic development. These projects were generally discouraged during the Carter administration because they usually

[36]Paul R. Dommel et al., *Targeting Community Development*, p. 15.

[37]Neal R. Peirce and Robert Guskind, "Reagan Budget Cutters Eye Community Block Grant Program on Its 10th Birthday," *National Journal* (January 5, 1985):13; and Paul R. Dommel, Michael J. Rich, and Leonard Rubinowitz, *Deregulating Community Development* (Washington, DC: U.S. Government Printing Office, 1983), pp. 73–75.

[38]U.S. Department of Housing and Urban Development, *1981 Annual Report* (Washington, DC: U.S. Government Printing Office, 1982), p. 7.

[39]Paul R. Dommel et al., *Deregulating Community Development*, pp. vii–xii. Most of CDBG's housing rehabilitation funds are spent on owner-occupied housing, not rental housing. See Neal R. Peirce and Robert Guskind, "Reagan Budget Cutters Eye Community Development Block Grants on Its 10th Birthday," p. 12. Cities also were required to reduce their expenditures on public works projects to a maximum of 10 percent in 1985.

yielded a lower level of direct benefits to low-income persons than most other community development projects. Cities began to focus more attention on economic development projects during the early 1980s, primarily because the national economic recession at that time had heightened intercity competition for business investment.[40] The percentage of CDBG funds used for economic development more than doubled, from 5 percent in 1980 to 12 percent in 1983.[41]

Mayors were particularly proud of CDBG's economic development projects during the early 1980s. They argued that while most economic development projects may not be located in low- or moderate-income neighborhoods, these projects often result in large private capital investments that produce jobs for the poor and a stronger city tax base to supply the poor with social services. The National League of Cities, for example, argued that CDBG's economic development projects often "leveraged" private investment that was 1.5 times greater than the CDBG expenditure.[42] Critics of these projects complained that they take needed funds away from economically distressed neighborhoods and put them into business enterprises that primarily benefit the wealthy.[43]

BLOCK GRANTS VERSUS CATEGORICAL GRANTS: WHICH ARE BETTER?

Advocates of block grants and general revenue sharing argue that categorical grants fail to target funds to areas of greatest need because they are subject to grantsmanship. Under the categorical, project grant approach, states and localities compete for funding by applying to the national bureaucracy administering the program. National bureaucrats then determine the merits of the applications and decide which of the applicants receive funding. The bureaucrats' decision is based either on criteria established by Congress or, if Congress' criteria are vague, according to their own criteria. Since Congress often leaves considerable discretion to the national bureaucracy, states and localities that have superior grantsmanship skills (the ability to write winning application proposals) tend to receive greater funding than states and localities with similar needs that do not have good grantsmanship skills. Block grants and general revenue sharing are immune from this "defect" because they allocate their funds according to a predetermined needs formula. Since the program's

[40]Paul R. Dommel et al., *Deregulating Community Development*, pp. vii–xii.

[41]Neal R. Peirce and Robert Guskind, "Reagan Budget Cutters Eye Community Block Grant Program on Its 10th Birthday," p. 14.

[42]Ibid., p. 13.

[43]Ibid., p. 15.

funds are allocated automatically according to the objective criteria of need in the formula, interstate and intercommunity competition is eliminated and grantsmanship's influence is ended.[44]

The political battle over CDBG's needs formula in 1977 suggests that formula-based grants do not eliminate interstate and intercommunity competition. Instead of competition in the halls of the bureaucracy through written applications, competition is in the halls of the Congress through elected representatives. Moreover, while grantsmanship's influence over the flow of money is eliminated, that flow is still being influenced by factors other than objective need. Instead of grantsmanship influencing the allocation of funds, formulamanship (the ability to manipulate the needs formula to target funds to your area) does.

As mentioned earlier, CDBG's original needs formula was based on population (as determined by the U.S. Census Bureau), amount of housing overcrowding (defined as the number of housing units with an average of 1.01 or more persons per room), and poverty (weighted twice). In addition, a "hold harmless" provision was in force during FYs 1975–1977 that guaranteed eligible cities and counties at least the average annual amount they had received in FYs 1968–1972 under the old categorical grant programs. After 1977, the "hold harmless" provision was scheduled to be phased out by thirds, so that all allocations would be made under the needs formula starting in 1980.

As FY 1978 approached and the CDBG proposal was scheduled to be introduced by the Carter administration, HUD received the report of an in-house study and an analysis from the Brookings Institution's Monitoring Studies Group on the ramifications of phasing out the "hold harmless" provision. Both reports indicated that as the "hold harmless" provision was phased out, the amount of funds provided to recipients located in the West and South would increase while the amount provided to recipients in the Northeast and Great Lakes region would decrease. Both reports also concluded that the major factor causing this shift was that the designation of poverty, which is weighted twice in the needs formula, did not take into account a cost-of-living factor.

Since the cost of attaining a particular living style is generally higher in the northeastern and midwestern states than elsewhere, northeastern and midwestern residents tend to have higher per capita income levels than residents of other regions. Since poverty is determined by per capita income level, the 1974 needs formula counted many residents of the South and West as being in poverty, even though their living style was comparable

---

[44]U.S. Advisory Commission on Intergovernmental Relations, *Categorical Grants: Their Role and Design* (Washington, DC: U.S. Government Printing Office, 1978), pp. 109–111; and Robert Jay Dilger, "Grantsmanship, Formulamanship, and Other Allocational Principles: Wastewater Treatment Construction Grants," *Journal of Urban Affairs* 5:4 (Fall 1983):269–286.

with, or even better than, many residents of the Northeast and Great Lakes region who were not counted as being in poverty.[45] The reports also determined that overcrowded housing conditions and poverty were highly correlated, leading to increased funding for the South if the "hold harmless" provision was eliminated.

The two reports also indicated that the formula's use of population as a criterion of need favored recipients with growing populations; many of these were located in the South and West. The Brooking Institution's report argued that a community's population change over a period of time was a better indicator of economic need than its current population level. It suggested that if population loss instead of current population level was used in the needs formula, the older cities of the Northeast, which were (and generally still are) losing population, would justifiably receive a larger portion of the program's funds.

Representatives of cities located in the Northeast and Great Lakes regions recognized that the phasing out of "hold harmless" meant that their funding levels would decline. They urged HUD to support either an extension of the "hold harmless" provision or the creation of a new formula that targeted more CDBG funds to their cities and counties.[46] The Carter administration's CDBG proposal was announced on February 24, 1977. It recommended that CDBG's total funding be increased from $8.3 billion to $10.95 billion over FYs 1978–1980 and that a new, dual needs formula be used to allocate its funds. Eligible cities and counties would have the option of selecting whichever formula gave them a greater allotment of funds.

This new, dual formula consisted of the original 1974 needs formula and another that provided aid according to each eligible communities' age of housing (weighted 50 percent), poverty (weighted 30 percent), and growth lag (weighted 20 percent). The age-of-housing factor referred to the number of existing housing units built prior to 1940 and represented the administration's concern for the physical deterioration of the infrastructure within the nation's older cities. Growth lag referred to the extent to which a city's population growth rate between 1960 and 1973 fell short of the average population growth rate for all metropolitan cities during the period.[47]

All interested parties recognized that this new, dual formula would allocate more funds to the larger cities of the Northeast-Great Lakes region. Many of these cities experienced growth lag during the 1960–1973 period and have a relatively old housing stock. The 748 small cities (under 50,000 persons) that received approximately $400 million annually during

[45]Richard Nathan et al., *Block Grants for Community Development*, p. 140.

[46]Robert Jay Dilger, *The Sunbelt/Snowbelt Controversy* (New York: New York University Press, 1982), p. 28.

[47]Ibid., p. 30.

the 1974–1977 period because of the existence of the "hold harmless" provision, however, would continue to be allocated funding under the original 1974 needs formula.

Recognizing that the omission of small cities from the new formula would cost the small cities of the Northeast-Great Lakes region millions of dollars in lost revenue, congressmen from the Northeast-Midwest Congressional Coalition lobbied HUD to revise its proposal so that small cities were covered by the dual formula. HUD subsequently agreed to support a dual formula, similar to the dual formula for large cities, for small cities. Congressmen from the Coalition, led by Michael Harrington (D-MA), Paul Tsongas (D-MA), and Stanley Lundine (D-NY), then lobbied members of the House Banking, Finance, and Urban Affairs Committee to accept both the dual formula for large cities and the dual formula for small cities. The committee subsequently approved both formulas, but two Democratic members of the committee from California, Mark Hannaford and Jerry Patterson, decided to appeal its decision on the House floor.

On May 4, 1977, they sent a "Dear Colleague" letter to all congressmen representing districts that would "lose" funds under the new, dual formula. They urged their colleagues to reject the two dual formulas and to keep the existing one for both large and small cities. They charged in their letter that the two dual needs formulas had created "gross inequities" because they increased funding to cities and counties with older housing stocks, regardless of the condition of that housing stock.[48]

Anticipating a difficult political battle, the Northeast-Midwest Congressional Coalition's staff commissioned a computer analysis of the formula changes' impact upon the funding level of all 435 congressional districts. The Coalition then sent its own "Dear Colleague" letter to all of the congressmen who represented districts that would gain funds under the two new, dual formulas. Mayors of major cities located in the Northeast-Great Lakes region also were informed and urged to lobby their local congressmen on behalf of the two dual formulas.

The Hannaford-Patterson Amendment to keep the original needs formula was defeated on the House floor on May 10, 1977, by a vote of 149–261. Representatives from the Northeast-Great Lakes region voted overwhelmingly (189–5) to kill the amendment. Their solidarity was partly a reflection of the administration's advocacy of the dual formula approach and partly a reflection of the efforts of the Northeast-Midwest Congressional Coalition.[49]

Now that the needs formula had been changed in the House, all eyes now turned to the Senate Banking, Housing, and Urban Affairs Commit-

[48]Since CDBG's funding was to be increased and recipients could choose between the 1974 formula and the new formula, most recipients would not lose funds in an absolute sense. Cities and counties in the Northeast-Great Lakes region, however, would receive most of the programs added revenue. See ibid., pp. 31–34.

[49]Ibid., pp. 36–39.

tee. It also decided to change the needs formula to benefit the Northeast-Great Lakes region. Senators Harrison Williams (D-NJ) and Edward Burke (R-MA) advocated the creation of three formulas for the program, each community picking the one that gave it the most funds. In addition to the two formulas presented by the Carter administration, they advocated a third formula that was identical to the administration's second formula except that instead of counting the number of pre-1940 housing units in a metropolitan area, it compared the proportion of pre-1940 housing stock in a specific metropolitan area with the average proportion of pre-1940 housing stock in all metroplitan areas. This change, called the impaction adjustment amendment, would have targeted an even larger proportion of the available funding to cities and counties located in the Northeast-Great Lakes region. Since the Senate Banking Committee was composed primarily of senators from the Northeast-Great Lakes area, it approved the three formulas without controversy, and the Senate routinely adopted the committee's bill 79–9 on June 7, 1977.[50]

In recognition of the bruising political battle that occurred on the House floor over CDBG's dual formula, Thomas Ashley (D-OH), who headed the House delegation in the conference committee, refused to accept the Senate's impaction adjustment formula. The Senate conference committee's members initially insisted on the three formulas, but after several months they gave in. The conference report supporting the House's two dual needs formulas was adopted by the Senate on October 1, 1977, and by the House on October 4. President Carter signed the bill into law on October 12, 1977.

With the memory of the bitter formula fight of 1977 still relatively fresh, Congress decided to leave the dual needs formulas intact when CDBG came up for its three-year renewal in 1981, and it remains in force today. Congress' attempt to restructure the needs formula during 1977, however, clearly indicates that while formula-based grants may be free of the grantsmanship defect, they have their own political problems when it comes to targeting aid to recipients of greatest need. With the advance of computer technology, Congress has discovered that it is very difficult to target economic resources when congressmen and constituents of the communities not receiving funds know that they are being excluded.

SOME NEW CONTROVERSIES

The political controversy over what constitutes the best needs formula began to lose some its significance after the Reagan administration took office in 1981. Instead of battling over who got what portion of the program's funds, Congress was forced to justify why the program should get

[50]Ibid., p. 39.

any money. In an effort to move toward a balanced national budget, President Reagan requested a reduction in CDBG's budget in every budget proposal he submitted to Congress. His lack of commitment to the program was further evidenced by his listing it as one of the programs to be turned back to the states in his 1982 New Federalism "swap" proposal.[51] Congress has kept the program's funding at the $3 billion level, but many officials are concerned that inflation is eroding its ability to meet the nation's community development needs.

Moreover, an analysis of CDBG's effectiveness in combating urban decline has suggested that while community development conditions in many entitlement communities have improved since the late 1970s because of CDBG, conditions in the nation's most distressed communities have declined in both absolute and relative terms. This decline is attributed primarily to an expansion in the number of entitlement communities in recent years, which has spread CDBG's funds among many cities and counties instead of concentrating the funds on the cities and counties most in need. The number of entitlement communities increased from 590 in 1975 to 814 in 1985, primarily because revised regulations adopted in 1980 made it easier for smaller cities to achieve designation as central cities within new metropolitan areas. Of the 224 entitlement communities added to the program since 1975, only 31 had populations exceeding 100,000. In 1985 more than one-quarter of all entitlement communities (216 out of 814) had populations under 50,000.[52] Since larger cities tend to have the greatest community development needs, this new trend has seriously weakened CDBG's ability to help the communities that are most in need.

CONCLUSIONS

CDBG was repeatedly targeted for budgetary reductions and funding rescissions during the 1980s. Yet the program has survived, because mayors have lobbied hard to save it and congressional representatives of large cities have been willing to sacrifice some targeting objectives in order to gather enough political support from congressmen representing suburban and rural areas to keep the program alive. Although the pork-barrel aspects of the program's formula are troubling to academics, given the national government's budgetary problems and the emergence of the macroeconomic theory of intergovernmental relations, the strategy of sac-

[51]See Timothy J. Conlan and David B. Walker, "Reagan's New Federalism," in *American Intergovernmental Relations Today: Perspectives and Controversies*, ed. Robert Jay Dilger (Englewood Cliffs, NJ: Prentice-Hall Inc., 1986), pp. 189–200.

[52]Paul R. Dommel and Michael J. Rich, "The Distributional Impacts of the Community Development Block Grant Program: Options for Increased Targeting on Community Need," Discussion Paper, Brown University, Providence, RI, March 1986, pp. iv–v, 48.

rificing the allocation principle of need to the allocation principle of politi cal fair shares is probably the only way to keep the program alive.

It is clear that it does matter if a program is operating as a categorical grant or a block grant. States and localities did behave differently once they were freed from the administrative restrictions under the categorical grant approach to community development. How one judges the impact of these changes in behavior is determined, at least in part, by one's values. Liberals are concerned that the recent trend toward using CDBG funds to finance local economic development projects is not consistent with the program's emphasis on helping the poor. Conservatives are convinced that local economic development projects will help the poor by creating additional job opportunities.

In either case, it is highly unlikely that the CDBG program will ever go back to the categorical format. There is a chance, however, depending on the future composition of Congress that the program's recipients will be subjected to administrative guidelines such as the ones imposed by the Carter administration during the late 1970s to target aid to poor neighborhoods. Although CDBG is currently one of the least administratively restrictive intergovernmental programs offered by the national government, Congress did take its first step toward adding more administrative red tape to the program in 1983 when it required communities to demonstrate that at least half of their CDBG funds benefited low- and moderate-income individuals over a period of one to three years. The debate over the appropriate role of the national government in guiding local community development efforts will continue to be a central political issue in the years to come.

CHAPTER 9

Wastewater Treatment Construction Grants

The Wastewater Treatment Construction Grants program was created in 1972 by the Federal Water Pollution Control Act. It currently provides states $2.5 billion annually to subsidize up to 55 percent of the cost of building wastewater treatment plants.[1] The funds are distributed among the states according to a multifaceted formula that is loosely tied to a needs assessment put together by the Environmental Protection Agency.[2] Cities apply to their state governments for funding of their particular projects.

The Wastewater Treatment Construction Grants program was designed to help cities meet the cost of complying with national water quality standards. City officials appreciate the national government's effort to subsidize wastewater treatment plant construction, but argue that since the national government sets the water quality standards, it should pay all of the cost of meeting those standards. Environmental groups also welcome the national government's funding of wastewater treatment plants but complain that the $2.5 billion annually committed to the program is just not enough to continue to make progress against water pollution. Economic conservatives, on the other hand, believe that state and local governments should assume full financial responsibility for building these plants because the national government's deficit precludes funding for programs whose benefits are primarily local.

This chapter examines the national government's role in determining water pollution policy and the arguments put forth by city officials, environmentalists, liberals, and conservatives concerning the national government's water quality standards and its Wastewater Treatment Construction Grants program. As was often the case during the 1980s, the size of the national government's budget deficit and the emergence of the

---

[1]U.S. Office of Management and Budget, *The Budget of the United States Government, FY 1988, Supplement* (Washington, DC: U.S. Government Printing Office, 1987), p. 5-46.

[2]Robert Jay Dilger, "Grantsmanship, Formulamanship, and Other Allocational Principles: Wastewater Treatment Construction Grants," *Journal of Urban Affairs* 5:4 (Fall 1983):251–267.

macroeconomic view of intergovernmental grants focused much of the political debate on the program's cost.

CLEAN WATER: A NATIONAL OR STATE AND LOCAL CONCERN?

Until 1972 water pollution was primarily a state and local issue. Each state determined its own water quality standards, and most public sewage treatment systems were financed by state and local governments through local property taxes or water and sewer bills. The national government's role in water pollution policy was very limited. In 1948 the Water Pollution Control Act gave the U.S. Department of Justice the authority to sue anyone polluting an interstate body of water. However, it could sue only if the governor of the state where the pollution originated consented to the legal action. The act also authorized the establishment of a $110 million fund that would be used to make low-interest (2 percent) loans to states and localities to help them build sewage treatment plants, but Congress failed to appropriate any money for the fund and no loans were ever made.[3] In 1956 the Water Pollution Control Act was amended to allow the expenditure of $50 million annually for ten years to help localities build wastewater treatment plants and interceptor sewers (large-diameter pipes designed to carry wastewater from large geographic areas to the treatment plant).[4] Only small communities participated in the program, because grants were limited to 30 percent of construction costs or $250,000, whichever was less.

At the same time the national government began to play a limited role in subsidizing wastewater treatment plant construction, it also expanded its role in determining and enforcing water quality standards. In 1961 the requirement for state consent to bring a legal action against polluters of interstate bodies of water was dropped if the national government determined that the pollution endangered the health and welfare of persons outside the state where it originated. The Department of Justice was also authorized to prosecute polluters of coastal areas and navigable intrastate streams and rivers.[5] In 1965 the Water Quality Act required states to set water quality standards for interstate waters that crossed their state bound-

[3]"Chronology of Legislation on Water and Power," in *Congress and the Nation, 1945–1964* (Washington, DC: Congressional Quarterly Service, 1965), p. 1132.

[4]In 1959 President Eisenhower asked Congress to phase out the Wastewater Treatment Construction Grants program. He argued that sewage treatment was a state and local responsibility. The Democratic Congress refused to eliminate the program, and voted in 1960 to renew it for an additional ten years at $90 million a year. President Eisenhower vetoed the bill and Congress was unable to override it. See "Environmental Programs," in *Congress and the Nation, 1969–1972* (Washington, DC: Congressional Quarterly Service, 1973), p. 750.

[5]"Chronology of Legislation on Water and Power," in *Congress and the Nation, 1965–1968* (Washington, DC: Congressional Quarterly Service, 1969), p. 498.

aries and established the Federal Water Pollution Control Administration within the Department of Health, Education, and Welfare to set those water quality standards if the states failed to do so.

To help cities pay the costs of meeting these new water quality standards, the Clean Water Restoration Act of 1966 opened the wastewater treatment construction grants program to cities of all sizes by removing the $250,000 per project ceiling, increasing the national government's share of construction costs to 40 percent, and increasing the program's authorization to $3.5 billion over the FY 1967–1971 period.[6]

The national government's new efforts in controlling water pollution resulted, at least in part, from the public's increased awareness and concern over environmental hazards that followed the airing of the televised documentaries by French oceanographer Jacques Cousteau, the publication of Rachael Carson's book *The Silent Spring*, and the writings of biologist Barry Commoner. Moreover, a number of environmental disasters during the late 1960s pushed the public's growing awareness and concern about the environment into a galvanized political movement. In 1969 an oil well located on land leased by the national government off the coast of Santa Barbara, California, burst its seams and pumped hundreds of thousands of gallons of crude oil into the Pacific Ocean. The oil spill formed an 800-square-mile oil slick that coated 30 miles of southern California beaches.[7] Later that year, the Cuyahoga River at Cleveland, Ohio, caught fire, arsenic was found in the Kansas River, mercury pollution ended fishing in Lake Erie, and millions of fish died in Lake Superior as a result of industrial pollutants.[8]

The General Accounting Office reported in November 1969 that despite the expenditure of approximately $15 billion by national, state, and local governments between 1952 and 1969 to clean up the nation's waters, over 1,400 cities and thousands of industrial plants still dropped untreated waste into the nation's waters. Moreover, only 140 million of the country's 200 million persons in 1969 were served by any kind of sewer system. Popular interest in the environment reached its peak on April 22, 1970, as millions of Americans celebrated Earth Day by marching to protest pollution and participating in local cleanup projects.[9]

The leaders of the environmental movement demanded that the national government be much more aggressive against water pollution. Representatives of the leading environmental groups, including the Sierra Club, the Audubon Society, the Izaak Walton League, and the National Wildlife Federation, lobbied Congress to expand funding for the Waste-

[6]"Environmental Programs," in *Congress and the Nation, 1969–1972*, p. 750; and Robert Jay Dilger, "Grantsmanship, Formulamanship, and Other Allocational Principles," p. 272.

[7]"Environmental Programs," in *Congress and the Nation, 1969–1972*, p. 745.

[8]"Magnitude of Water Pollution Problem in 1970," in *Congress and the Nation, 1969–1972*, p. 767.

[9]Ibid.

water Treatment Construction Grants program and to tighten the national government's water quality standards. They were particularly opposed to allowing the states to set water quality standards because most states were reluctant to set rigorous standards for fear of losing business to neighboring states.[10]

The U.S. Conference of Mayors and the National League of Cities also took strong stands at this time in favor of a more active role for the national government in cleaning up the nation's water. They were particularly interested in getting the national government to help cities pay for the construction of wastewater treatment plants. Claiming that local financing was already strained to the breaking point, they asked Congress to increase funding for the Wastewater Treatment Construction Grants program to at least $2.5 billion annually, to increase the national government's matching ratio to at least 50 percent and preferably to 70 percent of construction costs, and to create long-term funding commitments so that local governments would be assured of continued national assistance once they started construction of a sewage treatment plant.[11]

Responding to the public's desire to clean up the environment, President Nixon created the Environmental Protection Agency (EPA) in 1970 as part of a reorganization of the executive branch. It combined 15 offices and agencies from 5 executive departments into a single agency, and was given the responsibility to oversee enforcement of water and air pollution standards as well as efforts to control toxic substances, radiation, and solid wastes.[12] Environmentalists and liberals generally approved of the bureaucratic reorganization as a means of streamlining the national government's enforcement procedures. However, they were disappointed that the Nixon administration opposed the creation of national water quality standards on the grounds that such standards were a violation of the principles of American federalism.

Environmentalists, city officials, and most Democrats in Congress were also disappointed when the Nixon administration announced its strong opposition to Congress' intention to increase funding for the Wastewater Treatment Construction Grants program beyond the administration's recommended level of $2 billion per year. The Nixon administration argued that wastewater treatment is a local concern that ought to be paid for by local citizens through user fees and state and local taxes, particularly given the pressures on the national government's budget caused by the war in Vietnam.

Overriding a presidential veto, Congress in 1972 adopted the most

[10]Clarke E. Cochran, Lawrence C. Mayer, T. R. Carr, and N. Joseph Cayer, *American Public Policy: An Introduction* (New York: St. Martin's Press, 1982), p. 104.

[11]U.S. Congress, Senate, Committee on Public Works, Subcommittee on Air and Water Pollution, *Water Pollution—1970*, Hearings, pt. 2, 91st Cong., 2nd sess. (Washington, DC: U.S. Government Printing Office, April 28, 1970), pp. 409–442.

[12]Ibid., p. 108.

sweeping environmental law in American history. The Federal Water Pollution Control Act of 1972 required an end to the untreated discharge of debris, organic wastes, and chemical effluents into the nation's waters by 1985 and set as an interim goal the making of all waters safe for fish, shellfish, wildlife, and people by 1983. To reach these goals, private industry was required to meet effluent limitations (the amount, rate, and concentration of pollutants discharged from a given source) based on the "best practicable control technology" by July 1, 1977, and to meet effluent limitations based on the "best available control technology" by July 1, 1983. Similar, but somewhat less stringent, standards were established for municipal wastewater treatment systems. Cities had to meet effluent limitations based on secondary treatment by July 1, 1977, and to use the best practicable control technology by July 1, 1983. The EPA was given the power to define what constituted the best practicable or the best available technology. Thus, by forcing cities and private industry to use the most modern technologies available to clean up their discharges, Congress hoped to permanently clean up the nation's water.

At that time, most industries did not treat their effluent, and most cities used the relatively inexpensive primary sewage treatment system to clean up its effluent. That system employs screens and settling chambers to remove sticks, papers, and dust from wastewater. The residue of this process is sludge that can be used as a fertilizer. The more expensive secondary treatment system required by the new law also utilizes a trickling filter, usually in the form of a bed of rocks three to ten feet deep, covered with bacteria that consume organic matter in the wastewater. This process removes approximately 90 percent of degradable organic wastes. Chlorination of the residue kills up to 99 percent of the germs in the water.[13]

To help cities meet the cost of building wastewater treatment plants, Congress authorized the expenditure of $18 billion over FYs 1973–1975 for the program and increased the national government's share of each project's cost to 75 percent. It also expanded funding eligibility from the construction of the treatment plant and interceptor sewers to include collectors (small-diameter pipes that carry wastewater to the main interceptor pipes), sewer rehabilitation, correction of infiltration/inflow problems (leaky pipes), combined sewer overflow problems (prevalent in older cities in the East that have systems that mix storm water with wastewater, causing temporary system overloads during prolonged rainy periods), and certain land acquisition costs. In addition, funding was made available for facility planning (step 1 planning grant), design and specification (step 2 engineering grant), and actual construction (step 3 construction grant).[14]

Environmentalists were ecstatic about the prospects of cleaning up

[13]"Environmental Programs," in *Congress and the Nation, 1969–1972*, p. 767.

[14]Robert Jay Dilger, "Grantsmanship, Formulamanship, and Other Allocational Principles," p. 272.

the nation's waters by 1985. However, implementing the law turned into a nightmare. First, municipal treatment needs to meet the law's water quality and effluent standards were vastly underestimated by Congress. This meant that funding for the program had to be expanded or the deadline for having fishable and swimmable water would have to be pushed back. Second, inflation rates soared during the 1970s, escalating construction costs. Third, President Nixon ordered the EPA to impound over $9 billion of the wastewater treatment plants funds in FYs 1973–1975 as a means of reducing the national government's budget deficit and controlling inflation. EPA did release the funds to the states in 1975, after the U.S. Supreme Court ruled that the impoundments were illegal; but the delay in their distribution, coupled with the twin cost problems of underestimated needs and inflation, made compliance with the law's water quality deadlines impossible.

Fourth, extensive paperwork at all three levels of government slowed the program's progress. A 1981 survey conducted by the National League of Cities revealed that 86 percent of city officials indicated that it was either urgent or important for the national government to reform the Wastewater Treatment Construction Grants program's regulations.[15] Part of this administrative "red tape" problem concerned disagreements between the EPA and the states over the technology employed in proposed construction projects. Since the law did not indicate exactly what constituted the best practicable technology available or precisely how cities were to meet the secondary treatment standard, private industry representatives, state officials, local planners, and environmentalists were forced to negotiate with EPA officials concerning the appropriateness of the technologies employed in each proposed wastewater treatment plant. These negotiations took time and led to construction delays.

Fifth, the EPA and state officials often disagreed over the states' determination of their wastewater treatment needs. Under the law, states are required to submit to the EPA their plans for meeting the national government's water quality standards and to make cost estimates for each category of eligible treatment works. The EPA uses this data to put together its annual needs survey. A problem arose because the national government's relatively generous 75 percent matching grant provided an incentive to the states to inflate their estimated needs. EPA routinely rejected many of the states' need estimates and would ask them to resubmit new plans. This constant haggling over each state's wastewater treatment needs and cost estimates delayed work on hundreds of construction projects during the 1970s and continues to plague the program today.[16]

[15]David R. Beam, "Washington's Regulation of States and Localities: Origins and Issues," in *American Intergovernmental Relations Today*, ed. Robert Jay Dilger (Englewood Cliffs, NJ: Prentice-Hall, Inc., 1986), p. 236.

[16]For example, the EPA approved only 57,000 of the 210,000 estimates of wastewater treatment needs submitted to it by the states in 1980. See Robert Jay Dilger, "Grantsmanship, Formulamanship, and Other Allocational Principles," p. 273.

Recognizing the program's implementation problems, Congress decided in 1977 to extend the cities' secondary treatment deadline to July 1, 1983, and to increase the Wastewater Treatment Construction Grants funding to $4.5 billion in FY 1978 and to $5 billion per year over FYs 1979–1982, making the program the nation's second largest nondefense public works program, exceeded only by highway construction. It also made the program a prime target for budget reductions when the Reagan administration came to office in 1981.[17]

A MACROECONOMIC VIEW OF WATER POLLUTION

When the Reagan administration took office, the EPA had already awarded nearly 17,000 planning, engineering, and construction grants, the national government had spent $33 billion between 1972 and 1981 for Wastewater Treatment Construction Grants, and over 3,200 treatment plants were in operation. Yet nearly every major interest group involved in the program criticized it. City officials argued that since the national government set the water quality standards and forced them to build expensive secondary wastewater treatment plants to meet those standards, the national government ought to pay 100 percent of the treatment plants' construction costs, not just a partial percentage. They also argued that the national government should pay the cost of operating these mandated treatment plants after they are built. City officials also complained that the national government failed to fund the program at sufficient levels to pay for all of the wastewater treatment plants that needed to be built to meet the national government's water quality standards. According to a study by the EPA in 1980, it would cost $120 billion to build all of the wastewater treatment plants necessary to meet the law's water quality standards by the year 2000.[18]

Faced with declining national assistance in other intergovernmental programs and a general tax revolt by residents, city officials asked where the national government expected them to get the money to meet their share of the cost of building these wastewater treatment plants. Officials of large cities also complained that they were often overlooked by their state governments when they distributed the Wastewater Treatment Construction Grant's money within the state. One study indicated that large cities treated approximately 70 percent of the nation's wastewater yet received only 40 percent of the Wastewater Treatment Construction Grant's funds. Officials of large cities claimed that states give most of the funds to small cities for political reasons. By spreading the money around, more state legislators are able to claim political credit for the program.[19]

[17]Ibid.

[18]Ibid., p. 274.

[19]Rochelle L. Stanfield, "EPA Debates Switch from the Carrot To the Stick in Sewage Treatment," *National Journal* (February 9, 1985):315.

Environmentalists also were not enamored of the program. They were pleased that dramatic progress had been made against the most severe cases of water pollution. The Potomac River, for example, was no longer full of huge globs of smelly algae, and fish kills measured by the square mile were no longer evident in Florida's waters.[20] But they complained that neither the national government nor the cities had lived up to the spirit of the law. Instead of funding the program at sufficient levels to enable cities to meet the water quality standards by the 1983 and 1985 deadlines, the national government had continually pushed back the date for meeting them.

Environmentalists also claimed that many cities decided to reduce their own pollution control expenditures after the national government's Wastewater Treatment Construction Grants program was adopted. In 1970 states and localities spent approximately $2.3 billion to build wastewater treatment plants. In 1982 they spent less than $1 billion on projects that received no national assistance.[21] Instead of increasing their expenditures for sewage cleanup to meet the law's water quality standards, many cities were obviously substituting national dollars for local dollars, putting their own sewage treatment funds to other uses, and betting that the national government would not impose fines and imprisonment sanctions when they failed to meet national water quality standards. Fewer than one-third of the 12,800 municipalities met the July 1, 1977, deadline for upgrading their wastewater treatment systems to the secondary standard.[22]

Another claim by environmentalists was that many cities used the national government's 75 percent subsidy to build super-large wastewater treatment plants that had the capacity to treat much greater amounts of effluent than they needed.[23] In this way, cities could continue to promote economic development without fear of violating the clean water standards. Although this made city politicians popular with the real estate and construction industries, it did little to improve the nation's water quality. While the total amount of water treated by municipal wastewater treatment plants increased by 7 billion gallons between 1972 and 1982, the total amount of pollutants discharged into the water system remained the same. The frustrations felt by most environmentalists in the early 1980s were best reflected in a statement made in 1985 by a member of the Sierra Club who complained that making progress against water pollution was like running up a down escalator.[24]

[20]Ibid., p. 313.

[21]Ibid.

[22]"Energy and Environment," Congressional Quarterly *Almanac, 1977* (Washington, DC: Congressional Quarterly, 1978), p. 705.

[23]Rochelle L. Stanfield, "EPA Debates Switch from the Carrot To the Stick in Sewage Treatment," p. 315.

[24]Ibid.

Private industry was not happy with the program, complaining that the cost of meeting the effluent discharge standards was prohibitively expensive. The petroleum industry, for example, estimated that it spent $5.5 billion between 1972 and 1977 to meet the Water Pollution Control Act's requirement to use the "best practicable technology" to reach the secondary treatment standard.[25] Total private industrial expenditures to meet the secondary treatment standards from 1972 to 1984 has been estimated at $13 billion.[26] To reduce costs, industries located in coastal regions argued that they should be exempt from the effluent discharge standards because oceans have a very large capacity to clean themselves. Other industries argued that they should be allowed to use the less expensive primary treatment process if the use of that process did not cause the water being polluted to fall below the national government's water quality standard.

President Reagan did not like the Wastewater Treatment Construction Grants program. An advocate of states' rights, he argued that water pollution was a local issue that ought to be dealt with by local citizens in consultation with state and local government officials. Instead of having the EPA tell them what their local water quality standards were, he preferred to let local citizens decide for themselves what was an acceptable water quality standard for their area. Instead of forcing business and city governments to install expensive pollution control equipment to meet stringent water quality standards, he preferred to let local citizens determine for themselves if the trade-off between better water quality and higher taxes and reduced business growth was in their best interest. He was convinced that letting the people decide what they wanted to do about water pollution would encourage citizen participation in the political process, result in better-informed citizens, and promote accountability in the political system. He was also convinced that letting the public decide the fate of water controls would not result in rampant environmental spoilage.[27]

Liberals and environmentalists disagreed with President Reagan's views. They felt that the public tends to purchase the least expensive product when quality is similar. Therefore, industry would never voluntarily install pollution control equipment that would increase the cost of products and put it at a competitive disadvantage. They were equally convinced that most local governments would never force local businesses to install expensive pollution control equipment. In their view, local governments almost always bow to the pressures of local businesses because the latter always threaten to relocate to other cities if they are not provided with incentives to stay. Letting the people decide for themselves may sound democratic,

[25] "Energy and Environment," Congressional Quarterly *Almanac, 1977*, p. 702.

[26] Rochelle L. Stanfield, "Enough and Clean Enough?" *National Journal* (August 17, 1985):1878.

[27] Clark E. Cochran, Lawrence C. Mayer, T. R. Carr, and N. Joseph Cayer, *American Public Policy*; p. 117.

but given the influence of business groups in local politics and the reluctance of the public to tax itself, most liberals and environmentalists were convinced that letting the public decide the fate of wastewater treatment plants would lead to increased water pollution levels in most areas of the country.[28]

Another reason President Reagan did not like the Wastewater Treatment Construction Grants program was its projected cost of $120 billion through the year 2000. Since the national government was providing 75 percent of construction costs, the national government's share of future costs was $90 billion. Given this expense; his belief in the public's right to decide how much to spend for pollution control; the relative weakness of the political support for the program, given the divisions over its methods; his pledge (subsequently withdrawn) to balance the national budget by FY 1984; his desire to increase defense expenditures and decrease domestic expenditures; and his lack of empathy for the environmental movement, President Reagan proposed a major overhaul of the program on March 10, 1981.

He asked for, and subsequently received, a rescission of $1.7 billion in the program's FY 1980 and 1981 funds. He also proposed funding the program at $2.4 billion a year instead of $5 billion a year, and announced that he would veto even that amount if the national government's future obligation to the program was not reduced from $90 billion to $23 billion. To achieve these savings, he proposed eliminating funding for treatment plants with excess capacity beyond 1980 population needs, sewer rehabilitation, and combined sewer overflow projects. Only secondary and tertiary sewage treatment plants (which are more expensive and effective than secondary treatment plants) and interceptor sewers would be funded, and then only if they were targeted to large cities where expenditures would produce the greatest improvement in water quality for each dollar spent.[29]

Recognizing that the president's veto would be upheld by the Republican Senate, Democrats in Congress reluctantly agree to reduce the program's authorization over FYs 1983–1986 to $2.4 billion annually. They also provided an additional $200 million annually to correct combined sewer overflows into marine bays and estuaries. To meet the president's demand to reduce the national government's future obligation to the program to $23 billion, Congress limited funding to the construction of wastewater treatment plants, the correction of infiltration/inflow, and new interceptor sewers. In addition, the national government's share of costs

28Ibid.

29Another issue involved the allocation of the program's $2.4 billion among the states. For an analysis of the congressional battle over the program's allocation formula, see Robert Jay Dilger, "Grantsmanship, Formulamanship, and Other Allocational Principles," pp. 269–286.

would remain at 75 percent only until 1984, when it would be reduced to 55 percent of costs. Moreover, funding would be allowed for wastewater treatment plants that had up to 20 years of excess capacity only if they were approved by the EPA by October 1, 1984. After that, no grant could be made for wastewater treatment needs in excess of the population needs of the community being served as of the date the step 3 construction grant was awarded by the EPA—and in no event would there be grants for needs in excess of those as of October 1, 1990.

In an effort to appease the distraught intergovernmental lobby, each state's governor was allowed to spend up to 20 percent of his or her state's funds on categories of treatment works that were ineligible for funding after 1984. Also, although it was not written into the law, the governors were led to believe that an informal agreement existed between Congress and the Reagan administration that the national government would continue to fund the remaining $23 billion in obligations at the $2.4 billion level for the next ten years.[30]

When the Clean Water Act came up for renewal in 1985, environmentalists, liberals, and city officials were surprised when the Reagan administration announced its plan to phase out the Wastewater Treatment Construction Grants program over a four-year period. Citing the need to reduce domestic expenditures and to strengthen state and local governmental responsibilities, it asked Congress to provide only $6 billion for the Wastewater Treatment Construction Grants program through FY 1989. After that, all funding for new projects would end. City officials were quick to point out that the national mandate to clean up the nation's water would remain in force. Using EPA estimates, they argued that they did not have the fiscal capacity to raise the $108 billion necessary to build all of the wastewater treatment plants that had to be built between 1986 and the year 2000 to meet the national water quality standards.[31] State officials joined city officials in opposition to the proposal. They argued that they did not have the fiscal capacity to help their cities build the required plants.

Environmentalists were outraged. They were hoping to expand the scope of the wastewater treatment plants program to include the elimination of toxic pollutants from raw sewage and to push for more national funding to control groundwater contamination and nonpoint pollution (water pollution that does not originate from the end of a pipe, such as pollution carried by rainwater and snowmelt that runs off large land areas).[32]

The Democratic House and the Republican Senate battled for almost

[30]Ibid., pp. 282, 283.

[31]W. John Moore, "Mandates Without Money," *National Journal* (October 4, 1986):2370.

[32]Rochelle L. Stanfield, "Enough and Clean Enough?" pp. 1876–1880.

two years before reaching an agreement late in 1986 to renew the Clean Water Act.[33] Part of the delay was caused by a vicious regional battle in the Senate over the state-by-state allocation of available funds. Another factor was a battle between environmentalists and members of the House Public Works Committee who wanted to reinstate funding eligibility for collector sewers. Environmentalists complained that these sewers subsidize residential housing growth and, as a result, lead to more water pollution. The House Committee dropped its support for the provision in 1986.[34] Finally, the House-Senate conference committee took more than a year to resolve several major differences between the House- and Senate-passed bills involving funding levels and the program's allocation formula.[35]

Congress' bill to renew the Clean Water Act was unanimously adopted by the House and the Senate during the last week of the 99th Congress. It authorized $9.6 billion for Wastewater Treatment Construction Grants through FY 1990 and $8.4 billion to set up a state-run revolving loan fund for treatment plant construction over FYs 1989–1994. An additional $400 million over four years was allotted for efforts to control pollution from nonpoint sources such as streets, fields, and forests. The current formula for allocating available funds among the states, which was viewed as benefiting states in the Northeast, was retained with only minor revisions that gave Texas an additional $18 million annually.[36]

It appeared that the Wastewater Treatment Construction Grants program would survive at least for an additional eight years, but while Congress was adjourned for the 1986 elections, President Reagan pocket vetoed the bill. He claimed that it "far exceeds acceptable levels of intended budgetary commitments."[37] Following the 1986 congressional elections, Democrats held the majority of seats in both the House and the Senate. Recognizing that Congress would now be able to override his vetoes, President Reagan offered a compromise $12 billion proposal that did not include loans for wastewater treatment plant construction or funds for nonpoint pollution control projects. However, the new Congress quickly approved a bill that was identical to the one the president had vetoed earlier. Although he knew he would probably be overridden, President

[33]Congress continued to authorize $2.4 billion annually for the Wastewater Treatment Construction Grants program through annual appropriations as the debate over its reauthorization continued. See Joseph A. Davis, "Clean Water Debate to Focus on Sewage Grant Program," Congressional Quarterly, *Weekly Report* (March 16, 1985):491.

[34]Joseph A. Davis, "Clean Water Act Renewal Awaits House, Senate Action," Congressional Quarterly, *Weekly Report* (May 25, 1985):1009.

[35]Joseph A. Davis, "House Action Sought Soon on Clean Water Act Renewal," Congressional Quarterly, *Weekly Report* (June 22, 1985):1217; and Joseph A. Davis, "House Refuses FY '86 Freeze on Spending for Clean Water," ibid. (July 27, 1985):1482.

[36]Joseph A. Davis, "Congress Votes Unaminously for $20 billion Water Cleanup," Congressional Quarterly, *Weekly Report* (October 18, 1986):2623.

[37]Joseph A. Davis, "Reagan Vetoes Clean Water Bill; Members Vow to Pass It Again," Congressional Quarterly, *Weekly Report* (November 8, 1986):2874.

Reagan decided to veto the bill anyway, claiming that it was loaded with waste and larded with pork. As expected, Congress overrode the veto.

CONCLUSIONS

The Wastewater Treatment Construction Grants program's days are numbered. The only question concerning its death is when. The weight of the national deficit and the feuding among its advocates made it very vulnerable to the Reagan administration's decision, based on its macroeconomic theory of intergovernmental relations, to eliminate the program. The only conceivable way that Wastewater Treatment Construction Grants can survive the 1990s is if the national elections in 1988 and 1992 produce a Democratic president committed to the program and an overwhelmingly Democratic House and Senate. Even if this were to occur, state and local officials recognize that the national deficit will force Congress to hold the program's funding far beneath the $108 billion necessary to meet the national water quality standards by the year 2000. Thus, it is very likely that local governments are going to have to raise at least $90 billion between 1987 and 2000 to meet the national government's water quality standard.

None of the options available to city officials to raise this money are politically popular. Many communities will increase local property taxes and user fees to pay for their wastewater treatment plants, while others will increase or impose for the first time local sales and income taxes to pay for them. City officials will also look to their state legislatures for additional assistance. Some state legislatures will provide extra funding, but many of them will be forced to increase taxes or to reduce expenditures in other areas to do so. In short, wastewater treatment plant construction and how to pay for it will be a hot political item in state and local election campaigns during the 1990s.

Environmentalists are concerned that if, as appears likely, the Wastewater Treatment Construction Grants program is terminated in the mid-1990s, many state and local officials who currently support the national government's water quality standards on philosophical grounds will be forced by budgetary realities to start lobbying for a weakening of those standards. Given current budgetary constraints at all governmental levels, the environmentalists' worst fear is that once the national government withdraws its funding for water pollution equipment, many states and localities will refuse to fund it.

A study of state and local funding decisions concerning wastewater treatment plant construction during FYs 1981–1984 revealed that most states did not increase their expenditures on wastewater treatment needs to compensate for the national government's cuts in the Wastewater Treatment Construction Grants program. The study concluded that most states decided that they had more pressing needs, including higher education, health care, and housing, and were unwilling to increase state and local taxes to compensate for the national government's decision to reduce its funding for Wastewater Treatment Construction Grants.[38]

Environmentalists recognize that it is extremely unlikely that the national government will prosecute state and local officials for not funding an activity that the national government itself refuses to fund. A likely scenario for the future is that the national government will continue to push back the compliance deadline for meeting its water quality standards and that the environmentalists' hopes for additional national controls for groundwater contamination and nonpoint pollution will probably not be realized.

[38]James P. Lester, "New Federalism and Environmental Policy," *Publius: The Journal of Federalism* 16 (Winter 1986):149–165.

CHAPTER 10

National Tax Expenditures

National tax expenditures are items in the national income tax code that encourage individuals either to invest in or to engage in certain designated activities by giving those activities a favored tax status. The Congressional Budget Act of 1974 defined tax expenditures as "revenue losses attributable to provisions of the Federal tax laws which allow a special exclusion, exemption, or deduction from gross income or which provide a special credit, a preferential rate of tax, or a deferral of liability."[1] The public tends to call these items "tax breaks" or "tax loopholes."

People often disagree over the desirability of specific tax expenditures. As one author explained it, "One person's loophole is another person's good tax policy."[2] The national government's two most expensive tax expenditures, the tax exclusion of contributions to employer-sponsored pension plans and the deduction of home mortgage interest from taxable income, have widespread public support throughout the nation. These tax "loopholes" encourage people to undertake desirable activities: to save for retirement and to buy homes. The cost of these two tax expenditures alone is staggering. The U.S. Office of Management and Budget has estimated that they will cost the national treasury over $76 billion in FY 1989.[3]

Prior to the enactment of the sweeping *Tax Reform Act of 1986*, there were 102 tax expenditures in the national government's income tax code. In FY 1986 they cost the national government over $400 billion annually in revenues that would have been collected if they had not been created by Congress. Although many of these tax expenditures were eliminated in

[1] William R. Barnes, "What Are Tax Expenditures and Why Are They Important?" in *Tax Breaks: An Introduction to Tax Expenditures*, ed. William R. Barnes (Washington, DC: National League of Cities, 1985), p. 1. Many conservatives do not like the use of the term "tax expenditure." They feel that the term assumes that national tax dollars are the property of the national government rather than of the taxpayers.

[2] Ibid.

[3] U.S. Office of Management and Budget, *Special Analyses: Budget of the United States Government, FY 1989* (Washington, DC: U.S. Government Printing Office, 1988), pp. G–42, G–44.

1986, tax expenditures continue to play an important role in affecting investment decisions and the flow of capital within the nation.

All tax expenditures have an indirect impact on states and localities because they affect the size of the national government's deficit (which influences interest rates and the overall level of economic activity) and channel investments into or away from economic activities that directly affect the lives of individuals who are likely to rely heavily on state and local governmental services. The deductibility of charitable contributions, for example, cost the national government over $12 billion in FY 1989.[4] This tax expenditure not only encourages people to donate to charity but also helps to relieve some of the pressure on state and local governments to assist the needy. If the deduction for charitable giving were eliminated, state and local governments would probably be forced to expand their services to compensate for an expected decrease in charitable giving and in the activities of charitable organizations.[5] Similarly, the special tax benefits accorded investments in low-income, multifamily (rental) housing construction projects not only provide an economic subsidy to the investors sponsoring these projects but also supplement state and local governments' efforts to provide decent, affordable housing for the poor.

There are two very expensive tax expenditures that have a direct impact on the ability of state and local governments to provide public services: the deductibility of state and local taxes, and the tax-exempt status of state and local government bonds. The rest of this chapter is devoted to examining these two programs' historical development, their rationales, the political controversies surrounding them, their impact on state and local revenue systems, and the way the Tax Reform Act of 1986 changed them.

THE DEDUCTIBILITY OF STATE AND LOCAL TAXES

Taxpayers who itemize their deductions on their national income tax forms can deduct selected state and local taxes from the amount of income subject to the national income tax. The deductibility of state and local taxes was included in U.S. Income Tax Code when it was enacted in 1913. Until 1986 there were very few major changes in this tax expenditure. In 1964 the deductibility of motor vehicle operators' license fees and state and local excise taxes, other than gasoline, were eliminated. In 1978 the deductibility of state and local excise taxes on gasoline was eliminated. This left four major state and local taxes that had been eligible for deduction since 1913:

---

[4]Ibid., pp. G–43, G–44.

[5]The Tax Reform Act of 1986 limited the deduction for charitable giving to individuals who itemize their deductions.

individual income, retail sales, real estate, and personal property.[6] Collectively, the deductibility of these four state and local taxes cost the national government approximately $36 billion in uncollected revenue in FY 1987.[7]

Prior to the enactment of the Tax Reform Act of 1986, the deductibility of state and local taxes had been challenged from a number of sources. During congressional deliberations on the *Tax Equity and Fiscal Responsibility Act of 1982*, both the House and the Senate seriously considered eliminating the deductibility of state and local sales and personal property taxes as a means to reduce the size of the national government's budget deficit. The House also considered eliminating the deductibility of all nonbusiness state and local income taxes. In 1985 President Reagan proposed the elimination of the deductibility of all state and local taxes for individual taxpayers. Businesses would continue to deduct state and local taxes as a business expense.[8]

The original argument supporting the deductibility of state and local taxes rested on the belief that the Tenth Amendment to the U.S. Constitution protected state taxing powers from any interference by the national government.[9] The modern debate over the deductibility of state and local taxes, however, never centered on constitutional issues involving federalism. Instead, it focused on the more technical aspects of the program's impact on the national government's tax revenues and on state and local funding decisions.

In 1985 and 1986 five major arguments were raised to continue the deductibility of state and local taxes. The first was that individuals should not be taxed on a tax. This argument rested on the premise that taxes, other than user fees levied on beneficiaries of specific programs, ought to be collected in accordance with a taxpayer's ability to pay them. Since individuals must pay their state and local tax obligations, it was argued that the deductibility of state and local taxes made the national income tax more equitable by ensuring that it more closely reflected the taxpayers' ability to pay.[10]

Opponents of the deductibility of state and local taxes countered this

[6]Nonna A. Noto and Dennis Zimmerman, *Limiting State-Local Tax Deductibility in Exchange for Increased General Revenue Sharing: An Analysis of the Economic Effects* (Washington, DC: U.S. Government Printing Office, 1983), p. 3.

[7]U.S. Office of Management and Budget, *Special Analyses: Budget of the United States Government, FY 1987* (Washington, DC: U.S. Government Printing Office, 1986), p. H16.

[8]Robert Jay Dilger, *The Deductibility of State and Local Taxes: Implications of Proposed Policy Changes* (Washington, DC: National League of Cities, 1985), p. 4.

[9]Daniel Patrick Moynihan, "Constitutional Dimensions of State and Local Tax Deductibility," *Publius: The Journal of Federalism* 16 (Summer 1986):74–77.

[10]Daphne A. Kenyon, "Federal Income Tax Deductibility of State and Local Taxes: What Are Its Effects? Should It Be Modified or Eliminated?" in *Strengthening the Federal Revenue System: Implications for State and Local Taxing and Borrowing* (Washington, DC: U.S. Advisory Commission on Intergovernmental Relations, 1984), p. 38.

argument by claiming that state and local taxes are not completely involuntary. Although everyone must pay state and local taxes, local taxpayers influence their state and local tax rates through the election process and have "ultimate control over the taxes they pay through their ability to locate in jurisdictions with amenable tax and fiscal policies."[11]

The second argument defending the deductibility of state and local taxes was that it justifiably enhances the revenue-raising ability of state and local governments. Itemizers who deduct their state and local tax obligations from their national taxable income receive a rebate from the national government (proportioned to their marginal income tax rate) for every dollar paid in state and local taxes. In economic terms, itemizers realize a reduction in the price they pay for state and local public goods. As a result, state and local governments find revenue raising easier because itemizers who claim a deduction for state and local tax obligations are able to pass a portion of the cost of their state and local public goods and services on to taxpayers who do not itemize and/or reside in other states and localities.[12]

The economic justification for enhancing the revenue-raising ability of state and local governments was that many state and local programs have benefits that spill over into neighboring jurisdictions, especially programs in the transportation, health, and environmental areas. Since the residents of the city or state providing these services do not receive all of these programs' benefits, they might be reluctant to finance them if the deductibility of state and local taxes were eliminated or its value significantly reduced.[13]

Opponents of the deductibility of state and local taxes agreed that it enhances the ability of state and local governments to raise revenues. They argued, however, that deductibility encourages state and local officials to keep state and local taxes at unnecessarily high levels. High taxes, in turn, hurt business investment and the national economy. Moreover, they argued that there was no solid evidence that the added revenues provided to state and local governments were being used to fund programs whose benefits spilled over into neighboring jurisdictions. Even if solid evidence did exist, they argued, a direct spending program, such as general revenue sharing, would be a much more cost efficient way to help state and local governments finance these programs. A direct spending program would place the funds into the hands of state and local officials instead of reaching them through the taxpayers' willingness to pay state and local taxes.

The third argument used to defend the deductibility of state and local taxes was that it narrows interstate and intercity tax differences and, as a result, reduces the incentive for individuals and businesses to migrate from

[11]Office of the President of the United States, *The President's Tax Proposal to the Congress for Fairness, Growth, and Simplicity* (Washington, DC: U.S. Government Printing Office, 1985), p. 63.

[12]Daphne A. Kenyon, "Federal Income Tax Deductibility of State and Local Taxes," pp. 38, 39.

[13]Robert Jay Dilger, *The Deductibility of State and Local Taxes*, p. 5.

one jurisdiction to another in an attempt to seek their optimal tax situation.[14] It narrows interstate and intercity tax differences because it rebates to individuals who itemize on their national income tax forms a percentage (equal to their national marginal income tax rate) of their state and local tax bill. Since taxpayers living in states and localities with high state and local taxes will have more state and local taxes to deduct than taxpayers with identical incomes who live in states and localities with relatively low state and local taxes, the former receive a larger tax subsidy from the national government than the latter. Thus, the deductibility of state and local taxes reduces the economic incentive for the people living in states or localities with high state and local taxes to move to states or localities with low taxes.

Opponents of the deductibility of state and local taxes argued that interjurisdictional tax competition is, in the long run, healthy for both the national economy and state and local governments. They repeated their argument that this tax expenditure encouraged states and localities to have artificially high tax rates that inhibit business investment and weaken the national economy. They also argued that deductibility's proponents overstated its impact on interjurisdictional tax competition because many taxpayers would decide to locate in the higher-taxing jurisdictions even if deductibility were eliminated because they placed a high value on the governmental services offered by those jurisdictions.[15]

The fourth argument raised in support of continuing the deductibility of state and local taxes was that it helped to increase national productivity by avoiding "excessive" cumulative national/state/local income tax rates. This argument was especially prominent when national marginal income tax rates were very high (peaking at 94 percent in 1944–1945). At that time, there was a very real possibility that cumulative marginal income tax rates could reach 100 percent, thereby removing all incentive for continued investment or earnings. It was argued that the national government should provide fiscal relief to taxpayers by allowing them to deduct state and local taxes because it had a larger tax base than either the states or localities. The lowering of the maximum national marginal income tax rate to 70 percent in 1971, to 50 percent in 1982, and to 28 percent in 1988 has removed much of the concern underlying this argument.[16]

The fifth argument raised in defense of the deductibility of state and local taxes was the nearly total autonomy it offers state and local governments in the use of its benefits. Unlike grants-in-aid spending programs,

[14]George F. Break and Joseph A. Pechman, *Federal Tax Reform: The Impossible Dream?* (Washington, DC: Brookings Institution, 1975), pp. 22, 23; and Daphne A. Kenyon, "Federal Income Tax Deductibility of State and Local Taxes," pp. 48–51.

[15]Daphne A. Kenyon, "Implicit Aid to State and Local Governments Through Federal Tax Deductibility," in *Intergovernmental Fiscal Relations in an Era of New Federalism*, ed. Michael Bell (Greenwich, CT: JAI Press, forthcoming), pp. 10–14.

[16]Richard Goode, *The Individual Income Tax* (Washington, DC: Brookings Institution, 1964), p. 177; Nonna A. Noto and Dennis Zimmerman, "Limiting State-Local Tax Deductibility," p. 18; and Robert Jay Dilger, *The Deductibility of State and Local Taxes*, p. 5.

there are no administrative strings, crossover, or other intergovernmental sanctions attached to the benefits that accrue to state and local governments because of the existence of this tax expenditure.[17]

Opponents of the deduction for state and local taxes agreed that it has few administrative strings, but argued that it is a very inefficient way to subsidize state and local governments. They added that the national government's large budget deficit forced them to advocate the elimination of this costly and inefficient subsidy. Some of its opponents argued in 1985, for example, that it should be eliminated and its revenue (over $36 billion annually at that time) used to help reduce the national government's deficit. Others, including the Reagan administration, proposed that it be eliminated and its revenue used to reduce the national government's marginal income tax rates. This not only would increase national productivity and economic growth but also would provide additional revenue to the national, state, and local governments' treasuries as new employment opportunities increased the number of people paying taxes and reduced the number of people dependent on governmental assistance. The Treasury Department estimated that eliminating the deductibility of state and local taxes would enable national marginal income tax rates to be reduced by 8 percent, across the board.[18]

Opponents of the deductibility of state and local taxes also argued that it violated the concept of economic neutrality. Economists argue that, theoretically, the best taxing system is one that raises revenue without causing anyone to change his or her economic behavior simply because of the way that behavior is taxed. A neutral tax would not lead anyone to work fewer or more hours, to save more or less resources, to decide to invest in certain securities and not in others, or to buy one type of consumer good rather than another. Similarly, a "good" national tax policy would not cause states and localities to alter their own taxing decisions. The deductibility of state and local taxes, however, encourages states and localities to use taxes that are eligible for deduction and to avoid taxes that are ineligible—specifically user fees, special assessments for improvements to property, and excise taxes. They are also encouraged to employ progressive, as opposed to proportional or regressive, tax structures because progressive taxes produce greater potential national tax subsidies for state and local taxpayers. This is the case because higher-income taxpayers are more likely to itemize and face higher national marginal income tax rates than lower-income taxpayers.[19]

[17]Robert Jay Dilger, *The Deductibility of State and Local Taxes*, p. 5.

[18]Ibid., p. 6.

[19]Ibid., p. 7; George F. Break and Joseph Pechman, *Federal Tax Reform: The Impossible Dream?*, pp. 7, 8; and Daphne A. Kenyon, "Implicit Aid to State and Local Governments Through Federal Tax Deductibililty," pp. 24–31. One early study that is no longer supported by most economists argued that the deductibility of state and local taxes has little impact on state and local decisions concerning the income tax. See Walter Hettich and Stanley Winer, "A Positive Model of Tax Structure," *Journal of Public Economics* (1984): 67–87.

Another criticism of the deductibility of state and local taxes was that it has an adverse impact on the progressivity of the national income tax. Since itemizers tend to be in families with middle or upper incomes, and only itemizers are allowed to deduct their state and local taxes, most of the benefits from the deductibility of state and local taxes accrue to middle- and upper-income taxpayers.[20]

THE POLITICAL BATTLE OVER STATE AND LOCAL TAX DEDUCTIONS

The political battle over the deductibililty of state and local taxes began in August 1982 when Sen. Bill Bradley (D-NJ) and Rep. Richard A. Gephardt (D-MO) introduced their "fair tax" bills into the Senate and House. Their purpose was to increase economic productivity and fairness in the tax system by reducing the number of "inefficient" tax expenditures and using the revenues from those tax expenditures to reduce marginal income tax rates. Their plan was revenue neutral. That is, the amount of revenue collected by the U.S. Treasury after the changes were implemented would raise virtually the same amount of revenue as current law. Taxpayers and corporations that used the tax expenditures targeted for elimination would generally pay more national income tax, and taxpayers and corporations that did not use tax expenditures would pay less.

Bradley and Gephardt proposed to reduce the national income tax system's 15 marginal income tax brackets, ranging from 11 percent to 50 percent, to 3 brackets of 14, 26, and 30 percent. One of the many "inefficient" tax expenditures targeted for adjustment to realize this reduction in marginal income tax rates was the deductibility of state and local taxes. The Bradley-Gephardt plan proposed the elimination of the deductibility of state and local sales and personal property taxes.

The Bradley-Gephardt "fair tax" plan generated a lot of media attention. Although economists disagree over the desirability of all of the plan's specific changes, there was a consensus among economists of all political persuasions that tax reform efforts that reduced marginal income tax rates by eliminating "inefficient" tax expenditures would lead to a more productive and robust economy.

In January 1984, President Reagan jumped on the tax reform bandwagon when he announced in his State of the Union Address that he was going to propose a simplification of the national income tax. He directed Secretary of the Treasury Donald T. Regan to put together a comprehensive tax reform package by December 1984 that was revenue neutral and

---

[20]U.S. Internal Revenue Service, *Statistics of Income, 1982: Individual Income Tax Returns* (Washington, DC: U.S. Government Printing Office, 1984), pp. 39, 60; and Office of Tax Analysis, Office of the Secretary of the Treasury, "Tabulations from the 1982 Statistics of Income File for the Fiscal Relations Study" (December 14, 1984), Table 1. (Mimeographed.)

significantly reduced marginal income tax rates. The president indicated that all tax expenditures were to be analyzed and subject to elimination or modification.

State and local officials were not directly involved in the Treasury Department's deliberations. Staff from several of the state and local lobby organizations, including the National League of Cities, the National Governors' Association, and the U.S. Advisory Commission on Intergovernmental Relations, closely monitored the Treasury Department's position on the deductibility of state and local taxes. They were members of the Treasury Department's State and Local Working Group. Although the working group was established by the Treasury Department to obtain input concerning reauthorization of the general revenue-sharing program, it quickly became the forum for state and local input into its tax reform plans.

The U.S. Conference of Mayors, the National League of Cities, and the National Association of Counties vigorously objected to any changes in the deductibility of state and local taxes. They argued that the Reagan administration was already advocating deep cuts in domestic spending programs that benefited the nation's cities. Many local officials felt that these cuts would force them to ask their constituents to accept higher state and local taxes just to maintain current service levels. They believed that if the deductibility of state and local taxes was eliminated at the same time that these cuts took place, their political futures were in serious jeopardy. The National League of Cities called it the "double whammy."

The National Governors' Association took a more moderate position. Its members felt that they could accept some reduction in the value of state and local tax deductions in exchange for reduced marginal income tax rates and the economic growth that would accompany the lower rates. They insisted, however, that their support was contingent on the administration's providing additional direct spending assistance to high-tax states that have a disproportionate number of itemizers, such as New York, Massachusetts, and California.

Despite the objections of the state and local lobby organizations, the Treasury Department recommended in its November 1984 tax reform plan that the deductibility of state and local taxes be eliminated. Leaders of the various state and local lobby organizations then appealed directly to President Reagan to save the deductibility provision. Several members of a delegation of state and local officials that met with the president in January 1985 indicated that he said he believed it was unfair to tax a tax, and the elimination of the provision was counter to his own personal views on federalism. Nevertheless, when he announced his tax reform plan to Congress on May 28, 1985, he recommended that the deductibility of state and local taxes be eliminated in its entirety.[21]

Lobbyists from the intergovernmental interest groups worked very

[21]Office of the President of the United States, *The President's Tax Proposals to the Congress for Fairness, Growth, and Simplicity*, pp. 62–69.

hard to convince Congress that this was not a good time to eliminate the deductibility of state and local taxes. They were joined by lobbyists from organized labor (which felt that state and local public employees' jobs were threatened by the elimination of state and local tax deductions), education groups (most school districts rely on the property tax for revenue), and the housing industry (which wanted to protect the deductibility of the real estate property tax). In addition, New York's state, local, and national officials made the protection of the deductibility of state and local taxes its number-one priority.

Recognizing the growing chorus of voices opposing any change in the deductibility of state and local taxes, the House Ways and Means Committee decided not to eliminate or alter it in any way. They then spent more than a month fighting over what additional tax expenditures would be eliminated or modified to compensate for the $36 billion lost when state and local tax deductions were reinstated. They finally decided to reduce the value of several tax expenditures used by business and sent their tax reform bill to the House floor, where it was approved and sent to the Senate for action.[22]

The Senate Finance Committee, chaired by Robert Packwood (R-OR), scheduled markup on the tax reform bill to begin in mid-March 1986. In the meantime, Packwood was asked by his colleagues on the Finance Committee to draft a proposal that reinstated the business-related tax expenditures deleted by the House Ways and Means Committee while maintaining the bill's revenue neutrality. Senator Packwood subsequently recommended a number of changes in the House bill, including the elimination of state and local sales and personal property taxes. He also recommended limiting the deduction for state and local income taxes to the first two of his proposal's three tax rates of 15, 25, and 35 percent. This would significantly reduce the deduction's value to high-income taxpayers (over $70,000) who would be subject to the proposed top income tax rate of 35 percent. These taxpayers would be allowed to deduct only 25 percent, instead of 35 percent, of their state and local income tax obligations. Only the deduction for state and local real estate property taxes would remain fully deductible for all taxpayers.

The members of the Senate Finance Committee did not embrace Packwood's tax reform package.[23] Several members, led by David Durenberger (R-MN), announced that they would oppose any proposal to elimi-

[22]Objecting to the bill's treatment of business tax incentives, Republicans and conservative Democrats almost defeated the bill. For details on the floor fight, see Dick Kirschten, "Tax Reform Dodges Another Bullet . . . but May Have Winged the GOP," *National Journal* (December 21, 1985):2919; and Pamela Fessler, "House Reverses Self, Passes Major Tax Overhaul," Congressional Quarterly, *Weekly Report* (December 21, 1985):2705–2711. The House bill created four income tax brackets: 15 percent on taxable income up to $22,500, 25 percent on taxable income between $22,500 and $43,000, 35 percent on taxable income between $43,000 and $100,000, and 38 percent on taxable income exceeding $100,000.

[23]Pamela Fessler, "Packwood's Senate Colleagues Already Fighting over Tax Bill," Congressional Quarterly, *Weekly Report* (March 22, 1986) p. 646.

nate or reduce the value of the deductibility of state and local taxes. Undaunted, Packwood scheduled votes on specific tax expenditures to commence on March 24, 1986. He knew that tax reform would probably die if he could not convince his committee to accept a reduction in the value of state and local tax deductions. But before the committee got to state and local taxes, it considered another tax expenditure of interest to state and local governments: the tax exemption of interest earned from state and local bonds. The committee's action on this issue nearly scuttled the whole tax reform movement.

THE TAX-EXEMPT STATUS OF STATE AND LOCAL BONDS

The interest collected by investors who purchase bonds issued by state and local governments to finance various public service projects has always been exempt from the national income tax. This enables state and local governments to borrow money at significantly lower interest rates than private business. Since investors do not have to pay either national or state income tax on the interest they receive from state and local bonds, they are willing to accept a lower interest rate from them, compared with bonds issued by private business. Since 1982 interest on tax-exempt bonds has been approximately 78 percent of the interest on nonexempt bonds.[24]

The tax-exempt status of state and local bonds stems from a series of Supreme Court decisions between 1819 and 1895 that established the doctrine of reciprocal immunity. This doctrine protected states from the national government's interference in their governmental affairs, just as the states were prevented from interfering in the affairs of the national government.[25] Since state and local bonds would be less valuable to investors if they were taxed by the national government, the investors would demand a higher interest rate before purchasing the bonds. Thus, the cost of financing state and local services would be raised. This would inhibit the ability of state and local governments to provide services to their people and was deemed by the courts an unconstitutional interference in the affairs of state and local governments.

Following the adoption of Sixteenth Amendment and the national income tax law in 1913, some analysts argued that the Sixteenth Amendment's right to collect taxes on income "from whatever source derived"

---

[24]Susannah E. Calkins, "Tax-Exempt Bonds," in *Strenghtening the Federal Revenue System: Implications for State and Local Taxing and Borrowing* (Washington, DC: U.S. Advisory Commission on Intergovernmental Relations, 1984), p. 127.

[25]Ibid., p. 116. The U.S. Supreme Court repudiated the doctrine of reciprocal immunity in *South Carolina vs. Bayer* (1988) arguing that states must look to the national political process and not to judicial enforcement of federalism principles embedded in the 10th Amendment for protection from the national government.

overturned the doctrine of reciprocal immunity. They argued that the interest from state and local bonds should now be taxed.[26] Although the courts would subsequently rule that state and local bonds can be taxed, the uncertainty of the legal justification for the tax exemption in the early 1980s made it a visible and tempting target for tax reformers even before the courts made their ruling.

THE POLITICAL BATTLE OVER STATE AND LOCAL TAX-EXEMPT BONDS

The move to restrict the tax-exempt status of state and local bonds began in the late 1960s. Many congressmen felt that state and local governments had the right to issue tax-exempt bonds to finance traditional governmental functions, such as school, road, and sewer construction. There was considerably less support for tax-exempt bonds that financed nontraditional governmental services, such as private housing projects, student loans, private hospital construction, sports stadiums, or industrial development projects.[27]

The volume of state and local bonds for nontraditional or private purposes expanded greatly during the 1970s and early 1980s (see Table 10.1). There are many reasons these bonds became so popular with state and local officials at this time. Many saw them as an additional tool to provide services to their constituents. As the number of jurisdictions issuing bonds grew, the practice became routine and accepted. Many state and local officials also viewed these bonds as a convenient means of compensating for funding cuts and freezes that occurred in many nationally financed intergovernmental grants during the late 1970s and early 1980s. Issuing a bond to maintain governmental services is much less politically controversial than asking constituents to accept a tax increase. Some officials used bonds to finance programs that could not be financed in any other way because of state and local tax, debt, or spending limitations such as California's Proposition 13. Others viewed the bonds as a means to make their cities and states more attractive for business expansion.[28]

Economic conservatives objected to the use of bonds for nontraditional purposes. They argued that these bonds had "anti-competitive and distortive effects on the economy," because private decisions on where to

[26]Ibid., p. 116, 117.

[27]In 1968, the Revenue and Expenditure Act imposed a dollar limit on the size of each "small issue" industrial development bond issued in each jurisdiction (now $10 million). However, the law did not restrict the size of industrial development bonds for legislatively specified projects, such as convention centers, sports stadiums, and airport facilities. See ibid , p. 119.

[28]Ibid., p. 120.

TABLE 10.1   Volume of Tax-Exempt State and Local Bonds, by Type of Activity: Selected Years, 1970–1985 (billions of dollars)

TYPE	1970	1976	1979	1982	1985
Total volume	18.1	36.5	48.7	87.5	218.2
Total public	17.2	24.1	21.9	39.8	101.8
Education	5.0	4.9	4.6	4.7	N/A
Transportation	3.2	3.0	2.4	6.2	N/A
Water & sewer	2.2	3.0	3.1	5.0	N/A
Public power	1.1	2.7	3.5	7.1	N/A
Other public	5.7	10.5	8.3	16.8	N/A
Total private	.8	9.2	25.6	43.4	116.4
Housing	.7	3.4	12.4	14.3	38.1
Industrial	.1	1.5	7.1	12.7	29.6
Pollution	—	1.9	2.1	5.3	7.4
Hospitals	—	2.3	3.4	9.5	37.3
Student loans	—	.1	.6	1.6	4.0
Refundings	.1	3.2	1.2	4.3	N/A

N/A = not available.
Sources: Daphne A. Kenyon, "Private Activity Tax-Exempt Bond Volume in 1985: Preliminary Data" (Washington, DC: U.S. Department of the Treasury, Office of Tax Analysis, July 15, 1986); and Susannah E. Calkins, "Tax-Exempt Bonds," in U.S. Advisory Commission on Intergovernmental Relations, *Strengthening the Federal Revenue System* (Washington, DC: U.S. Government Printing Office, 1984), p. 117.

invest were biased in favor of the activities supported by the bonds.[29] Moreover, much of the bond's value ended up in the hands of wealthy investors and those who administered the bond sale. It was estimated that the revenue loss to the national treasury from these bonds was between 33 and 50 percent higher than the benefits received by the borrower.[30]

Many in Congress also began to be concerned over the bonds' rising cost to the national treasury. To help keep costs down, restrictions were placed on the issuance of bonds to subsidize home mortgages in 1980, and the tax-exempt status of industrial development bonds was eliminated in 1982 if more than 25 percent of their proceeds were used for automobile sales or service, recreation or entertainment facilities, or food and retail establishments.[31]

State and local lobbyists were not surprised when the Treasury Department recommended, and President Reagan subsequently proposed, the elimination of the tax-exempt status of state and local bonds used for nontraditional, governmental purposes in his tax reform message to Con-

[29]Office of the President of the United States, *The President's Tax Proposals to the Congress for Fairness, Growth, and Simplicity*, p. 283.
[30]Ibid.
[31]Ibid., p. 119.

gress in 1986. Many state and local officials had already indicated that they were willing to negotiate on tax-exempt bonds. Some state and local officials viewed the loss of bonds used for nontraditional purposes (a subsidy value of $3 billion annually) as a small price to pay for the promised economic expansion that would follow the lowering of national marginal income tax rates. Others recognized that as the total volume of tax-exempt bonds increased as a result of the increasing use of nontraditional bonds, investors found tax-exempt bonds easier to get. Since they were easier to get, investors were able to negotiate a higher rate of return. This resulted in an overall increase in the cost of borrowing for all state and local activities. Thus, many state and local officials believed that a limitation on the volume of private purpose bonds would probably cause the overall cost of borrowing for traditional bonds to fall.

State and local lobby organizations recognized that their constituencies were generally willing to compromise on this issue, but were concerned by the lack of precision in the administration's proposal. It did list bonds used for student loans, mortgage subsidies, and industrial development as being no longer eligible for tax exemption. But it also indicated that bonds would lose their tax exempt status if more than 1 percent of the proceeds were used directly or indirectly by any entity other than a state or local government.[32] State and local lobby organizations argued that this provision would cause many state and local bonds used to finance traditional governmental purposes to lose their tax-exempt status.

The House Ways and Means Committee decided to compromise on the tax exemption of state and local bonds. Instead of eliminating the tax-exempt status of all bonds used for nontraditional or private purposes, the committee voted to eliminate the tax exemption for some of them and placed a volume cap on many of the remaining private-purpose bonds.[33] It also decided to relax the Reagan administration's 1 percent rule for losing tax-exempt status to 10 percent.[34]

The Ways and Means Committee's bill (H.R. 3838) was approved by

[32]Frank Shafroth, "The Reagan Tax Proposals," *Nation's Cities Weekly* (June 3, 1985):2.

[33]Bonds used to finance sports facilities, convention centers, parking lots, air or water pollution control activities, and hotels and retail outlets attached to airports lost their tax-exempt status. Bonds used for other private purposes, such as home mortgage subsidies, multifamily housing construction projects, and student loans, retained their tax-exempt status. The committee restricted existing annual state volume caps on bonds used for student loans, small issue industrial development, and single family mortgages by including them in total volume caps placed on bonds used for multifamily rental housing, mass commuting facilities, qualified veterans' mortgages, and nonprofit colleges and hospitals. The new cap was set at the greater of $200 million per state or $175 per state resident in 1986 and 1987, and $125 per state resident after that. See W. John Moore, "A Break for Bonds," *National Journal* (May 17, 1986): 1200.

[34]For other House Ways and Means action on bonds see "Major Provisions of Ways and Means Tax Bill," Congressional Quarterly, *Weekly Report* (November 30, 1985):2495; and James L. Rowe, Jr., "For Municipal Bond Issuers, the House Tax Bill Is Already Law," *Washington Post*, Weekly Edition (March 10, 1986):19.

the House and sent to the Senate ior consideration on December 17, 1985.[35] State and local lobby organizations were not pleased with the House's treatment of state and local bonds. They turned to Senate Finance Committee member David Durenberger (R-MN) for help. A long time member of the U.S. Advisory Commission on Intergovernmental Relations and the chairman of the Senate Governmental Affairs Committee's Subcommittee on Intergovernmental Relations, he not only knew the leaders of the state and local lobbies but also was very sympathetic to their needs and interests.

Durenberger subsequently led a successful fight against a proposal by Finance Committee Chairman Robert Packwood to subject all state and local bonds, including ones already purchased, to a proposed 20 percent alternative minimum income tax. Packwood had argued that his proposal would significantly increase the progressivity of the tax plan as nearly 80 percent of all tax-free bonds were held by individuals with incomes exceeding $100,000. News of Packwood's proposal brought the local bond market to a complete halt. Faced with a barrage of criticism from bond issuers, buyers, and dealers, the Senate Finance Committee voted 19–0 to subject only bonds issued after January 1, 1987, to the proposed national minimum income tax.

After this victory, Durenberger drafted a proposal to preserve the tax-exempt status of most state and local bonds used for private purposes. Packwood had recommended the enactment of a state-by-state volume cap for a limited number of private-purpose bonds. Even though his proposal would have had a relatively small impact on the volume of tax-exempt bonds and the revenue collected by the national government, the Finance Committee approved Durenberger's proposal on April 17, 1986.

Following this action, Packwood announced a suspension of the committee's markup on the tax reform bill. He was convinced that the committee's rejection of his proposal concerning state and local tax-exempt bonds was a clear signal that it was not going to accept his proposal on the deductibility of state and local taxes. This meant that the Finance Committee was not going to raise enough revenue to keep the proposal revenue neutral and to pay for the added tax incentives for business. It looked like the tax reform movement was dead.

Three weeks later, following a series of heated discussions behind closed doors, Senator Packwood announced to a stunned Senate that the Finance Committee had agreed to a tax reform bill. He was able to save the bill by proposing the elimination of nearly all tax expenditures used by individuals and using most of the saved revenue to slash the four marginal

---

[35]Anticipating the national government's restrictions on state and local tax exempt bonds, states and localities rushed to issue, as many bonds as possible in 1985. Total state and local bonds' volume was $93.4 billion in 1983, $101.9 billion in 1984, and $218.2 billion in 1985. See Frank Shafroth, "The Reagan Tax Proposals"; and Daphne Kenyon, "Private Activity Tax-Exempt Bond Volume in 1985: Preliminary Data," p. 5.

income tax rates in the House bill (15, 25, 35 and 38 percent) to just two rates of 15 and 27 percent. Among the few tax expenditures remaining for individuals would be the tax exemption of nearly all state and local bonds and the deductibility of state and local income, real estate property, and personal property taxes.[36] State and local sales taxes would no longer be eligible for deduction. Packwood also used some of the saved revenue to increase the value of depreciation for business machinery and equipment.

The committee approved the plan unanimously, 20–0. Liberals liked the proposal because it increased the standard deduction and personal exemption so much that it would eliminate millions of the working poor from the tax rolls. Conservatives liked the proposal because it significantly reduced the top marginal tax rate for individuals to 27 percent and reduced the value of business tax expenditures by approximately $20 billion annually, as opposed to the House bill, which would cut those tax expenditures by approximately $28 billion annually.[37]

State and local officials and lobbyists were delighted with the Finance Committee's bond decisions. Bond experts predicted that state and local bonds would thrive under the committee's proposal, even with a reduction in the top marginal tax rate to 27 percent, because almost every other tax shelter for individuals would be eliminated.[38] State and local officials and lobbyists were also relatively pleased with the committee's decision concerning the deductibility of state and local taxes. They were confident that the House would insist on keeping the deductibility of all state and local taxes. They also knew that they would have a good chance of saving the sales tax deduction on the Senate floor. They organized themselves into the Coalition Against Double Taxation and, with the support of Senators from the 11 states that rely on the sales tax for a large portion of their state revenue, began a massive lobbying effort to restore the deduction.

It is difficult to determine precisely why the Senate Finance Committee decided to eliminate the deductibility of state and local sales taxes because its negotiations were held behind closed doors. However, discussions with several representatives of state and local public interest groups and analysts at the U.S. Treasury Department indicated that the sales tax

---

[36]W. John Moore, "A Break for Bonds," pp. 1193, 1194. The House and the Senate bills would eliminate the tax exemption of bonds used to finance the construction of sports facilities, convention centers, parking lots, and retail outlets attached to airports. The Senate bill would keep the tax exemption for bonds used to construct hazardous-waste facilities and neighborhood heating plants. It also retained the House's volume cap on private-purpose bonds, but added multifamily housing bonds to the list of bonds exempt from the cap. The Senate bill also broadened the definition of a private-purpose bond. The 10 percent private use threshold in the House bill was changed to 25 percent. The Senate bill, unlike the House bill, exempted interest from state and local bonds from the bill's proposed minimum income tax on individuals.

[37]Timothy B. Clark and Richard E. Cohen, "Tax Reform Locomotive," *National Journal* (May 31, 1986):1300.

[38]W. John Moore, "A Break for Bonds," p. 1200.

was vulnerable because (1) Senator Packwood represents Oregon, which does not have a sales tax; (2) it ran counter to the idea of simplifying the national government's income tax forms, because under existing law it was difficult for individuals to deduct sales taxes—one either had to look up the permissible sales tax deduction on a relatively complicated table supplied in the 1040 income tax form or had to keep records of all purchases during the year; (3) many Democrats did not like the sales tax because it is more regressive than income taxes; and (4) the committee needed to raise additional revenue to keep the bill revenue neutral because it had already decided to provide business with more tax subsidies than had been provided by the House.

On June 20, 1986, the Coalition Against Double Taxation was able to convince the full Senate to agree to amend the Finance Committee's tax bill to allow a partial restoration of the sales tax deduction. The amendment allowed taxpayers to deduct 60 percent of the amount by which their state sales tax payments exceeded their state income tax payments. Although this fell short of the Coalition's desire to restore the full sales tax deduction, it was one of the very few amendments added to the Finance Committee's tax reform bill.[39]

The nation's attention was now focused on the House-Senate conference committee, which commenced work in July 1986. It was now apparent that the national government's income tax code would undergo significant revision. Taxpayers across the land tried to figure out if they would be better off or worse off under the House or the Senate version of the bill. Progress in the conference committee however, was slow. The House and Senate conferees were bitterly divided, especially over business tax expenditures. The House bill would have increased business taxes by nearly $140 billion over FYs 1986–1991, while the Senate bill would have increased business taxes by $100 billion over those years. The Republican Senate argued that its bill's $100 billion increase in business taxes (to pay for individual marginal income tax rate reductions) was as high as it was willing to go.[40]

The conferees also differed on the extent of tax relief offered to middle-income taxpayers. The House bill retained a number of tax expenditures used by middle-income taxpayers that had been eliminated or significantly reduced in value by the Senate, including the deductibility of state and local sales taxes. It was estimated that it would cost nearly $20 billion to reconcile the House and Senate bills' differing impacts on taxpayers earning less than $50,000 annually.

---

[39]Tom Redburn, "Senate Adopts Partial Tax Deduction for States Sales," *Los Angeles Times*, June 20, 1986, pp. 1, 15.

[40]Eileen Shanahan, "Conferees Progress Slowly Toward Tax Bill Compromise," Congressional Quarterly, *Weekly Report* (August 9, 1986):1782.

Progress in the conference committee stalled as Senators from oil-producing states threatened to filibuster any tax reform bill that increased taxes on the oil industry. The price of oil at that time was falling and many independent oil riggers were going bankrupt. As a result, it became increasingly difficult for the House conferees to find any tax expenditures to cut so that politically popular tax expenditures (such as individual retirement accounts and state sales tax deductions) that had been reduced in value by the Senate could be fully restored. As the deadlock dragged on, the tax reform bill's fate became subject to the calendar. The 99th Congress was due to recess in late August to prepare for the 1986 congressional elections. If the tax reform bill was not ready for action soon, it would die.

Furious negotiations ensued behind closed doors. On August 16, 1986, the House-Senate conference committee announced that it had reached an agreement. Starting in 1988, the national government's 15 individual income tax rates would be reduced to just 2. The top marginal income tax rate would be reduced from 50 percent to 28 percent of adjusted gross income (AGI). The other marginal income tax rate, which would apply to approximately 80 percent of all taxpayers, would be 15 percent of AGI. In addition, the top corporate income tax rate would be reduced from 46 percent to 34 percent of AGI. To achieve this dramatic reduction in marginal income tax rates, dozens of tax expenditures were eliminated entirely and dozens more were reduced in value.

To the surprise of state and local officials, the final compromise package included the elimination of the deductibility of state and local sales taxes. Moreover, it narrowed the definition of a public-purpose bond (no more than 10 percent of the proceeds can benefit a private company or developer), immediately eliminated several types of bonds available for tax-exempt status (pollution control equipment, sports and convention facilities, parking facilities, and industrial parks), scheduled the elimination of the tax-exempt status of two other types of bonds in future years (single-family mortgage on December 31, 1988, and small-issue industrial development bonds on December 31, 1989), tightened guidelines for using tax-exempt bonds for low-income multifamily housing projects, and placed a $250 million or $75 per capita cap on the volume of state tax-exempt bonds that are used for nontraditional purposes (single-family mortgages, multifamily housing, student loans, mass transportation, electricity and gas supply, and hazardous-waste facilities) in 1987. The state volume cap for bonds used to finance these nontraditional purposes was cut to $150 million or $50 per capita for 1988 and beyond.[41]

---

[41]Lawrence J. Hass, "Radical Alteration of Muni Market Seen if Tax Bill Is Enacted," *The Bond Buyer* (August 19, 1986): 1, 24; and Lawrence J. Hass, "Ready for Assessment: The Final Tax Bill," *Credit Markets* (August 25, 1986): 1, 36.

CONCLUSIONS

The Tax Reform Act of 1986 will have many anticipated and, no doubt, unanticipated impacts on state and local governments in the years to come. The direct impact of the elimination of the state and local sales tax deduction and the restrictions placed on state and local bonds are somewhat easier to gauge. States with a relatively high reliance on the sales tax for revenue (such as Louisiana, Nevada, Tennessee, Washington, and Wyoming) will experience some additional pressure from their taxpayers for a shift in state and local taxing mechanisms or a reduction in state and local taxes.[42] States that have traditionally floated large volumes of tax-exempt bonds for nontraditional purposes (such as Arizona, California, Florida, Illinois, Massachusetts, New York, Pennsylvania, and Texas) are going to have to raise taxes or stop providing those services.[43]

Congress' restrictions on nontraditional bonds had an immediate impact on the municipal bond market. The total volume of state and local tax-exempt bonds fell from $218 billion in 1985 to $147 billion in 1986 and to $100 billion in 1987. The largest drops, as expected, were for bonds used for private or nontraditional purposes. Tax-exempt bonds to finance multifamily housing for low-income individuals, for example, dropped from $20 billion in 1985 to $2.8 billion in 1987.[44]

Another direct impact of the new tax law was a revenue windfall for 33 states. They experienced a $6.3 billion increase in state income tax collections in 1987 because their definitions of adjusted gross income are tied to the national government's definition of taxable income.[45] Most taxpayers experienced an increase in the amount of their taxable income because the national government reduced both the number of available tax expenditures and the value of many of the remaining ones. These 33 states were faced with the choice of returning the windfall to taxpayers by reducing state marginal income tax rates or increasing state standard deductions or keeping the money to help fund state services. Fifteen states chose to keep all of the windfall, 13 states returned all of it to state taxpayers, and 5

---

[42]Some analysts have stated that the national government's elimination of the deductibility of state and local sales taxes may lead to the emergence of a more balanced and equitable state tax system. They argue that the sales tax, which is employed by 45 states and accounts for approximately 36 percent total state tax revenue, is a regressive tax that ought to be avoided. The income tax, on the other hand, which is used by 40 states and accounts for only 26 percent of total state tax revenue, is a progressive tax that ought to be encouraged. See Neal R. Peirce, "Sales Tax to Stay Despite Federal Tax Reform," *National Journal* (May 24, 1986):1276.

[43]U.S. Advisory Commission on Intergovernmental Relations, *Strengthening the Federal Revenue System: Implications for State and Local Taxing and Borrowing* (Washington, DC: U.S. Government Printing Office, 1984), p. 124.

[44]W. John Moore, "Bond Voyage," *National Journal* (January 23, 1988):189.

[45]W. John Moore, "Tax Reform Ripples," *National Journal* (September 12, 1987):2269.

states kept part of the windfall and rebated some of it to its taxpayers.[46]

Another impact of all of these changes in the states' income taxing systems was the emergence of more progressive taxing systems. Although most states still rely on regressive sales, excise, and severance taxes for the bulk of their revenue, 11 that imposed income taxes on poor families before national tax reform no longer do so.[47]

Finally, the fight over national tax reform once again indicated that the new macroeconomic theory of intergovernmental relations was having an impact on national policy. President Reagan indicated in the January 1985 meeting with state and local leaders that he was sympathetic to their desire to preserve the deductibility of state and local taxes because it strengthened federalism. However, after comparing its value to federalism with its value in reducing marginal income tax rates and spurring economic growth, federalism lost out to economic considerations.

[46]States keeping all of the windfall in 1987 were Alabama, Arkansas, Idaho, Illinois, Indiana, Kansas, Kentucky, Louisiana, Mississippi, Missouri, Montana, New Mexico, North Carolina, Oklahoma, and Utah. States returning all of the windfall were Arizona, California, Connecticut, Georgia, Hawaii, Maine, Massachusetts, Minnesota, New York, Ohio, Virginia, West Virginia and Wisconsin. States that kept part of the windfall and rebated part of it were Colorado, Delaware, Iowa, Maryland, and Oregon. See Ibid., p. 2271. States without income taxes and those not using the national government's definition of adjusted gross income did not experience a revenue windfall.

[47]Ibid., p. 2273.

CHAPTER 11

Conclusions

Three objectives were cited at the outset of this book: to examine ten important national intergovernmental programs in the context of a five-part sequential policymaking process, to analyze the emergence and influence of the macroeconomic theory of intergovernmental relations, and to provide enough information about these ten programs to help the reader determine which of the three leading prescriptive theories of intergovernmental relations theories is best. The following discussion is organized around these three objectives.

WHY DID THE NATIONAL GOVERNMENT PUT THESE TEN PROGRAMS ON THE PUBLIC AGENDA IN THE FIRST PLACE?

The enactment of all eight of the national grants-in-aid spending programs and both of the national tax expenditure items examined in this book were justified by proponents on the basis of one or more of the seven traditional arguments justifying national assistance for intergovernmental programs (see Introduction). The three most important and most used justifications employed were that the program fostered a national goal, that it perfected the imperfections in the economic marketplace brought about by the presence of economic spillovers (or externalities), and that it enhanced the fiscal capacity of state and local governments to attain either their own or the national government's goals. For example, all eight of the spending programs and both of the tax expenditures fostered a specific national goal. Medicaid, AFDC, Food Stamps, Job Training Partnership, and Compensatory Education for the Disadvantaged all reinforced the national government's commitment to fostering equal economic opportunity for the poor. Medicaid, AFDC, and Food Stamps reinforced this commitment directly through the provision of cash assistance or in-kind services. Job Training Partnership and Compensatory Education for the Disadvantaged reinforced this commitment indirectly by helping the poor obtain the skills necessary to compete in the private job market.

Federal Aid to Highways and Wastewater Treatment Construction Grants were designed to promote the national government's commitment to economic development and clean water, respectively. CDBG was designed to foster the national government's commitment to improve the nation's housing condition and the urban living environment. The deductibility of state and local taxes fostered equity in the national income tax code for both individuals and businesses. The tax-exempt status of state and local bonds for both traditional and nontraditional governmental services was designed to promote expenditures in those areas deemed of national interest. In addition, the Federal Aid to Highways and Wastewater Treatment Construction Grants programs were justified on the grounds that they helped to compensate for the propensity of state and local governments to underfund highway and wastewater construction projects because these activities are subject to economic spillovers.

Finally, all ten of these programs were designed to enhance, at least to some extent, the fiscal capacity of state and local governments to achieve either their own or the national government's goals. Medicaid, AFDC, and CDBG, for example, all have direct factors in their allotment mechanisms that are tied to the states' or localities' fiscal capacity.

WHAT WERE THE IDEOLOGICAL, POLITICAL, AND ECONOMIC FORCES THAT SHAPED THE FORMATION AND ADOPTION OF THESE TEN INTERGOVERNMENTAL PROGRAMS' ADMINISTRATIVE STRUCTURES, FINANCING MECHANISMS, AND PROGRAMMATIC OBJECTIVES?

Ideological Factors

Although thousands of bills to create various programs are introduced in Congress every year, most of them die in committee. Programs need strong and determined political support to survive in the corridors of Congress, the White House, and the bureaucracy. The initial political support for all of these programs examined in this book came from economic and social liberals (usually Democrats), as opposed to economic and social conservatives (usually Republicans).[1] In all of the programs examined, liberals demonstrated a broader vision of the national government's role in

[1]Republicans did initiate the reforms that led to the conversion of categorical grants into CDBG and the relaxation of stringent regulations in Chapter 1 and JTPA, but Democrats were primarily responsible for initiating the national government's role in promoting community development, education for the disadvantaged, and job training efforts.

promoting national goals than did conservatives.[2] They also expressed more firmly their belief in the necessity of enhancing the fiscal capacity of state and local governments to achieve minimum levels of governmental services.

Moreover, although both liberals and conservatives supported a national presence in programs when economic spillovers were involved, liberals generally advocated a strong role for the national government, while conservatives generally advocated a relatively minor role. Conservatives not only opposed the enactment of all of the spending programs examined in this book but repeatedly advocated budget restraint for all of them after they were adopted. They also sought the elimination or modification of tax-exempt bonds and the deductibility of state and local taxes.

These differences between liberals and conservatives have historically been derived from their fundamentally different cognitive understanding of liberty. Conservatives generally tend to view liberty as the freedom from governmental restraints on individual behavior. In their view, the best government is often the least government. Liberals, on the other hand, tend to view liberty as the freedom from restraints imposed by other individuals or economic and social forces. In their view, the best government is often an active government that uses its powers to protect individuals from exploitation by other institutions and authority figures such as corporations, unions, landlords, and other governmental bodies.[3]

Political Factors

The liberals' strong influence in the Democratic party, coupled with that party's status as the majority party in the House of Representatives throughout the post-World War II era and its usual position as the majority party in the Senate, was an important political factor that led to the adoption of the eight intergovernmental spending programs examined in this book and to the expansion of the national government's role in domestic governance throughout the postwar period. The political credit received by individual congressmen for creating specific categorical grants-in-aid programs also played a role. When asked by constituents what he had done for them lately, the response was that he had created a program to address perceived problems: to clean up the water, Congress created the Waste-

---

[2]At the time these programs were conceived, the current need (as discussed in the Introduction) to divide liberals and conservatives into economic and social subclassifications did not exist. Most liberals believed in Keynesian economics and the need for a strong national presence in promoting social and racial equality. Most conservatives believed in classical, laissez-faire economics and did not believe that the national government should infringe on the rights of the states and localities to determine their own policies concerning social and racial equality.

[3]James MacGregor Burns, J. W. Peltason, and Thomas E. Cronin, *Government by the People*, 13th ed. (Englewood Cliffs, NJ: Prentice-Hall, Inc., 1987), pp. 5–7.

water Treatment Construction Grants program; to combat poverty, Food Stamps and AFDC; and so on.

The belief, shared by most Democrats, that state and local governments were either fiscally unable or politically unwilling to assist minorities and the poor was also an important political factor contributing to the adoption of intergovernmental programs that provide assistance to these groups. Collectively, these political factors help to explain why nearly all intergovernmental grants created between World War II and 1980 were categorical grants and had financing mechanisms that encouraged state and local participation by paying for at least half of total program costs.[4]

Another important political factor that helps to explain why these programs were adopted was the fiscal inability and political paralysis that prevented many state and local governments from responding adequately to the economic calamity of the Great Depression and the social unheavals surrounding the civil rights and environmental movements during the 1960s. These historical events provided the crisis atmosphere that enabled liberals to push through AFDC, Food Stamps, Medicaid, Compensatory Education for the Disadvantaged, and Wastewater Treatment Construction Grants in the first place. Once these and other intergovernmental programs examined were started, each program's bureaucracy and its clientele interest groups (including state and local officials and industries and individuals receiving benefits from the programs) worked with supportive congressional members to preserve, protect, and defend the program against budgetary restrictions and consolidation throughout the postwar period. Clientele interest groups strongly opposed budgetary restrictions and grant consolidation (if it included budget cuts) because they viewed these efforts as threats to the continued national support for programs that provided them subsidies. These actions were influenced more by rational considerations of what they got out of the program than by ideological concerns.[5]

Economic Factors

The strength of the national economy and the relatively strong fiscal position of the national government during the 1945–1975 era made spending on intergovernmental grants a relatively painless task for liberals.

[4]U.S. Advisory Commission on Intergovernmental Relations, *Categorical Grants: Their Role and Design* (Washington, DC: U.S. Government Printing Office, 1978), pp. 61–90. The use of numerous congressional committees, segregated by subject area, was another factor that helped to account for Congress' tendency to rely on categorical grants. A decentralized decision-making process encouraged Congress to create intergovernmental programs that could be dealt with by individual committees. Consolidating categorical grants into block grants ran the risk of overlapping committee jurisdictions and opening up battles among committees for control over, and political credit for, the program.

[5]Ibid., p. 63. For a discussion of intergovernmental gamesmanship, see Deil S. Wright, *Understanding Intergovernmental Relations* 3rd ed. (Pacific Grove, CA: Brooks/Cole Publishing Co., 1988),pp. 79, 91–94, Appendix B.

They had at their disposal the economic resources to fulfill their ideological desire to help create a more equal society. Moreover, Keynesian economics suggested that spending on these programs would enhance national economic performance. As a result, it made perfect sense for them to continually fight for increased budgets for these programs, to encourage states and localities to participate in them by offering to pay for most of their costs, to package them as categorical grants to insist on stringent administrative conditions to ensure that states and localities spent the funds in a correct manner, and to resist efforts to consolidate them into block grants where states and localities would have an opportunity to choose their own funding priorities that could or could not reflect the liberals' priorities.

The national economy and the fiscal position of the national government have not fared particularly well since 1975. Economic competition from abroad, the change from an industry-based to a service-based economy, and dependence on foreign oil all contributed to a sluggish national economy. Many, including those who believed in Keynesian economics, blamed the national government's growing deficit for the economic downturn. In an attempt to reduce the national government's annual deficit, the Carter administration subjected all governmental programs, including intergovernmental grants-in-aid programs, to increased budgetary scrutiny during the late 1970s; and the Reagan administration targeted all domestic spending programs, particularly intergovernmental programs, for significant budgetary reductions during the 1980s. Despite the protests of clientele interest groups, total funding for national intergovernmental grants-in-aid leveled off during the mid-1980s at the $100 to $110 billion level. As a percentage of state and local expenditures, national intergovernmental expenditures peaked at 26 percent in 1978 and have continued to fall throughout the 1980s.[6]

during the 1980s, the national government's deficit is expected to pass the $3 trillion mark in the early 1990s. As the nation's population and life expectancy continue to increase, expenditures on entitlement programs (social security, Medicare, and others) will continue to rise and consume an increasingly large share of the national budget. Interest payments on the deficit (approaching $200 billion annually) will consume an increasingly high share of the budget. Assuming that defense expenditures will retain their high priority, both social and economic liberals are going to find it increasingly difficult to justify their demands for more intergovernmental expenditures. They are also going to be pressured to demonstrate that these programs are cost effective and worth keeping.

---

[6]John Shannon, "Federal and State-Local Spenders Go Their Separate Ways," in *American Intergovernmental Relations Today: Perspectives and Controversies*, ed. Robert Jay Dilger (Englewood Cliffs, N.J.: Prentice-Hall, Inc., 1986), p. 169–183.

DOES THE EXISTING LITERATURE INDICATE THAT
NATIONAL INTERGOVERNMENTAL PROGRAMS ARE COST
EFFECTIVE AND WORTH KEEPING?

Just as beauty is in the eye of the beholder, so the success or failure of the intergovernmental programs examined in this book is largely determined by the values and expectations of the person evaluating them. Although economic and social liberals did find faults in all of the programs examined in this book, they generally agreed that on the whole the programs were successful. Medicaid has saved thousands of lives by providing the poor with access to emergency medical assistance, prolonged the life of countless others by providing the poor with access to regular medical care, and saved millions of young families from having to exhaust their savings to pay for their parents' medical bills. AFDC, with all of its problems, has provided the most vulnerable members of our society with at least a subsistence income. It has also served to attenuate urban unrest. Food Stamps has significantly reduced hunger in America. The Job Training Partnership program has enabled thousands of poor people to gain the skills necessary to become productive members of society and to escape the misery of poverty. Compensatory Education for the Disadvantaged has raised the academic skills of millions of economically disadvantaged children as determined by standardized test scores.

Federal Aid to Highways has accelerated economic development throughout the nation. Community Development Block Grants has rejuvenated hundreds of low-income neighborhoods and dozens of downtown business centers. The Wastewater Treatment Construction Grants program has significantly reduced the pollution in the nation's waterways. The deductibility of state and local taxes has increased the equity of the national income tax system and enhanced the ability of state and local governments to provide needed governmental services. The tax-exempt status of state and local bonds has enhanced the fiscal capacity of state and local governments, which has made it easier for them to provide needed governmental services.

Many social and economic conservatives disagree. In their view, the benefits provided by these programs are outweighed by their costs. The three income-maintenance programs examined in this book (Medicaid, AFDC, and Food Stamps), for example, provide the poor with little incentive to work and cost too much, given the size of the national government's cumulative debt (nearly $3 trillion) and its annual deficits. Recent regulatory changes in the Job Training Partnership and Compensatory Education for the Disadvantaged programs have significantly improved them, but the high cost of providing the poor with skills necessary to compete in the private sector or to bring them up to the educational achievement of the average student is prohibitive. It would be better to eliminate these programs, reduce national spending levels, lower taxes, and let the private sector and state and local governments create their own training and education programs for the poor.

Now that the interstate highway system is nearing completion, it's time to close the Highway Trust Fund and to turn those tax resources and the responsibility for highways back to the states and localities. The regulatory relief offered to localities in the Community Development Block Grant program has enabled localities to use the funds for needed economic development projects, but the necessity to balance the national government's budget requires that this program be terminated. The Wastewater Treatment Construction Grants program has a noble cause and has been responsible for significant advances against water pollution. However, the need to balance the national government's budget requires that this program be terminated as well. Let the people in each locality decide for themselves if they are willing to pay the cost of constructing a wastewater treatment plant to clean up their local water supply. Finally, the deductibility of state and local taxes, and the tax-exempt status of state and local bonds used for nontraditional purposes, must be curtailed to promote a taxing system that is more conducive to economic growth.

WHAT DEMANDS FOR REFORM, IF ANY, HAVE RESULTED FROM EVALUATIVE STUDIES OF THE PROGRAM'S PERFORMANCE?

The arguments of lobbyists, academics, and politicians concerning the future of each of the ten programs featured in this book have been examined in each of the preceding chapters. The information provided by the Brookings Institution's Monitoring Studies Group, for example, was very influential in determining the outcome of CDBG's allocation formula, and the many studies conducted by both academics and the Department of Education concerning the Compensatory Education for the Disadvantaged program played an important role in the formation of what became the Chapter 1 program. It would be redundant to reiterate all that has been written within these chapters about the role of evaluative studies in the policymaking process, but it is important to note that despite all of the studies and reports written about these intergovernmental programs, there still were very strong disagreements among decision makers concerning how each of these programs should be structured, financed, and administered.

There were also strong disagreements over whether some of the programs should exist at all. These disagreements were primarily derived from strong ideological differences on the part of decision makers concerning the proper role of the national government in domestic policy, from different attitudes concerning the necessity of balancing the national government's budget, and from conflicting views concerning whether defense or domestic programs should shoulder the brunt of budget reductions to achieve a more balanced national budget.

This is not meant to diminish the importance of these evaluative studies. They do influence the structure and direction of intergovernmental programs. It must be remembered, however, that politicians base their decisions on many inputs, including the views of their constituencies, their fellow congressmen, their party's leadership and ranking committee members, interest groups, and their staff.[7]

THE MACROECONOMIC THEORY OF INTERGOVERNMENTAL RELATIONS

When Ronald Reagan became president of the United States in 1981, it was assumed that his stated support for states' rights would make federalism a central component of his administration's domestic agenda. The Reagan administration's efforts to create additional block grants in 1981, to return governmental responsibility to the states in the 1982 New Federalism swap proposal, and its efforts to reduce administrative rules and regulations throughout its two terms in office seemed to confirm its commitment to revitalizing the states' role in American federalism. However, when federalism goals conflicted with the competing goals of reducing the national government's budget deficit, deregulating the private sector, or advancing the conservative social agenda, federalism's goals did not prevail.[8]

The Reagan administration not only targeted categorical grants for funding reductions but also overrode state and local interests by also proposing funding reductions for most block grants and the now terminated general revenue-sharing program. It also overrode the interests of state and local governments when it proposed the elimination of the deductibility of state and local taxes and the tax-exempt status of state and local bonds used for nontraditional purposes, preempted state laws regulating double-trailer trucks, overrode state objections to increased offshore oil drilling and expanded use of nuclear power, advocated "workfare" requirements and a nationally mandated minimum drinking age, and filed suit against localities that sought to retain aggressive affirmative action hiring programs.[9]

[7]John W. Kingdon, *Congressmen's Voting Decisions*, 2nd ed. (New York: Harper & Row, 1981), pp. 3–224.

[8]Timothy J. Conlan, "Federalism and Competing Values in the Reagan Administration," *Publius: The Journal of Federalism* 16 (Winter 1986):30.

[9]Ibid.

All of these decisions, plus the proposed funding reductions and devolution plans examined in this book, are consistent with the macroeconomic theory of intergovernmental relations. The Reagan administration overruled the direct interests of state and local governments whenever it perceived that those interests were in conflict with its commitment to the supply-side theory of economics, which stresses the need for a balanced national budget and the lowest possible level of governmental taxes and spending to foster national economic growth. In theory, the Reagan administration believed that it was acting in the long-term interests of state and local governments when it proposed budget reductions for national intergovernmental programs.

According to the supply-side theory of economics, cutting national taxes and balancing the national budget will generate so many new jobs for the poor that most nationally financed, intergovernmental programs designed to provide economic support for individuals (such as Medicaid, AFDC, and Food Stamps) will become unnecessary. In addition, national economic growth will provide states and localities with an expanded tax base as businesses generate taxable profits and workers' taxable incomes increase. This, in turn, will make most national intergovernmental programs designed to help states and localities build public works projects (such as highways, bridges and wastewater treatment plants) unnecessary because state and local governments will no longer have relatively anemic fiscal capacities.

Moreover, the expansion of state and local tax bases will reduce the need for the national government to finance intergovernmental programs to correct for the tendency of state and local governments to underfund governmental services with economic spillovers. States and localities will be in a much stronger fiscal position to compensate for those economic spillovers without national government support.

It needs to be said that the Reagan administration and other economic conservatives have never articulated allegiance to a macroeconomic theory of intergovernmental relations. Critics of the administration may even argue that it did not possess the intellectual underpinnings to follow any theoretical guidelines of its decision-making process. Instead, they would suggest that the Reagan administration reacted to issues as they arose, one by one, and did not make an effort to relate one decision to another in a coherent, theoretical fashion. The evidence suggests, however, that the Reagan administration did follow a fairly consistent pattern in its decisions on domestic priorities.[10]

The macroeconomic theory of intergovernmental relations presents some very serious questions for the future of intergovernmental relations. Although it is currently embraced only by economic conservatives, and

[10]Ibid.

they remain in the minority, it creates an entirely new challenge to the seven basic theoretical justifications for intergovernmental relations. Unless the national government's budgetary difficulties disappear, the perceived need to balance the budget makes all intergovernmental programs vulnerable to budgetary reductions. The introduction of the macroeconomic theory of intergovernmental relations into the budgetary debate will weaken the position of intergovernmental programs when decisions are made concerning which domestic programs are eliminated or have their budgets reduced and which ones survive or experience budget increases.

WHO IS RIGHT: ELAZAR, WALKER OR ANTON/NATHAN?

The decision concerning whether Elazar's, Walker's, or Anton and Nathan's prescriptive theory of intergovernmental relations is the right one depends largely on one's values. All three theories were advanced by authors who are thoroughly familiar with the operations and structures of national intergovernmental programs and regulations, yet all three reach vastly different conclusions concerning the appropriate role of the national government in determining domestic policy.

Elazar concludes that the national government has overstepped the governmental boundaries established by the framers when they wrote the Constitution. He advocates national program devolution to the states and localities and significant regulatory reforms for programs that remain intergovernmental as a means to restore American federalism.

Walker does not believe that the national government has overstepped the boundaries established by the framers but is concerned that it has taken on too many responsibilities. He suggests that the national government should remain involved in programs that primarily involve national goals, such as helping the poor gain equal economic and social opportunities through Medicaid, AFDC, and Food Stamps, but should turn responsibility for programs that have primarily state or local impacts, such as CDBG, over to the states and localities.

Anton and Nathan agree with Walker that the national government has not overstepped the governmental boundaries established by the framers, but disagree concerning the need for the national government to devolve programs to the states and localities. In their view, the national government's intergovernmental programs have been, on balance, successful in achieving national goals, providing many opportunities for state and local input and influence on decision making, correcting for economic spillover impacts on state and local spending decisions, and enhancing the fiscal capacity of states and localities so that they are better able to accomplish both their own goals and the goals of the national government.

Instead of program turnbacks, they advocate more moderate reforms to improve governmental performance, such as regulatory changes to target resources to states, localities, and individuals having the greatest objective need for national financial assistance.

We have seen in this book how liberals and conservatives, holding different values, have reached different conclusions concerning how specific intergovernmental issues should be structured, financed, and administered. Economic and social liberals tended to emphasize the need for the national government to intervene in the affairs of state and local governments to protect minorities and the politically vulnerable, and to foster their vision of the national good. Economic and social conservatives tended to emphasize the need for the national government to leave state and local governments and the public alone. Moderates, neoliberals, and neoconservatives tended to swing from one side to the other depending on the specific issue at hand, or to seek compromise.

Although it is tempting to do so, it would be a mistake to label Elazar's theory as the conservative theory, Walker's theory as the moderate theory, and Anton/Nathan's theory as the liberal theory. These authors are among the very best scholars in the field of intergovernmental relations. They have gone to great lengths to analyze intergovernmental programs and regulations with the highest regard for academic rigor. It was their intention to reach an intellectually sound judgment concerning the current and future condition of intergovernmental relations that was not subject to either political or ideological bias. Nevertheless, many economic and social conservatives advocate the devolutionary prescriptions of Elazar's theory; many moderates, neoliberals, and neoconservatives advocate the sorting out of governmental responsibilities suggested by Walker's theory; and many economic and social liberals advocate the more incremental and moderate reforms suggested by Anton and Nathan's theory.

The lack of consensus among politicians, lobbyists, bureaucrats, and academics over which of these three theories of intergovernmental relations is the most appropriate one to guide future policy decisions is largely a result of the diversity of political values held in our society. I hope that reading this book has helped you to better define your own political values and to gain a better sense of where intergovernmental programs came from, the many factors that have influenced their development, the varying roles played by the national, state, and local governments in each of them, and the direction they are headed. I also hope that it has helped you to reach a judgment concerning which of these three leading prescriptive theories of intergovernmental relations, or the new macroeconomic theory of intergovernmental relations, is the most appropriate one for our times.

INDEX